I0560072

www.ingramcontent.com/pod-product-compliance
Lightning Source LLC
Chambersburg PA
CBHW051322120626
46547CB00015B/2357

* 9 7 8 1 9 5 7 1 0 9 2 8 2 *

וַיִּקְרָא

THE
ISRAEL
BIBLE

LEVITICUS

EDITED BY

Rabbi Tuly Weisz

The Israel Bible: Leviticus

First Edition, 2021

The Israel Bible was produced by Israel365 in cooperation with Teach for Israel and is used with permission from Teach for Israel. All rights reserved. The English translation was adapted by Israel365 from the JPS Tanakh. Copyright © 1985 by the Jewish Publication Society. All rights reserved.

Cover image used under license from Shutterstock.com

ISBN 978-1-957109-28-2

A CIP catalogue record for this title is available from the British Library

The Israel Bible: Leviticus is a holy book that contains the name of God and should be treated with respect.

Table of Contents

iv	Introduction to *The Israel Bible*
ix	Foreword
xiii	Introduction to *Sefer Vayikra* (Leviticus)
xiv	Chart of the *Korbanot Yachid* (Offerings Brought by an Individual)
1	*Sefer Vayikra* (Leviticus)
79	List of Transliterated Words in *The Israel Bible*
93	Photo Credits
94	Map of Modern-Day Israel and its Neighbors

Introduction

The Hebrew Bible is commonly known as the *Tanakh* which stands for *Torah* (the Five Books of Moses), *Neviim* (the Prophets) and *Ketuvim* (the Writings). The *Tanakh* consists of 24 books that are considered by Jews to be the word of God. While these books have been referred to as the "Old Testament," many Jews reject this label since it implies the replacement of the Hebrew Bible with something newer and prefer the more authentic Jewish name.

The *Tanakh* is not only the most important book known to man, it is God's word that is perfect and absolute. It is therefore a daunting undertaking to publish an edition of the *Tanakh,* and the responsibilities are awesome. There is no room for error or carelessness in dealing with the eternal word of God. Further, upon embarking on such a serious initiative, we ask ourselves if our efforts are gratuitous. Considering the many editions of the Bible in print, is there truly a need for yet another one?

While there are numerous Bibles in circulation today, its most central aspect – the Land of Israel – has often been overlooked. References to Israel appear on nearly every page, and the city of Jerusalem is specifically referred to hundreds of times throughout the Bible. The essential link between Israel and *Torah* is emphasized repeatedly in verses such as, "For instruction (*Torah*) shall come forth from *Tzion*, the word of *Hashem* from *Yerushalayim*" (Micah 4:2).

The miraculous return of the People of Israel to the Land of Israel in our own generation provides the perfect moment for a new volume to fill this void in biblical literature. *The Israel Bible* includes many special features elucidating God's focus on Israel throughout *Tanakh* and there are many additional, multimedia features available on our website **www.theisraelbible.com.**

Ordering and Presentation – In presenting *The Israel Bible*, our goal is to spread awareness of the biblical significance of the Land of Israel as well as the Jewish people's eternal connection to the land, based on the text of the *Tanakh*, the Hebrew Bible. We aim to honor "the God, the People and the Land of Israel" from an Orthodox Jewish perspective. To that end, *The Israel Bible* follows the traditional Jewish ordering of the books and the customary Hebrew division of chapters. Therefore, for example, we count 24 books of *Tanakh* with *Sefer Divrei Hayamim* (Chronicles) appearing last. It is our hope that our rich content will speak to all Jews and non-Jews who appreciate Israel as the God given land of the Jewish people.

English Translation – Throughout history, Jews have studied the Bible in Hebrew, as any form of translation would miss much of the nuance of the original holy tongue in which *Torah* has been transmitted since the days of Moses. However, as many Jews settled in America in the 19th Century, the need for an English translation became necessary. To be sure, there were already English translations prepared over the centuries by Christians, but in the words of the original editors of the Jewish Publication Society (JPS), "The Jew cannot afford to have his Bible translation prepared for him by others. He cannot have it as a gift, even as he cannot borrow his soul from others."

JPS set out in the late 1800s to publish an authoritative English translation "in the spirit of Jewish tradition." It was compiled over decades by some of the leading Jewish scholars of the time. They formed committees and subcommittees to compare existing English versions, considering medieval and modern Jewish commentators. The monumental JPS translation, originally published in 1917, has been updated in recent years, and *The Israel Bible* is proud to utilize the 1984 New Jewish Publication Society (NJPS) version with its modern, clear language, as well as its wide-ranging acceptance as an accurate and high-quality translation. We applied the NJPS translation verbatim, except for a select list of nouns which we replaced with their traditional Hebrew names. This is true even when we found the NJPS translation to be different than the popular translation of a word or phrase and when the NJPS switched the order of the text for the sake of clarity (see, for example, Ezekiel 24:22–24).

Hebrew Transliteration – To give our readers an authentic *Tanakh* experience, every verse that has commentary is transliterated from Hebrew into English. The Hebrew alphabet chart includes our standards for transliteration and pronunciation of Hebrew verses, enabling readers of *The Israel Bible* to decipher key biblical passages in the holy language. Readers can hear the entire Bible read in Hebrew on our website **www.theisraelbible.com**.

There are various standards when it comes to transliterating Hebrew words into English letters. While we have relied primarily on the classical Hebrew transliteration, we have occasionally deviated for the sake of simplicity, clarity and to reflect common usage.

In addition to whole verses, we have also transliterated many proper nouns in the English translation so that our readers can learn the names of key biblical figures and locations in their Hebrew form. As a rule, we chose to transliterate names of people that were central in the establishment and functioning of the nation of Israel, as well as significant places in the Holy Land. Therefore, regarding Adam's sons, for example, only *Shet* (Seth) is transliterated since it was from him that *Noach* (Noah), and ultimately *Avraham* (Abraham), descended. For this reason, there might be verses or sections of *The Israel Bible* that contains multiple names and only some of them are transliterated.

For the same reason, we have transliterated the names of the books of *Tanakh* when referring to them in our introductions and commentary. When referencing a specific chapter or verse, however, we use the English names of the books in our citations for clarity. We also transliterated ideas and concepts that are central to Judaism such as *Shabbat* (Sabbath), the names of the Jewish holidays and the *Beit Hamikdash* (Temple), as well as biblical measurements. Finally, the name of God is transliterated. Out of respect, Orthodox Jews generally refer to the Lord as *Hashem*, which literally means 'the Name.' Referring to God as *Hashem* reminds us that we feel close to Him but also recognize our distance at the same time. To stress this moniker, we transliterated both the Tetragrammaton as well as the name *Elohim* as *Hashem*.

Study Notes – Our unique commentary was compiled by Orthodox Jewish scholars who live in Israel. It is an anthology in the sense that most of the commentary is not original, but draws from traditional teachings of early Jewish Sages and modern rabbinic commentators. We also include quotations from individuals who have played a significant part in the past century of modern Israeli history including Israeli prime ministers, poets and military leaders.

Our commentary can be broken into four categories, three of which are identified by an icon at the beginning of the study note:

 Israel lessons are indicated with an icon bearing the map of Israel and focus on the Land of Israel and the modern State of Israel.

 Jewish lessons are indicated with a *Torah* scroll and teach a concept in Judaism or a classic idea from rabbinic thought.

 Hebrew lessons are represented by an icon bearing the letter *aleph* and focus on the meaning of a Hebrew word or phrase.

All other comments are considered general comments and are not assigned an icon.

Supplemental Material – In addition to our unique translation and original commentary, *The Israel Bible* offers supplementary material to enrich the learning experience of our readers. Before every book of *Tanakh*, we provide an introduction, as well as information, generally in the form of a map, a chart or a list, which is central to the specific book.

Maps – As the purpose of *The Israel Bible* is to highlight the biblical significance of the Land of Israel, significant time was spent researching and preparing maps to bring the physical contours of the holy land to life with great accuracy. However, since there is a lack of information regarding the precise locations of certain ancient cities, some of the places on our maps are approximate or subject to debate. In these cases, we followed the opinion that we are most comfortable with, but acknowledge that there is room for disagreement. We continue to produce new maps, which are available on our website **www.theisraelbible.com/maps**.

Torah **Readings** – The *Torah* is not just a work that is studied privately, it is also read out loud in synagogue. Every *Shabbat* and holiday a portion of the *Torah* is read, as well as a related section from *Neviim*, the prophets, called the *haftarah*. We included the blessings recited before and after the reading of the *Torah*, a list of the weekly *Torah* portions and their corresponding *haftarot*, and a chart of the *Torah* readings for special days with their corresponding *haftarot*. Readers can always find the current week's *Torah* portion by visiting **www.theisraelbible.com/weekly-torah-portion**. In this volume, we indicate where a new *Torah* portion begins by highlighting the Hebrew verse number with a gray box so readers can follow along with the communal *Torah* readings. Furthermore, we have included prayers for the State of Israel and the soldiers of the Israel Defense Forces (IDF) that are generally recited following the *Torah* reading in synagogue. It is our constant prayer that God watch over the State of Israel and the members of the IDF, who defend Israel every hour of every day.

In 1948, the State of Israel was created providing a modern answer to Isaiah's ancient question, "Is a nation born all at once?" (Isaiah 66:8). *The Israel Bible* was first published in the 70th year of God's miraculous restoration of the People of Israel to the Land of Israel. Jewish wisdom teaches that 70 is a significant number: *Moshe* (Moses) translated the *Torah* into 70 languages for all 70 nations of the world. From our very origins, the Jewish people were meant to be a light unto the 70 nations, spreading God's truth to the masses.

In the seven decades since the modern rebirth of the State of Israel, God's plan has been unfolding with unprecedented speed, dramatic highs and heartbreaking lows. Never has Israel been at the forefront of the world's attention as it is in our generation. Efforts to vilify the Jewish State seem to spread every day across the globe. At the same time, so does the growing movement of millions of non-Jewish biblical Zionists who stand with the nation of Israel as an expression of their commitment to God's word. As we seek to understand the clash of these two conflicting worldviews, the need for *The Israel Bible* has never been so important.

Standing on the great shoulders of those who came before us and emanating from the land that has always served as the birthplace for the Bible, we conclude with a heartfelt prayer: May the Almighty bless our efforts in offering this *Tanakh* to influence the hearts, minds and actions of its readers. In this way, it is our hope to spread God's name so that the publication of *The Israel Bible* brings us one step closer to the final redemption of Israel and the entire world.

Rabbi Tuly Weisz
Editor, *The Israel Bible*

Foreword

The mandate to study God's word daily is interestingly not found in the Five Books of Moses (Pentateuch), but rather in the first book of our prophetic writings: "Let not this Book of the Teaching cease from your lips, but recite it day and night, so that you may observe faithfully all that is written in it. Only then will you prosper in your undertakings and only then will you be successful" (Joshua 1:8). Charged with bringing the Israelites into the land covenantally promised to Abraham, Isaac and Jacob, God ensures Joshua of His protection if the nation observes His ways as dictated in the Divine constitution known as the *Torah*.

In Jewish tradition, Joshua (1:8) is directly linked with Deuteronomy (11:14), "You shall gather in your new grain and wine, and oil."[1] Our Sages deduced from this scriptural combination the importance of merging *Torah* study with a profession. Completely dedicating oneself to the study of *Torah* without having the financial means to sustain this lifestyle can lead one to eventually straying from observance of God's will. Poverty and crime can have an intimate relationship.

We must also be careful that our work does not affect our daily study of Scripture. The addiction of becoming a workaholic and not making *Torah* study a priority can also lead one into temptations that can violate our personal relationship with Him as well as our fellow human beings. The goal is to achieve a healthy balance between our study of God's word and our daily work.

The Deuteronomic verse quoted above is part of the second section of the Shema[2] that discusses the concept of reward and punishment. Sanctifying God by fulfilling His commandments results in the Land of Israel practically benefitting from rains that occur in the right season and reaping the abundance from the fields. However, if the nation follows pagan gods and practices, the consequences are devastating – famine and death. The Land of Israel is intrinsically linked with the keeping of the *Torah*. Covenant Land comes with covenant responsibility.

---

1. Talmud Bavli Berachot 35b
2. Consisting of three sections within the Five Books of Moses (Deut. 6:4–8; 11:13–22 and Numbers 15:37–42), the *Shema* is proclamation of accepting God's Kingdom in our lives, loyalty to His commandments and remembering His redemptive act of liberating us from Egypt. Jews recite the *Shema* twice a day as stated in Deut. 6:7.

Born into slavery, Joshua is now leading His people into the Promised Land. More than 500 years separates him from his ancestral forefather Abraham. The historical narratives that took place between Abraham leaving everything behind to follow God in Genesis 12 and the death of Moses in the last chapter of Deuteronomy are filled with intrigue, suspense, joy, sorrow and hope. What began as a family is now a nation actualizing its mission to be a kingdom of priests to the world. However, for the Israelites to succeed in the Land of Israel, they must see the *Torah* as the only compass to direct their lives.

The biblical episodes after our first entry into the land are well known. Our ancestors' triumphs and sins are all on public record. We learned the harsh reality of Leviticus (18:28) "So let not the land spew you out for defiling it as it spewed out the nation that came before you." Twice, we lost the privilege to be stewards of the Land of Israel and to fulfill our nation state mandate to be a light to the world. However, when the annals of history were ready to archive the Jewish people after the Holocaust, God kept His covenantal promise and gathered us from the four corners of the globe to come home. The year 1948 was a game changer. Biblical prophecies were and are being realized. We are now living in the birth pangs of the messianic era.

In our morning prayers, we recite a series of blessings over the *Torah* that include petitioning God to have a sweet tooth for His word, to study it without any ulterior motive and to have Him to teach it to us. They are some congregations that invoke the following liturgical prayer after the completion of these blessings: *May the Torah be my faith and El Shaddai my help. Blessed be the name of His glorious kingdom forever and all time.*

According to Jewish tradition, the neglect of not blessing the *Torah* before engaging in its study was one of the reasons for the destruction of the Temple.[3] This is deduced from the redundancy of words in Jeremiah (9:12) that talks about Israel not following God: "... Because they forsook the teaching I had set before them. They did not obey Me and they did not follow it [did not make a blessing before studying it]." Our inability to properly cherish God's greatest gift to the world, the *Torah*, led to our eventual exile from our land.

On Israel's Independence Day, Jews around the world recite Psalms 113–118 to express our gratitude to God for His Divine hand in helping establish the State of Israel. We have learned from our past and realize the privilege to see firsthand the land, people and *Torah* operating all together in our generation.

---

3. Babylonian Talmud Nedarim 81a

When Rabbi Tuly Weisz approached me about his intent to publish *The Israel Bible* that would highlight commentary about the special relationship between the land and people, I saw this project as another way to publicly demonstrate our appreciation to God for having the State of Israel. In addition, it is another educational tool to ensure biblical literacy. If we are to truly enjoy the Land of Israel, it is incumbent upon us to continually study the *Torah*. Isaiah once prophesied that the Jewish people would return to Zion with songs, "crowned with everlasting joy" (35:10). *The Israel Bible* provides us the lyrical content to express our joy in living in the land that God calls holy.

Rabbi Shlomo Riskin
Chief Rabbi of Efrat
Founder of the Center for Jewish-Christian
Understanding & Cooperation (CJCUC)

Introduction to Sefer Vayikra
The Book of Leviticus

Introduction and commentary by Shira Schechter

Following the inspirational narrative of *Sefer Bereishit* (Genesis) and the exciting stories of *Sefer Shemot* (Exodus), it may appear at first glance that *Sefer Vayikra* (Leviticus) fails to live up to the standard set by its two dramatic predecessors. The name "Leviticus" comes from *Levi*, the father of the priestly tribe, and much of its 27 chapters are devoted to describing the priestly rituals in great detail. Since most of these practices are not observed today, some modern readers have difficulty in finding practical significance in *Sefer Vayikra*, and thus miss out on its eternal values.

To be sure, it is possible to get lost in all the nuances of the various rituals and offerings described in *Sefer Vayikra*, but it is imperative that the reader not lose sight of the big picture. As we study the intricate details of the offerings, we discover that their overarching purpose is to bring the people closer to *Hashem* through His earthly dwelling place, as it says, "Make for Me a sanctuary, that I may dwell among them" (Exodus 25:8). *Sefer Vayikra*'s intricate details are necessary for us to bring God's presence into our lives in a very physical way, by serving Him in a very specific manner.

The *Mishkan* was a temporary edifice that paved the way for the *Beit Hamikdash* in *Yerushalayim*, which served as the permanent structure for worshipping the God of Israel. Today, even though we don't have the *Mishkan* (Tabernacle) to uplift us or the Temple to pray in, *Yerushalayim* remains mankind's special gateway between heaven and earth. Nowadays, our connection to *Eretz Yisrael* is still able to uplift our service to *Hashem*.

By delving deeper into the meaning behind the *Torah*'s ancient rituals and discovering their many fundamental truths, and by highlighting the role of Zion throughout the Book of *Vayikra*, it is our hope that *The Israel Bible* helps us fulfill the purpose of the *Mishkan*: to bring God's presence into our lives.

May our study of *The Israel Bible* infuse us with sanctity as if we were bringing the offerings described in *Sefer Vayikra*, and prepare us for the day when the *Beit Hamikdash* is rebuilt in *Yerushalayim* and we are able to fully feel God's presence in this world.

Chart of the *Korbanot Yachid* (Offerings Brought by an Individual)

While the end of *Sefer Shemot* describes the construction of the *Mishkan* (Tabernacle) at the foot of Mount Sinai, *Sefer Vayikra* focuses on the service performed in the *Mishkan*. It begins with the laws of *korbanot* (offerings) brought on the *Mizbayach* (altar). The following chart outlines *Sefer Vayikra* chapters 1–5, which describe the *korbanot yachid*, or offerings brought by an individual.

Voluntary Offerings (Leviticus Chapters 1–3)

Type of *korban*	Description	What is brought	Relevant verses
Korban Olah – Burnt Offering	An offering of an animal – the entire *korban* is burnt on the *Mizbayach*	Cattle, Sheep, Goats, Fowl	Leviticus 1:1–17
Korban Mincha – Meal Offering	An offering from flour – part of the offering is burnt on the *Mizbayach* and part is eaten by the *kohanim*.	a. Flour mixed with oil and frankincense b. Flour mixture baked in an oven c. Flour mixture fried on a griddle d. Flour mixture fried in a pan e. Flour taken from the first harvest	Leviticus 2:1–16
Korban Shelamim – Peace Offering	An animal offering that is partially burnt on the *Mizbayach*, partially eaten by the *kohanim* and partially eaten by the owner.	Cattle, Sheep, Goats	Leviticus 3:1–17

Mandatory Offerings (Leviticus Chapters 4–5)

Type of *Korban*	Reason for the *Korban*	What is brought	Relevant Verses
Korban Chatat – Sin Offering	To atone for unintentional sins	**For General Transgressions:** a. *Kohen* – bull b. The High Court – bull c. Prince – male goat d. Layman – a female goat or a female lamb	Leviticus 4:1–35
		For Specific Transgressions: a. Wealthy Person – a female goat or lamb b. Poor Person – two birds c. Very Poor Person – a plain flour offering	Leviticus 5:1–13
Korban Asham – Guilt Offering	To atone for taking from Temple property, if one is unsure he sinned, or for stealing from someone else	Ram	Leviticus 5:14–26

Leviticus

1 ¹ *Hashem* called to *Moshe* and spoke to him from the Tent of Meeting, saying:

א וַיִּקְרָא אֶל־מֹשֶׁה וַיְדַבֵּר יְהֹוָה אֵלָיו מֵאֹהֶל מוֹעֵד לֵאמֹר:

² Speak to *B'nei Yisrael*, and say to them: When any of you presents an offering of cattle to *Hashem*, he shall choose his offering from the herd or from the flock.

ב דַּבֵּר אֶל־בְּנֵי יִשְׂרָאֵל וְאָמַרְתָּ אֲלֵהֶם אָדָם כִּי־יַקְרִיב מִכֶּם קָרְבָּן לַיהֹוָה מִן־הַבְּהֵמָה מִן־הַבָּקָר וּמִן־הַצֹּאן תַּקְרִיבוּ אֶת־קָרְבַּנְכֶם:

da-BAYR el b'-NAY yis-ra-AYL v'-a-mar-TA a-lay-HEM a-DAM kee yak-REEV mi-KEM kor-BAN la-do-NAI min ha-b'-hay-MAH min ha-ba-KAR u-min ha-TZON tak-REE-vu et kor-ban-KHEM

³ If his offering is a burnt offering from the herd, he shall make his offering a male without blemish. He shall bring it to the entrance of the Tent of Meeting, for acceptance in his behalf before *Hashem*.

ג אִם־עֹלָה קָרְבָּנוֹ מִן־הַבָּקָר זָכָר תָּמִים יַקְרִיבֶנּוּ אֶל־פֶּתַח אֹהֶל מוֹעֵד יַקְרִיב אֹתוֹ לִרְצֹנוֹ לִפְנֵי יְהֹוָה:

⁴ He shall lay his hand upon the head of the burnt offering, that it may be acceptable in his behalf, in expiation for him.

ד וְסָמַךְ יָדוֹ עַל רֹאשׁ הָעֹלָה וְנִרְצָה לוֹ לְכַפֵּר עָלָיו:

⁵ The bull shall be slaughtered before *Hashem*; and *Aharon*'s sons, the *Kohanim*, shall offer the blood, dashing the blood against all sides of the *Mizbayach* which is at the entrance of the Tent of Meeting.

ה וְשָׁחַט אֶת־בֶּן הַבָּקָר לִפְנֵי יְהֹוָה וְהִקְרִיבוּ בְּנֵי אַהֲרֹן הַכֹּהֲנִים אֶת־הַדָּם וְזָרְקוּ אֶת־הַדָּם עַל־הַמִּזְבֵּחַ סָבִיב אֲשֶׁר־פֶּתַח אֹהֶל מוֹעֵד:

⁶ The burnt offering shall be flayed and cut up into sections.

ו וְהִפְשִׁיט אֶת־הָעֹלָה וְנִתַּח אֹתָהּ לִנְתָחֶיהָ:

⁷ The sons of *Aharon* the *Kohen* shall put fire on the *Mizbayach* and lay out wood upon the fire;

ז וְנָתְנוּ בְּנֵי אַהֲרֹן הַכֹּהֵן אֵשׁ עַל־הַמִּזְבֵּחַ וְעָרְכוּ עֵצִים עַל־הָאֵשׁ:

⁸ and *Aharon*'s sons, the *Kohanim*, shall lay out the sections, with the head and the suet, on the wood that is on the fire upon the *Mizbayach*.

ח וְעָרְכוּ בְּנֵי אַהֲרֹן הַכֹּהֲנִים אֵת הַנְּתָחִים אֶת־הָרֹאשׁ וְאֶת־הַפָּדֶר עַל־הָעֵצִים אֲשֶׁר עַל־הָאֵשׁ אֲשֶׁר עַל־הַמִּזְבֵּחַ:

⁹ Its entrails and legs shall be washed with water, and the *Kohen* shall turn the whole into smoke on the *Mizbayach* as a burnt offering, an offering by fire of pleasing odor to *Hashem*.

ט וְקִרְבּוֹ וּכְרָעָיו יִרְחַץ בַּמָּיִם וְהִקְטִיר הַכֹּהֵן אֶת־הַכֹּל הַמִּזְבֵּחָה עֹלָה אִשֵּׁה רֵיחַ־נִיחוֹחַ לַיהֹוָה:

¹⁰ If his offering for a burnt offering is from the flock, of sheep or of goats, he shall make his offering a male without blemish.

י וְאִם־מִן־הַצֹּאן קָרְבָּנוֹ מִן־הַכְּשָׂבִים אוֹ מִן־הָעִזִּים לְעֹלָה זָכָר תָּמִים יַקְרִיבֶנּוּ:

קרבן

א **1:2 When any of you presents an offering of cattle to *Hashem*** *Sefer Vayikra* describes the various offerings that were brought in the *Beit Hamikdash* in great detail. The Hebrew term for 'offering,' *korban* (קרבן), comes from the word *karov* (ק-ר-ב), meaning 'close,' since the offerings are meant to bring people closer to the Eternal One. For this reason, the common English translation of *korban*, 'sacrifice,' is insufficient, as it does not accurately portray the essence of the word. While the person bringing the offering might be giving something from his personal possessions, he gains much more than he gives. Now that we no longer have *korbanot*, prayer is the primary vehicle through which we come close to our Father in Heaven.

Early morning prayer at the Western Wall

¹¹ It shall be slaughtered before *Hashem* on the north side of the *Mizbayach*, and *Aharon*'s sons, the *Kohanim*, shall dash its blood against all sides of the *Mizbayach*.

יא וְשָׁחַט אֹתוֹ עַל יֶרֶךְ הַמִּזְבֵּחַ צָפֹנָה לִפְנֵי יְהוָה וְזָרְקוּ בְּנֵי אַהֲרֹן הַכֹּהֲנִים אֶת־דָּמוֹ עַל־הַמִּזְבֵּחַ סָבִיב:

¹² When it has been cut up into sections, the *Kohen* shall lay them out, with the head and the suet, on the wood that is on the fire upon the *Mizbayach*.

יב וְנִתַּח אֹתוֹ לִנְתָחָיו וְאֶת־רֹאשׁוֹ וְאֶת־פִּדְרוֹ וְעָרַךְ הַכֹּהֵן אֹתָם עַל־הָעֵצִים אֲשֶׁר עַל־הָאֵשׁ אֲשֶׁר עַל־הַמִּזְבֵּחַ:

¹³ The entrails and the legs shall be washed with water; the *Kohen* shall offer up and turn the whole into smoke on the *Mizbayach*. It is a burnt offering, an offering by fire, of pleasing odor to *Hashem*.

יג וְהַקֶּרֶב וְהַכְּרָעַיִם יִרְחַץ בַּמָּיִם וְהִקְרִיב הַכֹּהֵן אֶת־הַכֹּל וְהִקְטִיר הַמִּזְבֵּחָה עֹלָה הוּא אִשֵּׁה רֵיחַ נִיחֹחַ לַיהוָה:

¹⁴ If his offering to *Hashem* is a burnt offering of birds, he shall choose his offering from turtledoves or pigeons.

יד וְאִם מִן־הָעוֹף עֹלָה קָרְבָּנוֹ לַיהוָה וְהִקְרִיב מִן־הַתֹּרִים אוֹ מִן־בְּנֵי הַיּוֹנָה אֶת־קָרְבָּנוֹ:

¹⁵ The *Kohen* shall bring it to the *Mizbayach*, pinch off its head, and turn it into smoke on the *Mizbayach*; and its blood shall be drained out against the side of the *Mizbayach*.

טו וְהִקְרִיבוֹ הַכֹּהֵן אֶל־הַמִּזְבֵּחַ וּמָלַק אֶת־רֹאשׁוֹ וְהִקְטִיר הַמִּזְבֵּחָה וְנִמְצָה דָמוֹ עַל קִיר הַמִּזְבֵּחַ:

¹⁶ He shall remove its crop with its contents, and cast it into the place of the ashes, at the east side of the *Mizbayach*.

טז וְהֵסִיר אֶת־מֻרְאָתוֹ בְּנֹצָתָהּ וְהִשְׁלִיךְ אֹתָהּ אֵצֶל הַמִּזְבֵּחַ קֵדְמָה אֶל־מְקוֹם הַדָּשֶׁן:

¹⁷ The *Kohen* shall tear it open by its wings, without severing it, and turn it into smoke on the *Mizbayach*, upon the wood that is on the fire. It is a burnt offering, an offering by fire, of pleasing odor to *Hashem*.

יז וְשִׁסַּע אֹתוֹ בִכְנָפָיו לֹא יַבְדִּיל וְהִקְטִיר אֹתוֹ הַכֹּהֵן הַמִּזְבֵּחָה עַל־הָעֵצִים אֲשֶׁר עַל־הָאֵשׁ עֹלָה הוּא אִשֵּׁה רֵיחַ נִיחֹחַ לַיהוָה:

2 ¹ When a person presents an offering of meal to *Hashem*, his offering shall be of choice flour; he shall pour oil upon it, lay frankincense on it,

ב א וְנֶפֶשׁ כִּי־תַקְרִיב קָרְבַּן מִנְחָה לַיהוָה סֹלֶת יִהְיֶה קָרְבָּנוֹ וְיָצַק עָלֶיהָ שֶׁמֶן וְנָתַן עָלֶיהָ לְבֹנָה:

v'-NE-fesh kee tak-REEV kor-BAN min-KHAH la-do-NAI SO-let yih-YEH kor-ba-NO v'-ya-TZAK a-LE-ha SHE-men v'-na-TAN a-LE-ha l'-vo-NAH

A flour mill at the Tel Dan Nature Reserve

2:1 When a person presents an offering of meal to *Hashem* In this verse, the Bible uses the word *nefesh* (נפש), 'soul,' to describe the person bringing this offering. The Talmud (*Menachot* 104b) explains that the word "soul" is specifically chosen for the voluntary meal-offering, as opposed to any of the other sacrifices, because the meal-offering is comprised of flour, oil and frankincense. These ingredients are much less expensive than the animals brought for the other offerings, and therefore, this offering is often brought specifi-cally by poor people. When a poor person chooses to give from his meager means to *Hashem*, He considers it as if the person has offered his very soul. What matters to the Lord is not our material wealth, how much we have or even how much we give. It is the sincerity behind our actions that matters most.

2 and present it to *Aharon*'s sons, the *Kohanim*. The *Kohen* shall scoop out of it a handful of its choice flour and oil, as well as all of its frankincense; and this token portion he shall turn into smoke on the *Mizbayach*, as an offering by fire, of pleasing odor to *Hashem*.

ב וֶהֱבִיאָהּ אֶל־בְּנֵי אַהֲרֹן הַכֹּהֲנִים וְקָמַץ מִשָּׁם מְלֹא קֻמְצוֹ מִסָּלְתָּהּ וּמִשַּׁמְנָהּ עַל כָּל־לְבֹנָתָהּ וְהִקְטִיר הַכֹּהֵן אֶת־אַזְכָּרָתָהּ הַמִּזְבֵּחָה אִשֵּׁה רֵיחַ נִיחֹחַ לַיהוָה:

3 And the remainder of the meal offering shall be for *Aharon* and his sons, a most holy portion from *Hashem*'s offerings by fire.

ג וְהַנּוֹתֶרֶת מִן־הַמִּנְחָה לְאַהֲרֹן וּלְבָנָיו קֹדֶשׁ קָדָשִׁים מֵאִשֵּׁי יְהוָה:

4 When you present an offering of meal baked in the oven, [it shall be of] choice flour: unleavened cakes with oil mixed in, or unleavened wafers spread with oil.

ד וְכִי תַקְרִב קָרְבַּן מִנְחָה מַאֲפֵה תַנּוּר סֹלֶת חַלּוֹת מַצֹּת בְּלוּלֹת בַּשֶּׁמֶן וּרְקִיקֵי מַצּוֹת מְשֻׁחִים בַּשָּׁמֶן:

5 If your offering is a meal offering on a griddle, it shall be of choice flour with oil mixed in, unleavened.

ה וְאִם־מִנְחָה עַל־הַמַּחֲבַת קָרְבָּנֶךָ סֹלֶת בְּלוּלָה בַשֶּׁמֶן מַצָּה תִהְיֶה:

6 Break it into bits and pour oil on it; it is a meal offering.

ו פָּתוֹת אֹתָהּ פִּתִּים וְיָצַקְתָּ עָלֶיהָ שָׁמֶן מִנְחָה הִוא:

7 If your offering is a meal offering in a pan, it shall be made of choice flour in oil.

ז וְאִם־מִנְחַת מַרְחֶשֶׁת קָרְבָּנֶךָ סֹלֶת בַּשֶּׁמֶן תֵּעָשֶׂה:

8 When you present to *Hashem* a meal offering that is made in any of these ways, it shall be brought to the *Kohen* who shall take it up to the *Mizbayach*.

ח וְהֵבֵאתָ אֶת־הַמִּנְחָה אֲשֶׁר יֵעָשֶׂה מֵאֵלֶּה לַיהוָה וְהִקְרִיבָהּ אֶל־הַכֹּהֵן וְהִגִּישָׁהּ אֶל־הַמִּזְבֵּחַ:

9 The *Kohen* shall remove the token portion from the meal offering and turn it into smoke on the *Mizbayach* as an offering by fire, of pleasing odor to *Hashem*.

ט וְהֵרִים הַכֹּהֵן מִן־הַמִּנְחָה אֶת־אַזְכָּרָתָהּ וְהִקְטִיר הַמִּזְבֵּחָה אִשֵּׁה רֵיחַ נִיחֹחַ לַיהוָה:

10 And the remainder of the meal offering shall be for *Aharon* and his sons, a most holy portion from *Hashem*'s offerings by fire.

י וְהַנּוֹתֶרֶת מִן־הַמִּנְחָה לְאַהֲרֹן וּלְבָנָיו קֹדֶשׁ קָדָשִׁים מֵאִשֵּׁי יְהוָה:

11 No meal offering that you offer to *Hashem* shall be made with leaven, for no leaven or honey may be turned into smoke as an offering by fire to *Hashem*.

יא כָּל־הַמִּנְחָה אֲשֶׁר תַּקְרִיבוּ לַיהוָה לֹא תֵעָשֶׂה חָמֵץ כִּי כָל־שְׂאֹר וְכָל־דְּבַשׁ לֹא־תַקְטִירוּ מִמֶּנּוּ אִשֵּׁה לַיהוָה:

12 You may bring them to *Hashem* as an offering of choice products; but they shall not be offered up on the *Mizbayach* for a pleasing odor.

יב קָרְבַּן רֵאשִׁית תַּקְרִיבוּ אֹתָם לַיהוָה וְאֶל־הַמִּזְבֵּחַ לֹא־יַעֲלוּ לְרֵיחַ נִיחֹחַ:

13 You shall season your every offering of meal with salt; you shall not omit from your meal offering the salt of your covenant with *Hashem*; with all your offerings you must offer salt.

יג וְכָל־קָרְבַּן מִנְחָתְךָ בַּמֶּלַח תִּמְלָח וְלֹא תַשְׁבִּית מֶלַח בְּרִית אֱלֹהֶיךָ מֵעַל מִנְחָתֶךָ עַל כָּל־קָרְבָּנְךָ תַּקְרִיב מֶלַח:

14 If you bring a meal offering of first fruits to *Hashem*, you shall bring new ears parched with fire, grits of the fresh grain, as your meal offering of first fruits.

יד וְאִם־תַּקְרִיב מִנְחַת בִּכּוּרִים לַיהוָה אָבִיב קָלוּי בָּאֵשׁ גֶּרֶשׂ כַּרְמֶל תַּקְרִיב אֵת מִנְחַת בִּכּוּרֶיךָ:

15 You shall add oil to it and lay frankincense on it; it is a meal offering.

טו וְנָתַתָּ עָלֶיהָ שֶׁמֶן וְשַׂמְתָּ עָלֶיהָ לְבֹנָה מִנְחָה הִוא:

16 And the *Kohen* shall turn a token portion of it into smoke: some of the grits and oil, with all of the frankincense, as an offering by fire to *Hashem*.

טז וְהִקְטִיר הַכֹּהֵן אֶת־אַזְכָּרָתָהּ מִגִּרְשָׂהּ וּמִשַּׁמְנָהּ עַל כָּל־לְבֹנָתָהּ אִשֶּׁה לַיהוָה:

3 ¹ If his offering is a sacrifice of well-being – If he offers of the herd, whether a male or a female, he shall bring before *Hashem* one without blemish.

ג א וְאִם־זֶבַח שְׁלָמִים קָרְבָּנוֹ אִם מִן־ הַבָּקָר הוּא מַקְרִיב אִם־זָכָר אִם־נְקֵבָה תָּמִים יַקְרִיבֶנּוּ לִפְנֵי יְהוָה:

v'-im ZE-vakh sh'-la-MEEM kor-ba-NO im min ha-ba-KAR HU mak-REEV
im za-KHAR im n'-kay-VAH ta-MEEM yak-ree-VE-nu lif-NAY a-do-NAI

2 He shall lay his hand upon the head of his offering and slaughter it at the entrance of the Tent of Meeting; and *Aharon*'s sons, the *Kohanim*, shall dash the blood against all sides of the *Mizbayach*.

ב וְסָמַךְ יָדוֹ עַל־רֹאשׁ קָרְבָּנוֹ וּשְׁחָטוֹ פֶּתַח אֹהֶל מוֹעֵד וְזָרְקוּ בְּנֵי אַהֲרֹן הַכֹּהֲנִים אֶת־הַדָּם עַל־הַמִּזְבֵּחַ סָבִיב:

3 He shall then present from the sacrifice of well-being, as an offering by fire to *Hashem*, the fat that covers the entrails and all the fat that is about the entrails;

ג וְהִקְרִיב מִזֶּבַח הַשְּׁלָמִים אִשֶּׁה לַיהוָה אֶת־הַחֵלֶב הַמְכַסֶּה אֶת־הַקֶּרֶב וְאֵת כָּל־הַחֵלֶב אֲשֶׁר עַל־הַקֶּרֶב:

4 the two kidneys and the fat that is on them, that is at the loins; and the protuberance on the liver, which he shall remove with the kidneys.

ד וְאֵת שְׁתֵּי הַכְּלָיֹת וְאֶת־הַחֵלֶב אֲשֶׁר עֲלֵהֶן אֲשֶׁר עַל־הַכְּסָלִים וְאֶת־הַיֹּתֶרֶת עַל־הַכָּבֵד עַל־הַכְּלָיוֹת יְסִירֶנָּה:

5 *Aharon*'s sons shall turn these into smoke on the *Mizbayach*, with the burnt offering which is upon the wood that is on the fire, as an offering by fire, of pleasing odor to *Hashem*.

ה וְהִקְטִירוּ אֹתוֹ בְנֵי־אַהֲרֹן הַמִּזְבֵּחָה עַל־הָעֹלָה אֲשֶׁר עַל־הָעֵצִים אֲשֶׁר עַל־ הָאֵשׁ אִשֶּׁה רֵיחַ נִיחֹחַ לַיהוָה:

6 And if his offering for a sacrifice of well-being to *Hashem* is from the flock, whether a male or a female, he shall offer one without blemish.

ו וְאִם־מִן־הַצֹּאן קָרְבָּנוֹ לְזֶבַח שְׁלָמִים לַיהוָה זָכָר אוֹ נְקֵבָה תָּמִים יַקְרִיבֶנּוּ:

7 If he presents a sheep as his offering, he shall bring it before *Hashem*

ז אִם־כֶּשֶׂב הוּא־מַקְרִיב אֶת־קָרְבָּנוֹ וְהִקְרִיב אֹתוֹ לִפְנֵי יְהוָה:

Old City of *Yerushalayim*, "city of peace"

3:1 If his offering is a sacrifice of well-being The sacrifice of well-being is often called the 'peace-offering' based on its Hebrew name, *korban sh'lamim* (קרבן שלמים), which comes from the Hebrew word *shalom* (שלום), 'peace.' According to Jewish tradition, it is so called because the *korban sh'lamim* symbolizes peace and unity, as it is the only offering that is shared by everyone involved: *Hashem* (referring to the portions consumed on the altar), the priest and the owner of the sacrifice. It is perhaps not a coincidence that it is also the only offering that is not restricted to the *Beit Hamikdash*, but may be eaten anywhere in the city of *Yerushalayim*. *Yerushalayim*, the Hebrew name for Jerusalem, also has the word *shalom* at its root. It is known as the *eer shel shalom* (עיר של שלום), 'city of peace.' We pray for the time when peace and unity, symbolized by the *korban sh'lamim*, will return to Jerusalem, and to all of Israel.

4

Leviticus

8 and lay his hand upon the head of his offering. It shall be slaughtered before the Tent of Meeting, and *Aharon*'s sons shall dash its blood against all sides of the *Mizbayach*.

ח וְסָמַךְ אֶת־יָדוֹ עַל־רֹאשׁ קָרְבָּנוֹ וְשָׁחַט אֹתוֹ לִפְנֵי אֹהֶל מוֹעֵד וְזָרְקוּ בְּנֵי אַהֲרֹן אֶת־דָּמוֹ עַל־הַמִּזְבֵּחַ סָבִיב:

9 He shall then present, as an offering by fire to *Hashem*, the fat from the sacrifice of well-being: the whole broad tail, which shall be removed close to the backbone; the fat that covers the entrails and all the fat that is about the entrails;

ט וְהִקְרִיב מִזֶּבַח הַשְּׁלָמִים אִשֶּׁה לַיהֹוָה חֶלְבּוֹ הָאַלְיָה תְמִימָה לְעֻמַּת הֶעָצֶה יְסִירֶנָּה וְאֶת־הַחֵלֶב הַמְכַסֶּה אֶת־הַקֶּרֶב וְאֵת כָּל־הַחֵלֶב אֲשֶׁר עַל־הַקֶּרֶב:

10 the two kidneys and the fat that is on them, that is at the loins; and the protuberance on the liver, which he shall remove with the kidneys.

י וְאֵת שְׁתֵּי הַכְּלָיֹת וְאֶת־הַחֵלֶב אֲשֶׁר עֲלֵהֶן אֲשֶׁר עַל־הַכְּסָלִים וְאֶת־הַיֹּתֶרֶת עַל־הַכָּבֵד עַל־הַכְּלָיֹת יְסִירֶנָּה:

11 The *Kohen* shall turn these into smoke on the *Mizbayach* as food, an offering by fire to *Hashem*.

יא וְהִקְטִירוֹ הַכֹּהֵן הַמִּזְבֵּחָה לֶחֶם אִשֶּׁה לַיהֹוָה:

12 And if his offering is a goat, he shall bring it before *Hashem*

יב וְאִם־עֵז קָרְבָּנוֹ וְהִקְרִיבוֹ לִפְנֵי יְהֹוָה:

13 and lay his hand upon its head. It shall be slaughtered before the Tent of Meeting, and *Aharon*'s sons shall dash its blood against all sides of the *Mizbayach*.

יג וְסָמַךְ אֶת־יָדוֹ עַל־רֹאשׁוֹ וְשָׁחַט אֹתוֹ לִפְנֵי אֹהֶל מוֹעֵד וְזָרְקוּ בְּנֵי אַהֲרֹן אֶת־דָּמוֹ עַל־הַמִּזְבֵּחַ סָבִיב:

14 He shall then present as his offering from it, as an offering by fire to *Hashem*, the fat that covers the entrails and all the fat that is about the entrails;

יד וְהִקְרִיב מִמֶּנּוּ קָרְבָּנוֹ אִשֶּׁה לַיהֹוָה אֶת־הַחֵלֶב הַמְכַסֶּה אֶת־הַקֶּרֶב וְאֵת כָּל־הַחֵלֶב אֲשֶׁר עַל־הַקֶּרֶב:

15 the two kidneys and the fat that is on them, that is at the loins; and the protuberance on the liver, which he shall remove with the kidneys.

טו וְאֵת שְׁתֵּי הַכְּלָיֹת וְאֶת־הַחֵלֶב אֲשֶׁר עֲלֵהֶן אֲשֶׁר עַל־הַכְּסָלִים וְאֶת־הַיֹּתֶרֶת עַל־הַכָּבֵד עַל־הַכְּלָיֹת יְסִירֶנָּה:

16 The *Kohen* shall turn these into smoke on the *Mizbayach* as food, an offering by fire, of pleasing odor. All fat is *Hashem*'s.

טז וְהִקְטִירָם הַכֹּהֵן הַמִּזְבֵּחָה לֶחֶם אִשֶּׁה לְרֵיחַ נִיחֹחַ כָּל־חֵלֶב לַיהֹוָה:

17 It is a law for all time throughout the ages, in all your settlements: you must not eat any fat or any blood.

יז חֻקַּת עוֹלָם לְדֹרֹתֵיכֶם בְּכֹל מוֹשְׁבֹתֵיכֶם כָּל־חֵלֶב וְכָל־דָּם לֹא תֹאכֵלוּ:

4 1 *Hashem* spoke to *Moshe*, saying:

ד א וַיְדַבֵּר יְהֹוָה אֶל־מֹשֶׁה לֵּאמֹר:

2 Speak to *B'nei Yisrael* thus: When a person unwittingly incurs guilt in regard to any of *Hashem*'s commandments about things not to be done, and does one of them –

ב דַּבֵּר אֶל־בְּנֵי יִשְׂרָאֵל לֵאמֹר נֶפֶשׁ כִּי־תֶחֱטָא בִשְׁגָגָה מִכֹּל מִצְוֹת יְהֹוָה אֲשֶׁר לֹא תֵעָשֶׂינָה וְעָשָׂה מֵאַחַת מֵהֵנָּה:

3 If it is the anointed *Kohen* who has incurred guilt, so that blame falls upon the people, he shall offer for the sin of which he is guilty a bull of the herd without blemish as a sin offering to *Hashem*.

ג אִם הַכֹּהֵן הַמָּשִׁיחַ יֶחֱטָא לְאַשְׁמַת הָעָם וְהִקְרִיב עַל חַטָּאתוֹ אֲשֶׁר חָטָא פַּר בֶּן־בָּקָר תָּמִים לַיהֹוָה לְחַטָּאת:

4 He shall bring the bull to the entrance of the Tent
of Meeting, before *Hashem*, and lay his hand upon
the head of the bull. The bull shall be slaughtered
before *Hashem*,

5 and the anointed *Kohen* shall take some of the bull's
blood and bring it into the Tent of Meeting.

6 The *Kohen* shall dip his finger in the blood, and
sprinkle of the blood seven times before *Hashem*, in
front of the curtain of the Shrine.

7 The *Kohen* shall put some of the blood on the horns
of the *Mizbayach* of aromatic incense, which is in
the Tent of Meeting, before *Hashem*; and all the
rest of the bull's blood he shall pour out at the base
of the *Mizbayach* of burnt offering, which is at the
entrance of the Tent of Meeting.

8 He shall remove all the fat from the bull of sin
offering: the fat that covers the entrails and all the
fat that is about the entrails;

9 the two kidneys and the fat that is on them, that
is at the loins; and the protuberance on the liver,
which he shall remove with the kidneys

10 just as it is removed from the ox of the sacrifice of
well-being. The *Kohen* shall turn them into smoke
on the *Mizbayach* of burnt offering.

11 But the hide of the bull, and all its flesh, as well as
its head and legs, its entrails and its dung

12 all the rest of the bull – he shall carry to a clean
place outside the camp, to the ash heap, and burn it
up in a wood fire; it shall be burned on the ash heap.

13 If it is the whole community of *Yisrael* that has
erred and the matter escapes the notice of the
congregation, so that they do any of the things
which by *Hashem*'s commandments ought not to
be done, and they realize their guilt

ד וְהֵבִיא אֶת־הַפָּר אֶל־פֶּתַח אֹהֶל מוֹעֵד
לִפְנֵי יְהוָה וְסָמַךְ אֶת־יָדוֹ עַל־רֹאשׁ
הַפָּר וְשָׁחַט אֶת־הַפָּר לִפְנֵי יְהוָה:

ה וְלָקַח הַכֹּהֵן הַמָּשִׁיחַ מִדַּם הַפָּר וְהֵבִיא
אֹתוֹ אֶל־אֹהֶל מוֹעֵד:

ו וְטָבַל הַכֹּהֵן אֶת־אֶצְבָּעוֹ בַּדָּם וְהִזָּה מִן־
הַדָּם שֶׁבַע פְּעָמִים לִפְנֵי יְהוָה אֶת־פְּנֵי
פָּרֹכֶת הַקֹּדֶשׁ:

ז וְנָתַן הַכֹּהֵן מִן־הַדָּם עַל־קַרְנוֹת מִזְבַּח
קְטֹרֶת הַסַּמִּים לִפְנֵי יְהוָה אֲשֶׁר בְּאֹהֶל
מוֹעֵד וְאֵת כָּל־דַּם הַפָּר יִשְׁפֹּךְ אֶל־יְסוֹד
מִזְבַּח הָעֹלָה אֲשֶׁר־פֶּתַח אֹהֶל מוֹעֵד:

ח וְאֶת־כָּל־חֵלֶב פַּר הַחַטָּאת יָרִים מִמֶּנּוּ
אֶת־הַחֵלֶב הַמְכַסֶּה עַל־הַקֶּרֶב וְאֵת כָּל־
הַחֵלֶב אֲשֶׁר עַל־הַקֶּרֶב:

ט וְאֵת שְׁתֵּי הַכְּלָיֹת וְאֶת־הַחֵלֶב אֲשֶׁר
עֲלֵיהֶן אֲשֶׁר עַל־הַכְּסָלִים וְאֶת־הַיֹּתֶרֶת
עַל־הַכָּבֵד עַל־הַכְּלָיוֹת יְסִירֶנָּה:

י כַּאֲשֶׁר יוּרַם מִשּׁוֹר זֶבַח הַשְּׁלָמִים
וְהִקְטִירָם הַכֹּהֵן עַל מִזְבַּח הָעֹלָה:

יא וְאֶת־עוֹר הַפָּר וְאֶת־כָּל־בְּשָׂרוֹ עַל־
רֹאשׁוֹ וְעַל־כְּרָעָיו וְקִרְבּוֹ וּפִרְשׁוֹ:

יב וְהוֹצִיא אֶת־כָּל־הַפָּר אֶל־מִחוּץ לַמַּחֲנֶה
אֶל־מָקוֹם טָהוֹר אֶל־שֶׁפֶךְ הַדֶּשֶׁן וְשָׂרַף
אֹתוֹ עַל־עֵצִים בָּאֵשׁ עַל־שֶׁפֶךְ הַדֶּשֶׁן
יִשָּׂרֵף:

יג וְאִם כָּל־עֲדַת יִשְׂרָאֵל יִשְׁגּוּ וְנֶעְלַם
דָּבָר מֵעֵינֵי הַקָּהָל וְעָשׂוּ אַחַת מִכָּל־
מִצְוֹת יְהוָה אֲשֶׁר לֹא־תֵעָשֶׂינָה
וְאָשֵׁמוּ:

*v'-IM kol a-DAT yis-ra-AYL yish-GU v'-ne-e-LAM da-VAR
may-ay-NAY ha-ka-HAL v'-a-SU a-KHAT mi-kol mitz-VOT
a-do-NAI a-SHER lo tay-a-SE-na v'-a-SHAY-mu*

**4:13 If it is the whole community of *Yisrael* that
has erred** As opposed to the previous three
chapters which discuss the voluntary offerings
meant for spiritual elevation, chapter four discusses sin-
offerings, required to atone for unintentional transgressions, and lists different scenarios in which a person might

Leviticus

¹⁴ when the sin through which they incurred guilt becomes known, the congregation shall offer a bull of the herd as a sin offering, and bring it before the Tent of Meeting.

¹⁵ The elders of the community shall lay their hands upon the head of the bull before *Hashem*, and the bull shall be slaughtered before *Hashem*.

¹⁶ The anointed *Kohen* shall bring some of the blood of the bull into the Tent of Meeting,

¹⁷ and the *Kohen* shall dip his finger in the blood and sprinkle of it seven times before *Hashem*, in front of the curtain.

¹⁸ Some of the blood he shall put on the horns of the *Mizbayach* which is before *Hashem* in the Tent of Meeting, and all the rest of the blood he shall pour out at the base of the *Mizbayach* of burnt offering, which is at the entrance of the Tent of Meeting.

¹⁹ He shall remove all its fat from it and turn it into smoke on the *Mizbayach*.

²⁰ He shall do with this bull just as is done with the [*Kohen*'s] bull of sin offering; he shall do the same with it. Thus the *Kohen* shall make expiation for them, and they shall be forgiven.

²¹ He shall carry the bull outside the camp and burn it as he burned the first bull; it is the sin offering of the congregation.

²² In case it is a chieftain who incurs guilt by doing unwittingly any of the things which by the commandment of *Hashem* his God ought not to be done, and he realizes his guilt

²³ or the sin of which he is guilty is brought to his knowledge – he shall bring as his offering a male goat without blemish.

יד וְנוֹדְעָה הַחַטָּאת אֲשֶׁר חָטְאוּ עָלֶיהָ וְהִקְרִיבוּ הַקָּהָל פַּר בֶּן־בָּקָר לְחַטָּאת וְהֵבִיאוּ אֹתוֹ לִפְנֵי אֹהֶל מוֹעֵד:

טו וְסָמְכוּ זִקְנֵי הָעֵדָה אֶת־יְדֵיהֶם עַל־רֹאשׁ הַפָּר לִפְנֵי יְהֹוָה וְשָׁחַט אֶת־הַפָּר לִפְנֵי יְהֹוָה:

טז וְהֵבִיא הַכֹּהֵן הַמָּשִׁיחַ מִדַּם הַפָּר אֶל־אֹהֶל מוֹעֵד:

יז וְטָבַל הַכֹּהֵן אֶצְבָּעוֹ מִן־הַדָּם וְהִזָּה שֶׁבַע פְּעָמִים לִפְנֵי יְהֹוָה אֵת פְּנֵי הַפָּרֹכֶת:

יח וּמִן־הַדָּם יִתֵּן עַל־קַרְנֹת הַמִּזְבֵּחַ אֲשֶׁר לִפְנֵי יְהֹוָה אֲשֶׁר בְּאֹהֶל מוֹעֵד וְאֵת כָּל־הַדָּם יִשְׁפֹּךְ אֶל־יְסוֹד מִזְבַּח הָעֹלָה אֲשֶׁר־פֶּתַח אֹהֶל מוֹעֵד:

יט וְאֵת כָּל־חֶלְבּוֹ יָרִים מִמֶּנּוּ וְהִקְטִיר הַמִּזְבֵּחָה:

כ וְעָשָׂה לַפָּר כַּאֲשֶׁר עָשָׂה לְפַר הַחַטָּאת כֵּן יַעֲשֶׂה־לּוֹ וְכִפֶּר עֲלֵהֶם הַכֹּהֵן וְנִסְלַח לָהֶם:

כא וְהוֹצִיא אֶת־הַפָּר אֶל־מִחוּץ לַמַּחֲנֶה וְשָׂרַף אֹתוֹ כַּאֲשֶׁר שָׂרַף אֵת הַפָּר הָרִאשׁוֹן חַטַּאת הַקָּהָל הוּא:

כב אֲשֶׁר נָשִׂיא יֶחֱטָא וְעָשָׂה אַחַת מִכָּל־מִצְוֹת יְהֹוָה אֱלֹהָיו אֲשֶׁר לֹא־תֵעָשֶׂינָה בִּשְׁגָגָה וְאָשֵׁם:

כג אוֹ־הוֹדַע אֵלָיו חַטָּאתוֹ אֲשֶׁר חָטָא בָּהּ וְהֵבִיא אֶת־קָרְבָּנוֹ שְׂעִיר עִזִּים זָכָר תָּמִים:

אִם
כִּי

need to bring such an offering. The *Kli Yakar* points out that when introducing the offering brought to atone for a sin committed by the entire congregation, meaning the nation as a whole, the verse uses the Hebrew word *im* (אִם), 'if,' implying that such a situation is somewhat unlikely to occur. However, when referring to

Joining together with the Israeli flag

the offering brought by an individual, the Bible (verse 1) uses the word *kee* (כִּי), which can be translated as 'when,' suggesting that an individual person is much more likely to make a mistake. This underscores the fact that the Children of Israel are significantly strengthened when they join together as a people.

24 He shall lay his hand upon the goat's head, and it shall be slaughtered at the spot where the burnt offering is slaughtered before *Hashem*; it is a sin offering.

כד וְסָמַךְ יָדוֹ עַל־רֹאשׁ הַשָּׂעִיר וְשָׁחַט אֹתוֹ בִּמְקוֹם אֲשֶׁר־יִשְׁחַט אֶת־הָעֹלָה לִפְנֵי יְהֹוָה חַטָּאת הוּא:

25 The *Kohen* shall take with his finger some of the blood of the sin offering and put it on the horns of the *Mizbayach* of burnt offering; and the rest of its blood he shall pour out at the base of the *Mizbayach* of burnt offering.

כה וְלָקַח הַכֹּהֵן מִדַּם הַחַטָּאת בְּאֶצְבָּעוֹ וְנָתַן עַל־קַרְנֹת מִזְבַּח הָעֹלָה וְאֶת־דָּמוֹ יִשְׁפֹּךְ אֶל־יְסוֹד מִזְבַּח הָעֹלָה:

26 All its fat he shall turn into smoke on the *Mizbayach*, like the fat of the sacrifice of well-being. Thus the *Kohen* shall make expiation on his behalf for his sin, and he shall be forgiven.

כו וְאֶת־כָּל־חֶלְבּוֹ יַקְטִיר הַמִּזְבֵּחָה כְּחֵלֶב זֶבַח הַשְּׁלָמִים וְכִפֶּר עָלָיו הַכֹּהֵן מֵחַטָּאתוֹ וְנִסְלַח לוֹ:

27 If any person from among the populace unwittingly incurs guilt by doing any of the things which by *Hashem*'s commandments ought not to be done, and he realizes his guilt

כז וְאִם־נֶפֶשׁ אַחַת תֶּחֱטָא בִשְׁגָגָה מֵעַם הָאָרֶץ בַּעֲשֹׂתָהּ אַחַת מִמִּצְוֺת יְהֹוָה אֲשֶׁר לֹא־תֵעָשֶׂינָה וְאָשֵׁם:

28 or the sin of which he is guilty is brought to his knowledge – he shall bring a female goat without blemish as his offering for the sin of which he is guilty.

כח אוֹ הוֹדַע אֵלָיו חַטָּאתוֹ אֲשֶׁר חָטָא וְהֵבִיא קָרְבָּנוֹ שְׂעִירַת עִזִּים תְּמִימָה נְקֵבָה עַל־חַטָּאתוֹ אֲשֶׁר חָטָא:

29 He shall lay his hand upon the head of the sin offering, and the sin offering shall be slaughtered at the place of the burnt offering.

כט וְסָמַךְ אֶת־יָדוֹ עַל רֹאשׁ הַחַטָּאת וְשָׁחַט אֶת־הַחַטָּאת בִּמְקוֹם הָעֹלָה:

30 The *Kohen* shall take with his finger some of its blood and put it on the horns of the *Mizbayach* of burnt offering; and all the rest of its blood he shall pour out at the base of the *Mizbayach*.

ל וְלָקַח הַכֹּהֵן מִדָּמָהּ בְּאֶצְבָּעוֹ וְנָתַן עַל־קַרְנֹת מִזְבַּח הָעֹלָה וְאֶת־כָּל־דָּמָהּ יִשְׁפֹּךְ אֶל־יְסוֹד הַמִּזְבֵּחַ:

31 He shall remove all its fat, just as the fat is removed from the sacrifice of well-being; and the *Kohen* shall turn it into smoke on the *Mizbayach*, for a pleasing odor to *Hashem*. Thus the *Kohen* shall make expiation for him, and he shall be forgiven.

לא וְאֶת־כָּל־חֶלְבָּהּ יָסִיר כַּאֲשֶׁר הוּסַר חֵלֶב מֵעַל זֶבַח הַשְּׁלָמִים וְהִקְטִיר הַכֹּהֵן הַמִּזְבֵּחָה לְרֵיחַ נִיחֹחַ לַיהֹוָה וְכִפֶּר עָלָיו הַכֹּהֵן וְנִסְלַח לוֹ:

32 If the offering he brings as a sin offering is a sheep, he shall bring a female without blemish.

לב וְאִם־כֶּבֶשׂ יָבִיא קָרְבָּנוֹ לְחַטָּאת נְקֵבָה תְמִימָה יְבִיאֶנָּה:

33 He shall lay his hand upon the head of the sin offering, and it shall be slaughtered as a sin offering at the spot where the burnt offering is slaughtered.

לג וְסָמַךְ אֶת־יָדוֹ עַל רֹאשׁ הַחַטָּאת וְשָׁחַט אֹתָהּ לְחַטָּאת בִּמְקוֹם אֲשֶׁר יִשְׁחַט אֶת־הָעֹלָה:

34 The *Kohen* shall take with his finger some of the blood of the sin offering and put it on the horns of the *Mizbayach* of burnt offering, and all the rest of its blood he shall pour out at the base of the *Mizbayach*.

לד וְלָקַח הַכֹּהֵן מִדַּם הַחַטָּאת בְּאֶצְבָּעוֹ וְנָתַן עַל־קַרְנֹת מִזְבַּח הָעֹלָה וְאֶת־כָּל־דָּמָהּ יִשְׁפֹּךְ אֶל־יְסוֹד הַמִּזְבֵּחַ:

35 And all its fat he shall remove just as the fat of the sheep of the sacrifice of well-being is removed; and this the *Kohen* shall turn into smoke on the *Mizbayach*, over *Hashem*'s offering by fire. Thus the *Kohen* shall make expiation on his behalf for the sin of which he is guilty, and he shall be forgiven.

לה וְאֶת־כָּל־חֶלְבָּהּ יָסִיר כַּאֲשֶׁר יוּסַר חֵלֶב־הַכֶּשֶׂב מִזֶּבַח הַשְּׁלָמִים וְהִקְטִיר הַכֹּהֵן אֹתָם הַמִּזְבֵּחָה עַל אִשֵּׁי יְהֹוָה וְכִפֶּר עָלָיו הַכֹּהֵן עַל־חַטָּאתוֹ אֲשֶׁר־חָטָא וְנִסְלַח לוֹ:

5 ¹ If a person incurs guilt – When he has heard a public imprecation and – although able to testify as one who has either seen or learned of the matter – he does not give information, so that he is subject to punishment;

ה א וְנֶפֶשׁ כִּי־תֶחֱטָא וְשָׁמְעָה קוֹל אָלָה וְהוּא עֵד אוֹ רָאָה אוֹ יָדָע אִם־לוֹא יַגִּיד וְנָשָׂא עֲוֹנוֹ:

² Or when a person touches any unclean thing – be it the carcass of an unclean beast or the carcass of unclean cattle or the carcass of an unclean creeping thing – and the fact has escaped him, and then, being unclean, he realizes his guilt;

ב אוֹ נֶפֶשׁ אֲשֶׁר תִּגַּע בְּכָל־דָּבָר טָמֵא אוֹ בְנִבְלַת חַיָּה טְמֵאָה אוֹ בְּנִבְלַת בְּהֵמָה טְמֵאָה אוֹ בְּנִבְלַת שֶׁרֶץ טָמֵא וְנֶעְלַם מִמֶּנּוּ וְהוּא טָמֵא וְאָשֵׁם:

³ Or when he touches human uncleanness – any such uncleanness whereby one becomes unclean – and, though he has known it, the fact has escaped him, but later he realizes his guilt;

ג אוֹ כִי יִגַּע בְּטֻמְאַת אָדָם לְכֹל טֻמְאָתוֹ אֲשֶׁר יִטְמָא בָּהּ וְנֶעְלַם מִמֶּנּוּ וְהוּא יָדַע וְאָשֵׁם:

⁴ Or when a person utters an oath to bad or good purpose – whatever a man may utter in an oath – and, though he has known it, the fact has escaped him, but later he realizes his guilt in any of these matters –

ד אוֹ נֶפֶשׁ כִּי תִשָּׁבַע לְבַטֵּא בִשְׂפָתַיִם לְהָרַע אוֹ לְהֵיטִיב לְכֹל אֲשֶׁר יְבַטֵּא הָאָדָם בִּשְׁבֻעָה וְנֶעְלַם מִמֶּנּוּ וְהוּא־יָדַע וְאָשֵׁם לְאַחַת מֵאֵלֶּה:

⁵ when he realizes his guilt in any of these matters, he shall confess that wherein he has sinned.

ה וְהָיָה כִי־יֶאְשַׁם לְאַחַת מֵאֵלֶּה וְהִתְוַדָּה אֲשֶׁר חָטָא עָלֶיהָ:

⁶ And he shall bring as his penalty to *Hashem*, for the sin of which he is guilty, a female from the flock, sheep or goat, as a sin offering; and the *Kohen* shall make expiation on his behalf for his sin.

ו וְהֵבִיא אֶת־אֲשָׁמוֹ לַיהֹוָה עַל חַטָּאתוֹ אֲשֶׁר חָטָא נְקֵבָה מִן־הַצֹּאן כִּשְׂבָּה אוֹ־שְׂעִירַת עִזִּים לְחַטָּאת וְכִפֶּר עָלָיו הַכֹּהֵן מֵחַטָּאתוֹ:

⁷ But if his means do not suffice for a sheep, he shall bring to *Hashem*, as his penalty for that of which he is guilty, two turtledoves or two pigeons, one for a sin offering and the other for a burnt offering.

ז וְאִם־לֹא תַגִּיעַ יָדוֹ דֵּי שֶׂה וְהֵבִיא אֶת־אֲשָׁמוֹ אֲשֶׁר חָטָא שְׁתֵּי תֹרִים אוֹ־שְׁנֵי בְנֵי־יוֹנָה לַיהֹוָה אֶחָד לְחַטָּאת וְאֶחָד לְעֹלָה:

⁸ He shall bring them to the *Kohen*, who shall offer first the one for the sin offering, pinching its head at the nape without severing it.

ח וְהֵבִיא אֹתָם אֶל־הַכֹּהֵן וְהִקְרִיב אֶת־אֲשֶׁר לַחַטָּאת רִאשׁוֹנָה וּמָלַק אֶת־רֹאשׁוֹ מִמּוּל עָרְפּוֹ וְלֹא יַבְדִּיל:

⁹ He shall sprinkle some of the blood of the sin offering on the side of the *Mizbayach*, and what remains of the blood shall be drained out at the base of the *Mizbayach*; it is a sin offering.

ט וְהִזָּה מִדַּם הַחַטָּאת עַל־קִיר הַמִּזְבֵּחַ וְהַנִּשְׁאָר בַּדָּם יִמָּצֵה אֶל־יְסוֹד הַמִּזְבֵּחַ חַטָּאת הוּא:

10 And the second he shall prepare as a burnt offering, according to regulation. Thus the *Kohen* shall make expiation on his behalf for the sin of which he is guilty, and he shall be forgiven.

י וְאֶת־הַשֵּׁנִי יַעֲשֶׂה עֹלָה כַּמִּשְׁפָּט וְכִפֶּר עָלָיו הַכֹּהֵן מֵחַטָּאתוֹ אֲשֶׁר־חָטָא וְנִסְלַח לוֹ:

11 And if his means do not suffice for two turtledoves or two pigeons, he shall bring as his offering for that of which he is guilty a tenth of an *efah* of choice flour for a sin offering; he shall not add oil to it or lay frankincense on it, for it is a sin offering.

יא וְאִם־לֹא תַשִּׂיג יָדוֹ לִשְׁתֵּי תֹרִים אוֹ לִשְׁנֵי בְנֵי־יוֹנָה וְהֵבִיא אֶת־קָרְבָּנוֹ אֲשֶׁר חָטָא עֲשִׂירִת הָאֵפָה סֹלֶת לְחַטָּאת לֹא־יָשִׂים עָלֶיהָ שֶׁמֶן וְלֹא־יִתֵּן עָלֶיהָ לְבֹנָה כִּי חַטָּאת הִיא:

12 He shall bring it to the *Kohen*, and the *Kohen* shall scoop out of it a handful as a token portion of it and turn it into smoke on the *Mizbayach*, with *Hashem*'s offerings by fire; it is a sin offering.

יב וֶהֱבִיאָהּ אֶל־הַכֹּהֵן וְקָמַץ הַכֹּהֵן מִמֶּנָּה מְלוֹא קֻמְצוֹ אֶת־אַזְכָּרָתָהּ וְהִקְטִיר הַמִּזְבֵּחָה עַל אִשֵּׁי יְהֹוָה חַטָּאת הוּא:

13 Thus the *Kohen* shall make expiation on his behalf for whichever of these sins he is guilty, and he shall be forgiven. It shall belong to the *Kohen*, like the meal offering.

יג וְכִפֶּר עָלָיו הַכֹּהֵן עַל־חַטָּאתוֹ אֲשֶׁר־חָטָא מֵאַחַת מֵאֵלֶּה וְנִסְלַח לוֹ וְהָיְתָה לַכֹּהֵן כַּמִּנְחָה:

14 And *Hashem* spoke to *Moshe*, saying:

יד וַיְדַבֵּר יְהֹוָה אֶל־מֹשֶׁה לֵּאמֹר:

15 When a person commits a trespass, being unwittingly remiss about any of *Hashem*'s sacred things, he shall bring as his penalty to *Hashem* a ram without blemish from the flock, convertible into payment in silver by the sanctuary weight, as a guilt offering.

טו נֶפֶשׁ כִּי־תִמְעֹל מַעַל וְחָטְאָה בִּשְׁגָגָה מִקָּדְשֵׁי יְהֹוָה וְהֵבִיא אֶת־אֲשָׁמוֹ לַיהֹוָה אַיִל תָּמִים מִן־הַצֹּאן בְּעֶרְכְּךָ כֶּסֶף־שְׁקָלִים בְּשֶׁקֶל־הַקֹּדֶשׁ לְאָשָׁם:

NE-fesh kee tim-OL MA-al v'-kha-t'AH bish-ga-GAH mi-kod-SHAY a-do-NAI v'-hay-VEE et a-sha-MO la-do-NAI A-yil ta-MEEM min ha-TZON b'-er-k'KHA KE-sef sh'-ka-LEEM b'-SHE-kel ha-KO-desh l'-a-SHAM

16 He shall make restitution for that wherein he was remiss about the sacred things, and he shall add a fifth part to it and give it to the *Kohen*. The *Kohen* shall make expiation on his behalf with the ram of the guilt offering, and he shall be forgiven.

טז וְאֵת אֲשֶׁר חָטָא מִן־הַקֹּדֶשׁ יְשַׁלֵּם וְאֶת־חֲמִישִׁתוֹ יוֹסֵף עָלָיו וְנָתַן אֹתוֹ לַכֹּהֵן וְהַכֹּהֵן יְכַפֵּר עָלָיו בְּאֵיל הָאָשָׁם וְנִסְלַח לוֹ:

17 And when a person, without knowing it, sins in regard to any of *Hashem*'s commandments about things not to be done, and then realizes his guilt, he shall be subject to punishment.

יז וְאִם־נֶפֶשׁ כִּי תֶחֱטָא וְעָשְׂתָה אַחַת מִכָּל־מִצְוֹת יְהֹוָה אֲשֶׁר לֹא תֵעָשֶׂינָה וְלֹא־יָדַע וְאָשֵׁם וְנָשָׂא עֲוֹנוֹ:

5:15 When a person commits a trespass Chapter five contains a list of sins for which one is required to bring a guilt-offering. Among those listed is the transgression of benefiting from an object belonging to the *Beit Hamikdash*. This refers to someone who eats or derives other personal gain from food or property that belongs to the Temple, including its wood or stones, or who improperly eats part of a sacrifice. The verse calls this sin 'a trespass', an improper use of something holy. We must be careful to honor the sanctity, not only of the *Beit Hamikdash*, but of the entire Holy Land, and not to misuse any part of it.

Stones that were once part of the outer wall of the second *Beit Hamikdash*

18 He shall bring to the *Kohen* a ram without blemish from the flock, or the equivalent, as a guilt offering. The *Kohen* shall make expiation on his behalf for the error that he committed unwittingly, and he shall be forgiven.

יח וְהֵבִיא אַיִל תָּמִים מִן־הַצֹּאן בְּעֶרְכְּךָ לְאָשָׁם אֶל־הַכֹּהֵן וְכִפֶּר עָלָיו הַכֹּהֵן עַל שִׁגְגָתוֹ אֲשֶׁר־שָׁגַג וְהוּא לֹא־יָדַע וְנִסְלַח לוֹ:

19 It is a guilt offering; he has incurred guilt before *Hashem*.

יט אָשָׁם הוּא אָשֹׁם אָשַׁם לַיהוָה:

20 *Hashem* spoke to *Moshe*, saying:

כ וַיְדַבֵּר יְהוָה אֶל־מֹשֶׁה לֵּאמֹר:

21 When a person sins and commits a trespass against *Hashem* by dealing deceitfully with his fellow in the matter of a deposit or a pledge, or through robbery, or by defrauding his fellow,

כא נֶפֶשׁ כִּי תֶחֱטָא וּמָעֲלָה מַעַל בַּיהוָה וְכִחֵשׁ בַּעֲמִיתוֹ בְּפִקָּדוֹן אוֹ־בִתְשׂוּמֶת יָד אוֹ בְגָזֵל אוֹ עָשַׁק אֶת־עֲמִיתוֹ:

22 or by finding something lost and lying about it; if he swears falsely regarding any one of the various things that one may do and sin thereby

כב אוֹ־מָצָא אֲבֵדָה וְכִחֶשׁ בָּהּ וְנִשְׁבַּע עַל־שָׁקֶר עַל־אַחַת מִכֹּל אֲשֶׁר־יַעֲשֶׂה הָאָדָם לַחֲטֹא בָהֵנָּה:

23 when one has thus sinned and, realizing his guilt, would restore that which he got through robbery or fraud, or the deposit that was entrusted to him, or the lost thing that he found,

כג וְהָיָה כִּי־יֶחֱטָא וְאָשֵׁם וְהֵשִׁיב אֶת־הַגְּזֵלָה אֲשֶׁר גָּזָל אוֹ אֶת־הָעֹשֶׁק אֲשֶׁר עָשָׁק אוֹ אֶת־הַפִּקָּדוֹן אֲשֶׁר הָפְקַד אִתּוֹ אוֹ אֶת־הָאֲבֵדָה אֲשֶׁר מָצָא:

24 or anything else about which he swore falsely, he shall repay the principal amount and add a fifth part to it. He shall pay it to its owner when he realizes his guilt.

כד אוֹ מִכֹּל אֲשֶׁר־יִשָּׁבַע עָלָיו לַשֶּׁקֶר וְשִׁלַּם אֹתוֹ בְּרֹאשׁוֹ וַחֲמִשִׁתָיו יֹסֵף עָלָיו לַאֲשֶׁר הוּא לוֹ יִתְּנֶנּוּ בְּיוֹם אַשְׁמָתוֹ:

25 Then he shall bring to the *Kohen*, as his penalty to *Hashem*, a ram without blemish from the flock, or the equivalent, as a guilt offering.

כה וְאֶת־אֲשָׁמוֹ יָבִיא לַיהוָה אַיִל תָּמִים מִן־הַצֹּאן בְּעֶרְכְּךָ לְאָשָׁם אֶל־הַכֹּהֵן:

26 The *Kohen* shall make expiation on his behalf before *Hashem*, and he shall be forgiven for whatever he may have done to draw blame thereby.

כו וְכִפֶּר עָלָיו הַכֹּהֵן לִפְנֵי יְהוָה וְנִסְלַח לוֹ עַל־אַחַת מִכֹּל אֲשֶׁר־יַעֲשֶׂה לְאַשְׁמָה בָהּ:

6 ¹ *Hashem* spoke to *Moshe*, saying:

ו א וַיְדַבֵּר יְהוָה אֶל־מֹשֶׁה לֵּאמֹר:

2 Command *Aharon* and his sons thus: This is the ritual of the burnt offering: The burnt offering itself shall remain where it is burned upon the *Mizbayach* all night until morning, while the fire on the *Mizbayach* is kept going on it.

ב צַו אֶת־אַהֲרֹן וְאֶת־בָּנָיו לֵאמֹר זֹאת תּוֹרַת הָעֹלָה הִוא הָעֹלָה עַל מוֹקְדָה עַל־הַמִּזְבֵּחַ כָּל־הַלַּיְלָה עַד־הַבֹּקֶר וְאֵשׁ הַמִּזְבֵּחַ תּוּקַד בּוֹ:

3 The *Kohen* shall dress in linen raiment, with linen breeches next to his body; and he shall take up the ashes to which the fire has reduced the burnt offering on the *Mizbayach* and place them beside the *Mizbayach*.

ג וְלָבַשׁ הַכֹּהֵן מִדּוֹ בַד וּמִכְנְסֵי־בַד יִלְבַּשׁ עַל־בְּשָׂרוֹ וְהֵרִים אֶת־הַדֶּשֶׁן אֲשֶׁר תֹּאכַל הָאֵשׁ אֶת־הָעֹלָה עַל־הַמִּזְבֵּחַ וְשָׂמוֹ אֵצֶל הַמִּזְבֵּחַ:

4 He shall then take off his vestments and put on other vestments, and carry the ashes outside the camp to a clean place.

ד וּפָשַׁט אֶת־בְּגָדָיו וְלָבַשׁ בְּגָדִים אֲחֵרִים וְהוֹצִיא אֶת־הַדֶּשֶׁן אֶל־מִחוּץ לַמַּחֲנֶה אֶל־מָקוֹם טָהוֹר:

5 The fire on the *Mizbayach* shall be kept burning, not to go out: every morning the *Kohen* shall feed wood to it, lay out the burnt offering on it, and turn into smoke the fat parts of the offerings of well-being.

ה וְהָאֵשׁ עַל־הַמִּזְבֵּחַ תּוּקַד־בּוֹ לֹא תִכְבֶּה וּבִעֵר עָלֶיהָ הַכֹּהֵן עֵצִים בַּבֹּקֶר בַּבֹּקֶר וְעָרַךְ עָלֶיהָ הָעֹלָה וְהִקְטִיר עָלֶיהָ חֶלְבֵי הַשְּׁלָמִים:

v'-ha-AYSH al ha-miz-BAY-akh tu-kad BO LO tikh-BEH u-vi-AYR a-LE-ha ha-ko-HAYN ay-TZEEM ba-BO-ker ba-BO-ker v'-a-RAKH a-LE-ha ha-o-LAH v'-hik-TEER a-LE-ha khel-VAY ha-sh'-la-MEEM

6 A perpetual fire shall be kept burning on the *Mizbayach*, not to go out.

ו אֵשׁ תָּמִיד תּוּקַד עַל־הַמִּזְבֵּחַ לֹא תִכְבֶּה:

7 And this is the ritual of the meal offering: *Aharon's* sons shall present it before *Hashem*, in front of the *Mizbayach*.

ז וְזֹאת תּוֹרַת הַמִּנְחָה הַקְרֵב אֹתָהּ בְּנֵי־אַהֲרֹן לִפְנֵי יְהוָֹה אֶל־פְּנֵי הַמִּזְבֵּחַ:

8 A handful of the choice flour and oil of the meal offering shall be taken from it, with all the frankincense that is on the meal offering, and this token portion shall be turned into smoke on the *Mizbayach* as a pleasing odor to *Hashem*.

ח וְהֵרִים מִמֶּנּוּ בְּקֻמְצוֹ מִסֹּלֶת הַמִּנְחָה וּמִשַּׁמְנָהּ וְאֵת כָּל־הַלְּבֹנָה אֲשֶׁר עַל־הַמִּנְחָה וְהִקְטִיר הַמִּזְבֵּחַ רֵיחַ נִיחֹחַ אַזְכָּרָתָהּ לַיהוָֹה:

9 What is left of it shall be eaten by *Aharon* and his sons; it shall be eaten as unleavened cakes, in the sacred precinct; they shall eat it in the enclosure of the Tent of Meeting.

ט וְהַנּוֹתֶרֶת מִמֶּנָּה יֹאכְלוּ אַהֲרֹן וּבָנָיו מַצּוֹת תֵּאָכֵל בְּמָקוֹם קָדֹשׁ בַּחֲצַר אֹהֶל־מוֹעֵד יֹאכְלוּהָ:

10 It shall not be baked with leaven; I have given it as their portion from My offerings by fire; it is most holy, like the sin offering and the guilt offering.

י לֹא תֵאָפֶה חָמֵץ חֶלְקָם נָתַתִּי אֹתָהּ מֵאִשָּׁי קֹדֶשׁ קָדָשִׁים הִוא כַּחַטָּאת וְכָאָשָׁם:

11 Only the males among *Aharon's* descendants may eat of it, as their due for all time throughout the ages from *Hashem's* offerings by fire. Anything that touches these shall become holy.

יא כָּל־זָכָר בִּבְנֵי אַהֲרֹן יֹאכְלֶנָּה חָק־עוֹלָם לְדֹרֹתֵיכֶם מֵאִשֵּׁי יְהוָֹה כֹּל אֲשֶׁר־יִגַּע בָּהֶם יִקְדָּשׁ:

12 *Hashem* spoke to *Moshe*, saying:

יב וַיְדַבֵּר יְהוָֹה אֶל־מֹשֶׁה לֵּאמֹר:

6:5 The fire on the *Mizbayach* shall be kept burning The fire on the altar burns continuously, and is never extinguished. Although the priests were commanded to add two pieces of wood to the fire twice daily, the fire on the *Mizbayach* remained burning miraculously, lit by a heavenly fire. The Sages (*Ethics of the Fathers* 5:5) list this as one of ten miracles experienced each day in the *Beit Hamikdash*. The continual flame serves as a reminder of *Hashem's* constant presence among the People of Israel. While there is no longer a Temple nor an Altar, God's everlasting presence is signified today by hanging an eternal light above the ark in every synagogue, a reminder of the eternal flame first mentioned in this verse.

Eternal lamp above the ark, *Petach Tikva*

12

13 This is the offering that *Aharon* and his sons shall offer to *Hashem* on the occasion of his anointment: a tenth of an *efah* of choice flour as a regular meal offering, half of it in the morning and half of it in the evening,

יג זֶה קָרְבַּן אַהֲרֹן וּבָנָיו אֲשֶׁר־יַקְרִיבוּ לַיהוָה בְּיוֹם הִמָּשַׁח אֹתוֹ עֲשִׂירִת הָאֵפָה סֹלֶת מִנְחָה תָּמִיד מַחֲצִיתָהּ בַּבֹּקֶר וּמַחֲצִיתָהּ בָּעָרֶב:

14 shall be prepared with oil on a griddle. You shall bring it well soaked, and offer it as a meal offering of baked slices, of pleasing odor to *Hashem*.

יד עַל־מַחֲבַת בַּשֶּׁמֶן תֵּעָשֶׂה מֻרְבֶּכֶת תְּבִיאֶנָּה תֻּפִינֵי מִנְחַת פִּתִּים תַּקְרִיב רֵיחַ־נִיחֹחַ לַיהוָה:

15 And so shall the *Kohen*, anointed from among his sons to succeed him, prepare it; it is *Hashem*'s – a law for all time – to be turned entirely into smoke.

טו וְהַכֹּהֵן הַמָּשִׁיחַ תַּחְתָּיו מִבָּנָיו יַעֲשֶׂה אֹתָהּ חָק־עוֹלָם לַיהוָה כָּלִיל תָּקְטָר:

16 So, too, every meal offering of a *Kohen* shall be a whole offering: it shall not be eaten.

טז וְכָל־מִנְחַת כֹּהֵן כָּלִיל תִּהְיֶה לֹא תֵאָכֵל:

17 *Hashem* spoke to *Moshe*, saying:

יז וַיְדַבֵּר יְהוָה אֶל־מֹשֶׁה לֵּאמֹר:

18 Speak to *Aharon* and his sons thus: This is the ritual of the sin offering: the sin offering shall be slaughtered before *Hashem*, at the spot where the burnt offering is slaughtered: it is most holy.

יח דַּבֵּר אֶל־אַהֲרֹן וְאֶל־בָּנָיו לֵאמֹר זֹאת תּוֹרַת הַחַטָּאת בִּמְקוֹם אֲשֶׁר תִּשָּׁחֵט הָעֹלָה תִּשָּׁחֵט הַחַטָּאת לִפְנֵי יְהוָה קֹדֶשׁ קָדָשִׁים הִוא:

19 The *Kohen* who offers it as a sin offering shall eat of it; it shall be eaten in the sacred precinct, in the enclosure of the Tent of Meeting.

יט הַכֹּהֵן הַמְחַטֵּא אֹתָהּ יֹאכְלֶנָּה בְּמָקוֹם קָדֹשׁ תֵּאָכֵל בַּחֲצַר אֹהֶל מוֹעֵד:

20 Anything that touches its flesh shall become holy; and if any of its blood is spattered upon a garment, you shall wash the bespattered part in the sacred precinct.

כ כֹּל אֲשֶׁר־יִגַּע בִּבְשָׂרָהּ יִקְדָּשׁ וַאֲשֶׁר יִזֶּה מִדָּמָהּ עַל־הַבֶּגֶד אֲשֶׁר יִזֶּה עָלֶיהָ תְּכַבֵּס בְּמָקוֹם קָדֹשׁ:

21 An earthen vessel in which it was boiled shall be broken; if it was boiled in a copper vessel, [the vessel] shall be scoured and rinsed with water.

כא וּכְלִי־חֶרֶשׂ אֲשֶׁר תְּבֻשַּׁל־בּוֹ יִשָּׁבֵר וְאִם־בִּכְלִי נְחֹשֶׁת בֻּשָּׁלָה וּמֹרַק וְשֻׁטַּף בַּמָּיִם:

22 Only the males in the priestly line may eat of it: it is most holy.

כב כָּל־זָכָר בַּכֹּהֲנִים יֹאכַל אֹתָהּ קֹדֶשׁ קָדָשִׁים הִוא:

23 But no sin offering may be eaten from which any blood is brought into the Tent of Meeting for expiation in the sanctuary; any such shall be consumed in fire.

כג וְכָל־חַטָּאת אֲשֶׁר יוּבָא מִדָּמָהּ אֶל־אֹהֶל מוֹעֵד לְכַפֵּר בַּקֹּדֶשׁ לֹא תֵאָכֵל בָּאֵשׁ תִּשָּׂרֵף:

7 1 This is the ritual of the guilt offering: it is most holy.

ז א וְזֹאת תּוֹרַת הָאָשָׁם קֹדֶשׁ קָדָשִׁים הוּא:

2 The guilt offering shall be slaughtered at the spot where the burnt offering is slaughtered, and the blood shall be dashed on all sides of the *Mizbayach*.

ב בִּמְקוֹם אֲשֶׁר יִשְׁחֲטוּ אֶת־הָעֹלָה יִשְׁחֲטוּ אֶת־הָאָשָׁם וְאֶת־דָּמוֹ יִזְרֹק עַל־הַמִּזְבֵּחַ סָבִיב:

3 All its fat shall be offered: the broad tail; the fat that covers the entrails;

ג וְאֵת כָּל־חֶלְבּוֹ יַקְרִיב מִמֶּנּוּ אֵת הָאַלְיָה וְאֶת־הַחֵלֶב הַמְכַסֶּה אֶת־הַקֶּרֶב:

⁴ the two kidneys and the fat that is on them at the loins; and the protuberance on the liver, which shall be removed with the kidneys.

ד וְאֵת שְׁתֵּי הַכְּלָיֹת וְאֶת־הַחֵלֶב אֲשֶׁר עֲלֵיהֶן אֲשֶׁר עַל־הַכְּסָלִים וְאֶת־הַיֹּתֶרֶת עַל־הַכָּבֵד עַל־הַכְּלָיֹת יְסִירֶנָּה:

⁵ The *Kohen* shall turn them into smoke on the *Mizbayach* as an offering by fire to *Hashem*; it is a guilt offering.

ה וְהִקְטִיר אֹתָם הַכֹּהֵן הַמִּזְבֵּחָה אִשֶּׁה לַיהֹוָה אָשָׁם הוּא:

⁶ Only the males in the priestly line may eat of it; it shall be eaten in the sacred precinct: it is most holy.

ו כָּל־זָכָר בַּכֹּהֲנִים יֹאכְלֶנּוּ בְּמָקוֹם קָדֹשׁ יֵאָכֵל קֹדֶשׁ קָדָשִׁים הוּא:

⁷ The guilt offering is like the sin offering. The same rule applies to both: it shall belong to the *Kohen* who makes expiation thereby.

ז כַּחַטָּאת כָּאָשָׁם תּוֹרָה אַחַת לָהֶם הַכֹּהֵן אֲשֶׁר יְכַפֶּר־בּוֹ לוֹ יִהְיֶה:

⁸ So, too, the *Kohen* who offers a man's burnt offering shall keep the skin of the burnt offering that he offered.

ח וְהַכֹּהֵן הַמַּקְרִיב אֶת־עֹלַת אִישׁ עוֹר הָעֹלָה אֲשֶׁר הִקְרִיב לַכֹּהֵן לוֹ יִהְיֶה:

⁹ Further, any meal offering that is baked in an oven, and any that is prepared in a pan or on a griddle, shall belong to the *Kohen* who offers it.

ט וְכָל־מִנְחָה אֲשֶׁר תֵּאָפֶה בַּתַּנּוּר וְכָל־נַעֲשָׂה בַמַּרְחֶשֶׁת וְעַל־מַחֲבַת לַכֹּהֵן הַמַּקְרִיב אֹתָהּ לוֹ תִהְיֶה:

¹⁰ But every other meal offering, with oil mixed in or dry, shall go to the sons of *Aharon* all alike.

י וְכָל־מִנְחָה בְלוּלָה־בַשֶּׁמֶן וַחֲרֵבָה לְכָל־בְּנֵי אַהֲרֹן תִּהְיֶה אִישׁ כְּאָחִיו:

¹¹ This is the ritual of the sacrifice of well-being that one may offer to *Hashem*:

יא וְזֹאת תּוֹרַת זֶבַח הַשְּׁלָמִים אֲשֶׁר יַקְרִיב לַיהֹוָה:

¹² If he offers it for thanksgiving, he shall offer together with the sacrifice of thanksgiving unleavened cakes with oil mixed in, unleavened wafers spread with oil, and cakes of choice flour with oil mixed in, well soaked.

יב אִם עַל־תּוֹדָה יַקְרִיבֶנּוּ וְהִקְרִיב עַל־זֶבַח הַתּוֹדָה חַלּוֹת מַצּוֹת בְּלוּלֹת בַּשֶּׁמֶן וּרְקִיקֵי מַצּוֹת מְשֻׁחִים בַּשָּׁמֶן וְסֹלֶת מֻרְבֶּכֶת חַלֹּת בְּלוּלֹת בַּשָּׁמֶן:

IM al to-DAH yak-ree-VE-nu v'-hik-REEV al ZE-vakh ha-to-DAH kha-LOT ma-TZOT b'-lu-LOT ba-SHE-men u-r'-kee-KAY ma-TZOT m'-shu-KHIM ba-SHA-men v'-SO-let mur-BE-khet kha-LOT b'-lu-LOT ba-SHA-men

¹³ This offering, with cakes of leavened bread added, he shall offer along with his thanksgiving sacrifice of well-being.

יג עַל־חַלֹּת לֶחֶם חָמֵץ יַקְרִיב קָרְבָּנוֹ עַל־זֶבַח תּוֹדַת שְׁלָמָיו:

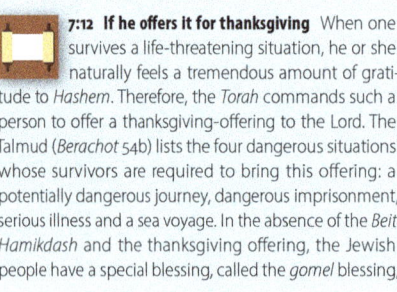

7:12 If he offers it for thanksgiving When one survives a life-threatening situation, he or she naturally feels a tremendous amount of gratitude to *Hashem*. Therefore, the *Torah* commands such a person to offer a thanksgiving-offering to the Lord. The Talmud (*Berachot* 54b) lists the four dangerous situations whose survivors are required to bring this offering: a potentially dangerous journey, dangerous imprisonment, serious illness and a sea voyage. In the absence of the *Beit Hamikdash* and the thanksgiving offering, the Jewish people have a special blessing, called the *gomel* blessing, recited to express thanks to *Hashem* when one overcomes a life-threatening situation. This idea of thanksgiving and being grateful is ingrained in the DNA of the Nation of Israel. In fact, the term *yehudi* (יהודי), 'Jew,' comes from the name of the tribe of *Yehuda*, which derives from the word *hoda'ah* (הודאה), 'thanksgiving.'

Ships on the sea in *Eilat*

14 Out of this he shall offer one of each kind as a gift to *Hashem*; it shall go to the *Kohen* who dashes the blood of the offering of well-being.

יד וְהִקְרִיב מִמֶּנּוּ אֶחָד מִכָּל־קָרְבָּן תְּרוּמָה לַיהֹוָה לַכֹּהֵן הַזֹּרֵק אֶת־דַּם הַשְּׁלָמִים לוֹ יִהְיֶה:

15 And the flesh of his thanksgiving sacrifice of well-being shall be eaten on the day that it is offered; none of it shall be set aside until morning.

טו וּבְשַׂר זֶבַח תּוֹדַת שְׁלָמָיו בְּיוֹם קָרְבָּנוֹ יֵאָכֵל לֹא־יַנִּיחַ מִמֶּנּוּ עַד־בֹּקֶר:

16 If, however, the sacrifice he offers is a votive or a freewill offering, it shall be eaten on the day that he offers his sacrifice, and what is left of it shall be eaten on the morrow.

טז וְאִם־נֶדֶר אוֹ נְדָבָה זֶבַח קָרְבָּנוֹ בְּיוֹם הַקְרִיבוֹ אֶת־זִבְחוֹ יֵאָכֵל וּמִמָּחֳרָת וְהַנּוֹתָר מִמֶּנּוּ יֵאָכֵל:

17 What is then left of the flesh of the sacrifice shall be consumed in fire on the third day.

יז וְהַנּוֹתָר מִבְּשַׂר הַזָּבַח בַּיּוֹם הַשְּׁלִישִׁי בָּאֵשׁ יִשָּׂרֵף:

18 If any of the flesh of his sacrifice of well-being is eaten on the third day, it shall not be acceptable; it shall not count for him who offered it. It is an offensive thing, and the person who eats of it shall bear his guilt.

יח וְאִם הֵאָכֹל יֵאָכֵל מִבְּשַׂר־זֶבַח שְׁלָמָיו בַּיּוֹם הַשְּׁלִישִׁי לֹא יֵרָצֶה הַמַּקְרִיב אֹתוֹ לֹא יֵחָשֵׁב לוֹ פִּגּוּל יִהְיֶה וְהַנֶּפֶשׁ הָאֹכֶלֶת מִמֶּנּוּ עֲוֹנָהּ תִּשָּׂא:

19 Flesh that touches anything unclean shall not be eaten; it shall be consumed in fire. As for other flesh, only he who is clean may eat such flesh.

יט וְהַבָּשָׂר אֲשֶׁר־יִגַּע בְּכָל־טָמֵא לֹא יֵאָכֵל בָּאֵשׁ יִשָּׂרֵף וְהַבָּשָׂר כָּל־טָהוֹר יֹאכַל בָּשָׂר:

20 But the person who, in a state of uncleanness, eats flesh from *Hashem*'s sacrifices of well-being, that person shall be cut off from his kin.

כ וְהַנֶּפֶשׁ אֲשֶׁר־תֹּאכַל בָּשָׂר מִזֶּבַח הַשְּׁלָמִים אֲשֶׁר לַיהֹוָה וְטֻמְאָתוֹ עָלָיו וְנִכְרְתָה הַנֶּפֶשׁ הַהִוא מֵעַמֶּיהָ:

21 When a person touches anything unclean, be it human uncleanness or an unclean animal or any unclean creature, and eats flesh from *Hashem*'s sacrifices of well-being, that person shall be cut off from his kin.

כא וְנֶפֶשׁ כִּי־תִגַּע בְּכָל־טָמֵא בְּטֻמְאַת אָדָם אוֹ בִּבְהֵמָה טְמֵאָה אוֹ בְּכָל־שֶׁקֶץ טָמֵא וְאָכַל מִבְּשַׂר־זֶבַח הַשְּׁלָמִים אֲשֶׁר לַיהֹוָה וְנִכְרְתָה הַנֶּפֶשׁ הַהִוא מֵעַמֶּיהָ:

22 And *Hashem* spoke to *Moshe*, saying:

כב וַיְדַבֵּר יְהֹוָה אֶל־מֹשֶׁה לֵּאמֹר:

23 Speak to *B'nei Yisrael* thus: You shall eat no fat of ox or sheep or goat.

כג דַּבֵּר אֶל־בְּנֵי יִשְׂרָאֵל לֵאמֹר כָּל־חֵלֶב שׁוֹר וְכֶשֶׂב וָעֵז לֹא תֹאכֵלוּ:

24 Fat from animals that died or were torn by beasts may be put to any use, but you must not eat it.

כד וְחֵלֶב נְבֵלָה וְחֵלֶב טְרֵפָה יֵעָשֶׂה לְכָל־מְלָאכָה וְאָכֹל לֹא תֹאכְלֻהוּ:

25 If anyone eats the fat of animals from which offerings by fire may be made to *Hashem*, the person who eats it shall be cut off from his kin.

כה כִּי כָּל־אֹכֵל חֵלֶב מִן־הַבְּהֵמָה אֲשֶׁר יַקְרִיב מִמֶּנָּה אִשֶּׁה לַיהֹוָה וְנִכְרְתָה הַנֶּפֶשׁ הָאֹכֶלֶת מֵעַמֶּיהָ:

26 And you must not consume any blood, either of bird or of animal, in any of your settlements.

כו וְכָל־דָּם לֹא תֹאכְלוּ בְּכֹל מוֹשְׁבֹתֵיכֶם לָעוֹף וְלַבְּהֵמָה:

27 Anyone who eats blood shall be cut off from his kin.

כז כָּל־נֶפֶשׁ אֲשֶׁר־תֹּאכַל כָּל־דָּם וְנִכְרְתָה הַנֶּפֶשׁ הַהִוא מֵעַמֶּיהָ:

28 And *Hashem* spoke to *Moshe*, saying:

כח וַיְדַבֵּר יְהֹוָה אֶל־מֹשֶׁה לֵּאמֹר:

29 Speak to *B'nei Yisrael* thus: The offering to *Hashem* from a sacrifice of well-being must be presented by him who offers his sacrifice of well-being to *Hashem*:

כט דַּבֵּ֞ר אֶל־בְּנֵ֤י יִשְׂרָאֵל֙ לֵאמֹ֔ר הַמַּקְרִ֞יב אֶת־זֶ֤בַח שְׁלָמָיו֙ לַֽיהֹוָ֔ה יָבִ֧יא אֶת־קָרְבָּנ֛וֹ לַֽיהֹוָ֖ה מִזֶּ֥בַח שְׁלָמָֽיו׃

30 his own hands shall present *Hashem*'s offerings by fire. He shall present the fat with the breast, the breast to be elevated as an elevation offering before *Hashem*;

ל יָדָ֣יו תְּבִיאֶ֔ינָה אֵ֖ת אִשֵּׁ֣י יְהֹוָ֑ה אֶת־הַחֵ֤לֶב עַל־הֶֽחָזֶה֙ יְבִיאֶ֔נּוּ אֵ֣ת הֶֽחָזֶ֗ה לְהָנִ֥יף אֹת֛וֹ תְּנוּפָ֖ה לִפְנֵ֥י יְהֹוָֽה׃

31 the *Kohen* shall turn the fat into smoke on the *Mizbeyach*, and the breast shall go to *Aharon* and his sons.

לא וְהִקְטִ֧יר הַכֹּהֵ֛ן אֶת־הַחֵ֖לֶב הַמִּזְבֵּ֑חָה וְהָיָה֙ הֶֽחָזֶ֔ה לְאַהֲרֹ֖ן וּלְבָנָֽיו׃

32 And the right thigh from your sacrifices of well-being you shall present to the *Kohen* as a gift;

לב וְאֵת֙ שׁ֣וֹק הַיָּמִ֔ין תִּתְּנ֥וּ תְרוּמָ֖ה לַכֹּהֵ֑ן מִזִּבְחֵ֖י שַׁלְמֵיכֶֽם׃

33 he from among *Aharon*'s sons who offers the blood and the fat of the offering of well-being shall get the right thigh as his portion.

לג הַמַּקְרִ֞יב אֶת־דַּ֧ם הַשְּׁלָמִ֛ים וְאֶת־הַחֵ֖לֶב מִבְּנֵ֣י אַהֲרֹ֑ן ל֧וֹ תִֽהְיֶ֛ה שׁ֥וֹק הַיָּמִ֖ין לְמָנָֽה׃

34 For I have taken the breast of elevation offering and the thigh of gift offering from the Israelites, from their sacrifices of well-being, and given them to *Aharon* the *Kohen* and to his sons as their due from the Israelites for all time.

לד כִּי֩ אֶת־חֲזֵ֨ה הַתְּנוּפָ֜ה וְאֵ֣ת ׀ שׁ֣וֹק הַתְּרוּמָ֗ה לָקַ֘חְתִּי֮ מֵאֵ֣ת בְּנֵֽי־יִשְׂרָאֵל֒ מִזִּבְחֵ֖י שַׁלְמֵיהֶ֑ם וָאֶתֵּ֣ן אֹתָ֡ם לְאַהֲרֹ֣ן הַכֹּהֵן֩ וּלְבָנָ֨יו לְחׇק־עוֹלָ֔ם מֵאֵ֖ת בְּנֵ֥י יִשְׂרָאֵֽל׃

35 Those shall be the perquisites of *Aharon* and the perquisites of his sons from *Hashem*'s offerings by fire, once they have been inducted to serve *Hashem* as *Kohanim*;

לה זֹ֣את מִשְׁחַ֤ת אַהֲרֹן֙ וּמִשְׁחַ֣ת בָּנָ֔יו מֵאִשֵּׁ֖י יְהֹוָ֑ה בְּיוֹם֙ הִקְרִ֣יב אֹתָ֔ם לְכַהֵ֖ן לַֽיהֹוָֽה׃

36 these *Hashem* commanded to be given them, once they had been anointed, as a due from the Israelites for all time throughout the ages.

לו אֲשֶׁר֩ צִוָּ֨ה יְהֹוָ֜ה לָתֵ֣ת לָהֶ֗ם בְּיוֹם֙ מׇשְׁח֣וֹ אֹתָ֔ם מֵאֵ֖ת בְּנֵ֣י יִשְׂרָאֵ֑ל חֻקַּ֥ת עוֹלָ֖ם לְדֹרֹתָֽם׃

37 Such are the rituals of the burnt offering, the meal offering, the sin offering, the guilt offering, the offering of ordination, and the sacrifice of well-being,

לז זֹ֣את הַתּוֹרָ֗ה לָֽעֹלָה֙ לַמִּנְחָ֔ה וְלַֽחַטָּ֖את וְלָאָשָׁ֑ם וְלַ֨מִּלּוּאִ֔ים וּלְזֶ֖בַח הַשְּׁלָמִֽים׃

38 with which *Hashem* charged *Moshe* on *Har Sinai*, when He commanded that the Israelites present their offerings to *Hashem*, in the wilderness of Sinai.

לח אֲשֶׁ֨ר צִוָּ֧ה יְהֹוָ֛ה אֶת־מֹשֶׁ֖ה בְּהַ֣ר סִינָ֑י בְּי֨וֹם צַוֺּת֜וֹ אֶת־בְּנֵ֤י יִשְׂרָאֵל֙ לְהַקְרִ֣יב אֶת־קׇרְבְּנֵיהֶ֔ם לַֽיהֹוָ֖ה בְּמִדְבַּ֥ר סִינָֽי׃

8 ¹ *Hashem* spoke to *Moshe*, saying:

ח א וַיְדַבֵּ֥ר יְהֹוָ֖ה אֶל־מֹשֶׁ֥ה לֵּאמֹֽר׃

² Take *Aharon* along with his sons, and the vestments, the anointing oil, the bull of sin offering, the two rams, and the basket of unleavened bread;

ב קַ֤ח אֶֽת־אַהֲרֹן֙ וְאֶת־בָּנָ֣יו אִתּ֔וֹ וְאֵת֙ הַבְּגָדִ֔ים וְאֵ֖ת שֶׁ֣מֶן הַמִּשְׁחָ֑ה וְאֵ֣ת ׀ פַּ֣ר הַֽחַטָּ֗את וְאֵת֙ שְׁנֵ֣י הָֽאֵילִ֔ים וְאֵ֖ת סַ֥ל הַמַּצּֽוֹת׃

3   and assemble the whole community at the entrance of the Tent of Meeting.

ג וְאֵת־כָּל־הָעֵדָה הַקְהֵל אֶל־פֶּתַח אֹהֶל מוֹעֵד:

v'-AYT kol ha-ay-DAH hak-HAYL el PE-takh O-hel mo-AYD

4   *Moshe* did as *Hashem* commanded him. And when the community was assembled at the entrance of the Tent of Meeting,

ד וַיַּעַשׂ מֹשֶׁה כַּאֲשֶׁר צִוָּה יְהוָה אֹתוֹ וַתִּקָּהֵל הָעֵדָה אֶל־פֶּתַח אֹהֶל מוֹעֵד:

5   *Moshe* said to the community, "This is what *Hashem* has commanded to be done."

ה וַיֹּאמֶר מֹשֶׁה אֶל־הָעֵדָה זֶה הַדָּבָר אֲשֶׁר־צִוָּה יְהוָה לַעֲשׂוֹת:

6   Then *Moshe* brought *Aharon* and his sons forward and washed them with water.

ו וַיַּקְרֵב מֹשֶׁה אֶת־אַהֲרֹן וְאֶת־בָּנָיו וַיִּרְחַץ אֹתָם בַּמָּיִם:

7   He put the tunic on him, girded him with the sash, clothed him with the robe, and put the ephod on him, girding him with the decorated band with which he tied it to him.

ז וַיִּתֵּן עָלָיו אֶת־הַכֻּתֹּנֶת וַיַּחְגֹּר אֹתוֹ בָּאַבְנֵט וַיַּלְבֵּשׁ אֹתוֹ אֶת־הַמְּעִיל וַיִּתֵּן עָלָיו אֶת־הָאֵפֹד וַיַּחְגֹּר אֹתוֹ בְּחֵשֶׁב הָאֵפֹד וַיֶּאְפֹּד לוֹ בּוֹ:

8   He put the breastpiece on him, and put into the breastpiece the Urim and Thummim.

ח וַיָּשֶׂם עָלָיו אֶת־הַחֹשֶׁן וַיִּתֵּן אֶל־הַחֹשֶׁן אֶת־הָאוּרִים וְאֶת־הַתֻּמִּים:

9   And he set the headdress on his head; and on the headdress, in front, he put the gold frontlet, the holy diadem – as *Hashem* had commanded *Moshe*.

ט וַיָּשֶׂם אֶת־הַמִּצְנֶפֶת עַל־רֹאשׁוֹ וַיָּשֶׂם עַל־הַמִּצְנֶפֶת אֶל־מוּל פָּנָיו אֵת צִיץ הַזָּהָב נֵזֶר הַקֹּדֶשׁ כַּאֲשֶׁר צִוָּה יְהוָה אֶת־מֹשֶׁה:

10   *Moshe* took the anointing oil and anointed the *Mishkan* and all that was in it, thus consecrating them.

י וַיִּקַּח מֹשֶׁה אֶת־שֶׁמֶן הַמִּשְׁחָה וַיִּמְשַׁח אֶת־הַמִּשְׁכָּן וְאֶת־כָּל־אֲשֶׁר־בּוֹ וַיְקַדֵּשׁ אֹתָם:

va-yi-KAKH mo-SHEH et SHE-men ha-mish-KHAH va-yim-SHAKH
et ha-mish-KAN v'-et kol a-sher BO vai-ka-DAYSH o-TAM

11   He sprinkled some of it on the *Mizbayach* seven times, anointing the *Mizbayach*, all its utensils, and the laver with its stand, to consecrate them.

יא וַיַּז מִמֶּנּוּ עַל־הַמִּזְבֵּחַ שֶׁבַע פְּעָמִים וַיִּמְשַׁח אֶת־הַמִּזְבֵּחַ וְאֶת־כָּל־כֵּלָיו וְאֶת־הַכִּיֹּר וְאֶת־כַּנּוֹ לְקַדְּשָׁם:

12   He poured some of the anointing oil upon *Aharon*'s head and anointed him, to consecrate him.

יב וַיִּצֹק מִשֶּׁמֶן הַמִּשְׁחָה עַל רֹאשׁ אַהֲרֹן וַיִּמְשַׁח אֹתוֹ לְקַדְּשׁוֹ:

va-yi-TZOK mi-SHE-men ha-mish-KHAH AL ROSH
a-ha-RON va-yim-SHAKH o-TO l'-ka-d'-SHO

8:3 And assemble the whole community at the entrance of the Tent of Meeting The entrance of the Tent of Meeting housed the *Mishkan*, the altar and the laver, and was not large enough to accommodate six hundred thousand people. *Rashi* comments that this is one of the miraculous instances where a small area contained many people. This miracle repeated itself daily in the *Beit Hamikdash*, and is one of the incredible features of *Eretz Yisrael* in general (see Ezekiel 20:6 and Daniel 11:41). The Sages (*Ethics of the Fathers* 5:7) recount that in the *Beit Hamikdash*, "the people stood pressed together, yet they found ample space to prostrate themselves…and no one ever said to his fellow, 'There is not enough room for me to spend the night in Jerusalem.'" One of the unique metaphysical properties of Israel in general, and *Yerushalayim* and the Temple Mount specifically, is that they expand to hold all their inhabitants and visitors.

The Temple Mount in *Yerushalayim*

13 *Moshe* then brought *Aharon's* sons forward, clothed them in tunics, girded them with sashes, and wound turbans upon them, as *Hashem* had commanded *Moshe.*

14 He led forward the bull of sin offering. *Aharon* and his sons laid their hands upon the head of the bull of sin offering,

15 and it was slaughtered. *Moshe* took the blood and with his finger put some on each of the horns of the *Mizbayach,* cleansing the *Mizbayach;* then he poured out the blood at the base of the *Mizbayach.* Thus he consecrated it in order to make expiation upon it.

16 *Moshe* then took all the fat that was about the entrails, and the protuberance of the liver, and the two kidneys and their fat, and turned them into smoke on the *Mizbayach.*

17 The rest of the bull, its hide, its flesh, and its dung, he put to the fire outside the camp – as *Hashem* had commanded *Moshe.*

18 Then he brought forward the ram of burnt offering. *Aharon* and his sons laid their hands upon the ram's head,

19 and it was slaughtered. *Moshe* dashed the blood against all sides of the *Mizbayach.*

20 The ram was cut up into sections and *Moshe* turned the head, the sections, and the suet into smoke on the *Mizbayach;*

21 *Moshe* washed the entrails and the legs with water and turned all of the ram into smoke. That was a burnt offering for a pleasing odor, an offering by fire to *Hashem* – as *Hashem* had commanded *Moshe.*

22 He brought forward the second ram, the ram of ordination. *Aharon* and his sons laid their hands upon the ram's head,

23 and it was slaughtered. *Moshe* took some of its blood and put it on the ridge of *Aharon's* right ear, and on the thumb of his right hand, and on the big toe of his right foot.

24 *Moshe* then brought forward the sons of *Aharon,* and put some of the blood on the ridges of their right ears, and on the thumbs of their right hands, and on the big toes of their right feet; and the rest of the blood *Moshe* dashed against every side of the *Mizbayach.*

יג וַיַּקְרֵב מֹשֶׁה אֶת־בְּנֵי אַהֲרֹן וַיַּלְבִּשֵׁם כֻּתֳּנֹת וַיַּחְגֹּר אֹתָם אַבְנֵט וַיַּחֲבֹשׁ לָהֶם מִגְבָּעוֹת כַּאֲשֶׁר צִוָּה יְהֹוָה אֶת־מֹשֶׁה:

יד וַיַּגֵּשׁ אֵת פַּר הַחַטָּאת וַיִּסְמֹךְ אַהֲרֹן וּבָנָיו אֶת־יְדֵיהֶם עַל־רֹאשׁ פַּר הַחַטָּאת:

טו וַיִּשְׁחָט וַיִּקַּח מֹשֶׁה אֶת־הַדָּם וַיִּתֵּן עַל־ קַרְנוֹת הַמִּזְבֵּחַ סָבִיב בְּאֶצְבָּעוֹ וַיְחַטֵּא אֶת־הַמִּזְבֵּחַ וְאֶת־הַדָּם יָצַק אֶל־יְסוֹד הַמִּזְבֵּחַ וַיְקַדְּשֵׁהוּ לְכַפֵּר עָלָיו:

טז וַיִּקַּח אֶת־כׇּל־הַחֵלֶב אֲשֶׁר עַל־הַקֶּרֶב וְאֵת יֹתֶרֶת הַכָּבֵד וְאֶת־שְׁתֵּי הַכְּלָיֹת וְאֶת־חֶלְבְּהֶן וַיַּקְטֵר מֹשֶׁה הַמִּזְבֵּחָה:

יז וְאֶת־הַפָּר וְאֶת־עֹרוֹ וְאֶת־בְּשָׂרוֹ וְאֶת־ פִּרְשׁוֹ שָׂרַף בָּאֵשׁ מִחוּץ לַמַּחֲנֶה כַּאֲשֶׁר צִוָּה יְהֹוָה אֶת־מֹשֶׁה:

יח וַיַּקְרֵב אֵת אֵיל הָעֹלָה וַיִּסְמְכוּ אַהֲרֹן וּבָנָיו אֶת־יְדֵיהֶם עַל־רֹאשׁ הָאָיִל:

יט וַיִּשְׁחָט וַיִּזְרֹק מֹשֶׁה אֶת־הַדָּם עַל־ הַמִּזְבֵּחַ סָבִיב:

כ וְאֶת־הָאַיִל נִתַּח לִנְתָחָיו וַיַּקְטֵר מֹשֶׁה אֶת־הָרֹאשׁ וְאֶת־הַנְּתָחִים וְאֶת־הַפָּדֶר:

כא וְאֶת־הַקֶּרֶב וְאֶת־הַכְּרָעַיִם רָחַץ בַּמָּיִם וַיַּקְטֵר מֹשֶׁה אֶת־כׇּל־הָאַיִל הַמִּזְבֵּחָה עֹלָה הוּא לְרֵיחַ־נִיחֹחַ אִשֶּׁה הוּא לַיהֹוָה כַּאֲשֶׁר צִוָּה יְהֹוָה אֶת־מֹשֶׁה:

כב וַיַּקְרֵב אֶת־הָאַיִל הַשֵּׁנִי אֵיל הַמִּלֻּאִים וַיִּסְמְכוּ אַהֲרֹן וּבָנָיו אֶת־יְדֵיהֶם עַל־ רֹאשׁ הָאָיִל:

כג וַיִּשְׁחָט וַיִּקַּח מֹשֶׁה מִדָּמוֹ וַיִּתֵּן עַל־ תְּנוּךְ אֹזֶן־אַהֲרֹן הַיְמָנִית וְעַל־בֹּהֶן יָדוֹ הַיְמָנִית וְעַל־בֹּהֶן רַגְלוֹ הַיְמָנִית:

כד וַיַּקְרֵב אֶת־בְּנֵי אַהֲרֹן וַיִּתֵּן מֹשֶׁה מִן־ הַדָּם עַל־תְּנוּךְ אׇזְנָם הַיְמָנִית וְעַל־בֹּהֶן יָדָם הַיְמָנִית וְעַל־בֹּהֶן רַגְלָם הַיְמָנִית וַיִּזְרֹק מֹשֶׁה אֶת־הַדָּם עַל־הַמִּזְבֵּחַ סָבִיב:

25 He took the fat – the broad tail, all the fat about the entrails, the protuberance of the liver, and the two kidneys and their fat – and the right thigh.

כה וַיִּקַּ֞ח אֶת־הַחֵ֣לֶב וְאֶת־הָ֣אַלְיָ֗ה וְאֶת־כׇּל־הַחֵ֙לֶב֙ אֲשֶׁ֣ר עַל־הַקֶּ֔רֶב וְאֵת֙ יֹתֶ֣רֶת הַכָּבֵ֔ד וְאֶת־שְׁתֵּ֥י הַכְּלָיֹ֖ת וְאֶת־חֶלְבְּהֶ֑ן וְאֵ֖ת שׁ֥וֹק הַיָּמִֽין׃

26 From the basket of unleavened bread that was before *Hashem*, he took one cake of unleavened bread, one cake of oil bread, and one wafer, and placed them on the fat parts and on the right thigh.

כו וּמִסַּ֨ל הַמַּצּ֜וֹת אֲשֶׁ֣ר ׀ לִפְנֵ֣י יְהֹוָ֗ה לָקַ֞ח חַלַּ֨ת מַצָּ֤ה אַחַת֙ וְֽחַלַּ֨ת לֶ֥חֶם שֶׁ֛מֶן אַחַ֖ת וְרָקִ֣יק אֶחָ֑ד וַיָּ֙שֶׂם֙ עַל־הַ֣חֲלָבִ֔ים וְעַ֖ל שׁ֥וֹק הַיָּמִֽין׃

27 He placed all these on the palms of *Aharon* and on the palms of his sons, and elevated them as an elevation offering before *Hashem*.

כז וַיִּתֵּ֣ן אֶת־הַכֹּ֔ל עַ֚ל כַּפֵּ֣י אַהֲרֹ֔ן וְעַ֖ל כַּפֵּ֣י בָנָ֑יו וַיָּ֧נֶף אֹתָ֛ם תְּנוּפָ֖ה לִפְנֵ֥י יְהֹוָֽה׃

28 Then *Moshe* took them from their hands and turned them into smoke on the *Mizbayach* with the burnt offering. This was an ordination offering for a pleasing odor; it was an offering by fire to *Hashem*.

כח וַיִּקַּ֨ח מֹשֶׁ֤ה אֹתָם֙ מֵעַ֣ל כַּפֵּיהֶ֔ם וַיַּקְטֵ֥ר הַמִּזְבֵּ֖חָה עַל־הָעֹלָ֑ה מִלֻּאִ֥ים הֵם֙ לְרֵ֣יחַ נִיחֹ֔חַ אִשֶּׁ֥ה ה֖וּא לַיהֹוָֽה׃

29 *Moshe* took the breast and elevated it as an elevation offering before *Hashem*; it was *Moshe*'s portion of the ram of ordination – as *Hashem* had commanded *Moshe*.

כט וַיִּקַּ֤ח מֹשֶׁה֙ אֶת־הֶ֣חָזֶ֔ה וַיְנִיפֵ֥הוּ תְנוּפָ֖ה לִפְנֵ֣י יְהֹוָ֑ה מֵאֵ֣יל הַמִּלֻּאִ֗ים לְמֹשֶׁ֤ה הָיָה֙ לְמָנָ֔ה כַּאֲשֶׁ֛ר צִוָּ֥ה יְהֹוָ֖ה אֶת־מֹשֶֽׁה׃

30 And *Moshe* took some of the anointing oil and some of the blood that was on the *Mizbayach* and sprinkled it upon *Aharon* and upon his vestments, and also upon his sons and upon their vestments. Thus he consecrated *Aharon* and his vestments, and also his sons and their vestments.

ל וַיִּקַּ֨ח מֹשֶׁ֜ה מִשֶּׁ֣מֶן הַמִּשְׁחָ֗ה וּמִן־הַדָּם֮ אֲשֶׁ֣ר עַל־הַמִּזְבֵּ֒חַ֒ וַיַּ֤ז עַֽל־אַהֲרֹן֙ עַל־בְּגָדָ֔יו וְעַל־בָּנָ֛יו וְעַל־בִּגְדֵ֥י בָנָ֖יו אִתּ֑וֹ וַיְקַדֵּ֤שׁ אֶֽת־אַהֲרֹן֙ אֶת־בְּגָדָ֔יו וְאֶת־בָּנָ֛יו וְאֶת־בִּגְדֵ֥י בָנָ֖יו אִתּֽוֹ׃

31 *Moshe* said to *Aharon* and his sons: Boil the flesh at the entrance of the Tent of Meeting and eat it there with the bread that is in the basket of ordination – as I commanded: *Aharon* and his sons shall eat it;

לא וַיֹּ֨אמֶר מֹשֶׁ֜ה אֶל־אַהֲרֹ֣ן וְאֶל־בָּנָ֗יו בַּשְּׁל֣וּ אֶת־הַבָּשָׂר֮ פֶּ֣תַח אֹ֣הֶל מוֹעֵד֒ וְשָׁם֙ תֹּאכְל֣וּ אֹת֔וֹ וְאֶ֨ת־הַלֶּ֔חֶם אֲשֶׁ֖ר בְּסַ֣ל הַמִּלֻּאִ֑ים כַּאֲשֶׁ֤ר צִוֵּ֙יתִי֙ לֵאמֹ֔ר אַהֲרֹ֥ן וּבָנָ֖יו יֹאכְלֻֽהוּ׃

32 and what is left over of the flesh and the bread you shall consume in fire.

לב וְהַנּוֹתָ֥ר בַּבָּשָׂ֖ר וּבַלָּ֑חֶם בָּאֵ֖שׁ תִּשְׂרֹֽפוּ׃

33 You shall not go outside the entrance of the Tent of Meeting for seven days, until the day that your period of ordination is completed. For your ordination will require seven days.

לג וּמִפֶּ֩תַח֩ אֹ֨הֶל מוֹעֵ֜ד לֹ֤א תֵֽצְאוּ֙ שִׁבְעַ֣ת יָמִ֔ים עַ֚ד י֣וֹם מְלֹ֔את יְמֵ֖י מִלֻּאֵיכֶ֑ם כִּ֚י שִׁבְעַ֣ת יָמִ֔ים יְמַלֵּ֖א אֶת־יֶדְכֶֽם׃

34 Everything done today, *Hashem* has commanded to be done [seven days], to make expiation for you.

לד כַּאֲשֶׁ֥ר עָשָׂ֖ה בַּיּ֣וֹם הַזֶּ֑ה צִוָּ֧ה יְהֹוָ֛ה לַעֲשֹׂ֖ת לְכַפֵּ֥ר עֲלֵיכֶֽם׃

35 You shall remain at the entrance of the Tent of Meeting day and night for seven days, keeping *Hashem*'s charge – that you may not die – for so I have been commanded.

לה וּפֶ֩תַח֩ אֹ֨הֶל מוֹעֵ֜ד תֵּשְׁב֨וּ יוֹמָ֤ם וָלַ֙יְלָה֙ שִׁבְעַ֣ת יָמִ֔ים וּשְׁמַרְתֶּ֛ם אֶת־מִשְׁמֶ֥רֶת יְהֹוָ֖ה וְלֹ֣א תָמ֑וּתוּ כִּי־כֵ֖ן צֻוֵּֽיתִי׃

36 And *Aharon* and his sons did all the things that *Hashem* had commanded through *Moshe*.

לו וַיַּ֥עַשׂ אַהֲרֹ֖ן וּבָנָ֑יו אֵ֚ת כׇּל־הַדְּבָרִ֔ים אֲשֶׁר־צִוָּ֥ה יְהֹוָ֖ה בְּיַד־מֹשֶֽׁה׃

9 ¹ On the eighth day *Moshe* called *Aharon* and his sons, and the elders of *Yisrael*.

² He said to *Aharon*: "Take a calf of the herd for a sin offering and a ram for a burnt offering, without blemish, and bring them before *Hashem*.

³ And speak to the Israelites, saying: Take a he-goat for a sin offering; a calf and a lamb, yearlings without blemish, for a burnt offering;

⁴ and an ox and a ram for an offering of well-being to sacrifice before *Hashem*; and a meal offering with oil mixed in. For today *Hashem* will appear to you."

⁵ They brought to the front of the Tent of Meeting the things that *Moshe* had commanded, and the whole community came forward and stood before *Hashem*.

⁶ *Moshe* said: "This is what *Hashem* has commanded that you do, that the Presence of *Hashem* may appear to you."

⁷ Then *Moshe* said to *Aharon*: "Come forward to the *Mizbayach* and sacrifice your sin offering and your burnt offering, making expiation for yourself and for the people; and sacrifice the people's offering and make expiation for them, as *Hashem* has commanded."

⁸ *Aharon* came forward to the *Mizbayach* and slaughtered his calf of sin offering.

⁹ *Aharon's* sons brought the blood to him; he dipped his finger in the blood and put it on the horns of the *Mizbayach*; and he poured out the rest of the blood at the base of the *Mizbayach*.

¹⁰ The fat, the kidneys, and the protuberance of the liver from the sin offering he turned into smoke on the *Mizbayach* – as *Hashem* had commanded *Moshe*;

¹¹ and the flesh and the skin were consumed in fire outside the camp.

¹² Then he slaughtered the burnt offering. *Aharon's* sons passed the blood to him, and he dashed it against all sides of the *Mizbayach*.

¹³ They passed the burnt offering to him in sections, as well as the head, and he turned it into smoke on the *Mizbayach*.

ט א וַיְהִי בַּיּוֹם הַשְּׁמִינִי קָרָא מֹשֶׁה לְאַהֲרֹן וּלְבָנָיו וּלְזִקְנֵי יִשְׂרָאֵל:

ב וַיֹּאמֶר אֶל־אַהֲרֹן קַח־לְךָ עֵגֶל בֶּן־בָּקָר לְחַטָּאת וְאַיִל לְעֹלָה תְּמִימִם וְהַקְרֵב לִפְנֵי יְהֹוָה:

ג וְאֶל־בְּנֵי יִשְׂרָאֵל תְּדַבֵּר לֵאמֹר קְחוּ שְׂעִיר־עִזִּים לְחַטָּאת וְעֵגֶל וָכֶבֶשׂ בְּנֵי־שָׁנָה תְּמִימִם לְעֹלָה:

ד וְשׁוֹר וָאַיִל לִשְׁלָמִים לִזְבֹּחַ לִפְנֵי יְהֹוָה וּמִנְחָה בְּלוּלָה בַשָּׁמֶן כִּי הַיּוֹם יְהֹוָה נִרְאָה אֲלֵיכֶם:

ה וַיִּקְחוּ אֵת אֲשֶׁר צִוָּה מֹשֶׁה אֶל־פְּנֵי אֹהֶל מוֹעֵד וַיִּקְרְבוּ כָּל־הָעֵדָה וַיַּעַמְדוּ לִפְנֵי יְהֹוָה:

ו וַיֹּאמֶר מֹשֶׁה זֶה הַדָּבָר אֲשֶׁר־צִוָּה יְהֹוָה תַּעֲשׂוּ וְיֵרָא אֲלֵיכֶם כְּבוֹד יְהֹוָה:

ז וַיֹּאמֶר מֹשֶׁה אֶל־אַהֲרֹן קְרַב אֶל־הַמִּזְבֵּחַ וַעֲשֵׂה אֶת־חַטָּאתְךָ וְאֶת־עֹלָתֶךָ וְכַפֵּר בַּעַדְךָ וּבְעַד הָעָם וַעֲשֵׂה אֶת־קָרְבַּן הָעָם וְכַפֵּר בַּעֲדָם כַּאֲשֶׁר צִוָּה יְהֹוָה:

ח וַיִּקְרַב אַהֲרֹן אֶל־הַמִּזְבֵּחַ וַיִּשְׁחַט אֶת־עֵגֶל הַחַטָּאת אֲשֶׁר־לוֹ:

ט וַיַּקְרִבוּ בְּנֵי אַהֲרֹן אֶת־הַדָּם אֵלָיו וַיִּטְבֹּל אֶצְבָּעוֹ בַּדָּם וַיִּתֵּן עַל־קַרְנוֹת הַמִּזְבֵּחַ וְאֶת־הַדָּם יָצַק אֶל־יְסוֹד הַמִּזְבֵּחַ:

י וְאֶת־הַחֵלֶב וְאֶת־הַכְּלָיֹת וְאֶת־הַיֹּתֶרֶת מִן־הַכָּבֵד מִן־הַחַטָּאת הִקְטִיר הַמִּזְבֵּחָה כַּאֲשֶׁר צִוָּה יְהֹוָה אֶת־מֹשֶׁה:

יא וְאֶת־הַבָּשָׂר וְאֶת־הָעוֹר שָׂרַף בָּאֵשׁ מִחוּץ לַמַּחֲנֶה:

יב וַיִּשְׁחַט אֶת־הָעֹלָה וַיַּמְצִאוּ בְּנֵי אַהֲרֹן אֵלָיו אֶת־הַדָּם וַיִּזְרְקֵהוּ עַל־הַמִּזְבֵּחַ סָבִיב:

יג וְאֶת־הָעֹלָה הִמְצִיאוּ אֵלָיו לִנְתָחֶיהָ וְאֶת־הָרֹאשׁ וַיַּקְטֵר עַל־הַמִּזְבֵּחַ:

14 He washed the entrails and the legs, and turned them into smoke on the *Mizbayach* with the burnt offering.

יד וַיִּרְחַץ אֶת־הַקֶּרֶב וְאֶת־הַכְּרָעָיִם וַיַּקְטֵר עַל־הָעֹלָה הַמִּזְבֵּחָה:

15 Next he brought forward the people's offering. He took the goat for the people's sin offering, and slaughtered it, and presented it as a sin offering like the previous one.

טו וַיַּקְרֵב אֵת קָרְבַּן הָעָם וַיִּקַּח אֶת־שְׂעִיר הַחַטָּאת אֲשֶׁר לָעָם וַיִּשְׁחָטֵהוּ וַיְחַטְּאֵהוּ כָּרִאשׁוֹן:

16 He brought forward the burnt offering and sacrificed it according to regulation.

טז וַיַּקְרֵב אֶת־הָעֹלָה וַיַּעֲשֶׂהָ כַּמִּשְׁפָּט:

17 He then brought forward the meal offering and, taking a handful of it, he turned it into smoke on the *Mizbayach* – in addition to the burnt offering of the morning.

יז וַיַּקְרֵב אֶת־הַמִּנְחָה וַיְמַלֵּא כַפּוֹ מִמֶּנָּה וַיַּקְטֵר עַל־הַמִּזְבֵּחַ מִלְּבַד עֹלַת הַבֹּקֶר:

18 He slaughtered the ox and the ram, the people's sacrifice of well-being. *Aharon*'s sons passed the blood to him – which he dashed against every side of the *Mizbayach*

יח וַיִּשְׁחַט אֶת־הַשּׁוֹר וְאֶת־הָאַיִל זֶבַח הַשְּׁלָמִים אֲשֶׁר לָעָם וַיַּמְצִאוּ בְּנֵי אַהֲרֹן אֶת־הַדָּם אֵלָיו וַיִּזְרְקֵהוּ עַל־הַמִּזְבֵּחַ סָבִיב:

19 and the fat parts of the ox and the ram: the broad tail, the covering [fat], the kidneys, and the protuberances of the livers.

יט וְאֶת־הַחֲלָבִים מִן־הַשּׁוֹר וּמִן־הָאַיִל הָאַלְיָה וְהַמְכַסֶּה וְהַכְּלָיֹת וְיֹתֶרֶת הַכָּבֵד:

20 They laid these fat parts over the breasts; and *Aharon** turned the fat parts into smoke on the *Mizbayach*,

כ וַיָּשִׂימוּ אֶת־הַחֲלָבִים עַל־הֶחָזוֹת וַיַּקְטֵר הַחֲלָבִים הַמִּזְבֵּחָה:

21 and elevated the breasts and the right thighs as an elevation offering before *Hashem* – as *Moshe* had commanded.

כא וְאֵת הֶחָזוֹת וְאֵת שׁוֹק הַיָּמִין הֵנִיף אַהֲרֹן תְּנוּפָה לִפְנֵי יְהוָה כַּאֲשֶׁר צִוָּה מֹשֶׁה:

22 *Aharon* lifted his hands toward the people and blessed them; and he stepped down after offering the sin offering, the burnt offering, and the offering of well-being.

כב וַיִּשָּׂא אַהֲרֹן אֶת־יָדֹו [יָדָיו] אֶל־הָעָם וַיְבָרְכֵם וַיֵּרֶד מֵעֲשֹׂת הַחַטָּאת וְהָעֹלָה וְהַשְּׁלָמִים:

23 *Moshe* and *Aharon* then went inside the Tent of Meeting. When they came out, they blessed the people; and the Presence of *Hashem* appeared to all the people.

כג וַיָּבֹא מֹשֶׁה וְאַהֲרֹן אֶל־אֹהֶל מוֹעֵד וַיֵּצְאוּ וַיְבָרְכוּ אֶת־הָעָם וַיֵּרָא כְבוֹד־יְהוָה אֶל־כָּל־הָעָם:

va-ya-VO mo-SHEH v'-a-ha-RON el O-hel mo-AYD va-YAY-tz'-U
vai-va-ra-KHU et ha-AM va-yay-RA kh'-vod a-do-NAI el kol ha-AM

---

* "*Aharon*" moved up from v. 21 for clarity

9:23 And the Presence of the Lord appeared to all the people The purpose of the *Mishkan* in the desert, and the *Beit Hamikdash* in Yerushalayim, is to serve as a fixed resting place for *Hashem*'s presence on earth. The commandment to build the *Mishkan* directly follows the revelation at Sinai, since, according to *Ramban*, the *Mishkan* constitutes the continuation of the revelation at Sinai. While the Divine Presence rested briefly on Mount Sinai, it found a long-term home in the *Mishkan*, and ultimately a permanent dwelling on the Temple Mount in *Yerushalayim*.

Model of the *Mishkan* in Timna Park

²⁴ Fire came forth from before *Hashem* and consumed the burnt offering and the fat parts on the *Mizbayach*. And all the people saw, and shouted, and fell on their faces.

כד וַתֵּ֤צֵא אֵשׁ֙ מִלִּפְנֵ֣י יְהֹוָ֔ה וַתֹּ֣אכַל עַל־הַמִּזְבֵּ֔חַ אֶת־הָעֹלָ֖ה וְאֶת־הַחֲלָבִ֑ים וַיַּ֤רְא כָּל־הָעָם֙ וַיָּרֹ֔נּוּ וַֽיִּפְּל֖וּ עַל־פְּנֵיהֶֽם׃

0 ¹ Now *Aharon's* sons *Nadav* and *Avihu* each took his fire pan, put fire in it, and laid incense on it; and they offered before *Hashem* alien fire, which He had not enjoined upon them.

א וַיִּקְח֣וּ בְנֵֽי־אַ֠הֲרֹ֠ן נָדָ֨ב וַאֲבִיה֜וּא אִ֣ישׁ מַחְתָּת֗וֹ וַיִּתְּנ֤וּ בָהֵן֙ אֵ֔שׁ וַיָּשִׂ֥ימוּ עָלֶ֖יהָ קְטֹ֑רֶת וַיַּקְרִ֜בוּ לִפְנֵ֤י יְהֹוָה֙ אֵ֣שׁ זָרָ֔ה אֲשֶׁ֧ר לֹ֦א צִוָּ֖ה אֹתָֽם׃

² And fire came forth from *Hashem* and consumed them; thus they died at the instance of *Hashem*.

ב וַתֵּ֤צֵא אֵשׁ֙ מִלִּפְנֵ֣י יְהֹוָ֔ה וַתֹּ֖אכַל אוֹתָ֑ם וַיָּמֻ֖תוּ לִפְנֵ֥י יְהֹוָֽה׃

³ Then *Moshe* said to *Aharon*, "This is what *Hashem* meant when He said: Through those near to Me I show Myself holy, And gain glory before all the people." And *Aharon* was silent.

ג וַיֹּ֨אמֶר מֹשֶׁ֜ה אֶֽל־אַהֲרֹ֗ן הוּא֩ אֲשֶׁר־דִּבֶּ֨ר יְהֹוָ֤ה ׀ לֵאמֹר֙ בִּקְרֹבַ֣י אֶקָּדֵ֔שׁ וְעַל־פְּנֵ֥י כָל־הָעָ֖ם אֶכָּבֵ֑ד וַיִּדֹּ֖ם אַהֲרֹֽן׃

*va-YO-mer mo-SHEH el a-ha-RON HU a-sher di-BER
a-do-NAI lay-MOR bik-ro-VAI e-ka-DAYSH v'-al p'-NAY
khol ha-AM e-ka-VAYD va-yi-DOM a-ha-RON*

⁴ *Moshe* called *Mishael* and Elzaphan, sons of Uzziel the uncle of *Aharon*, and said to them, "Come forward and carry your kinsmen away from the front of the sanctuary to a place outside the camp."

ד וַיִּקְרָ֣א מֹשֶׁ֗ה אֶל־מִֽישָׁאֵל֙ וְאֶ֣ל אֶלְצָפָ֔ן בְּנֵ֥י עֻזִּיאֵ֖ל דֹּ֣ד אַהֲרֹ֑ן וַיֹּ֣אמֶר אֲלֵהֶ֗ם קִ֠רְב֠וּ שְׂא֤וּ אֶת־אֲחֵיכֶם֙ מֵאֵ֣ת פְּנֵֽי־הַקֹּ֔דֶשׁ אֶל־מִח֖וּץ לַֽמַּחֲנֶֽה׃

⁵ They came forward and carried them out of the camp by their tunics, as *Moshe* had ordered.

ה וַֽיִּקְרְב֗וּ וַיִּשָּׂאֻם֙ בְּכֻתֳּנֹתָ֔ם אֶל־מִח֖וּץ לַֽמַּחֲנֶ֑ה כַּאֲשֶׁ֖ר דִּבֶּ֥ר מֹשֶֽׁה׃

⁶ And *Moshe* said to *Aharon* and to his sons *Elazar* and *Itamar*, "Do not bare your heads and do not rend your clothes, lest you die and anger strike the whole community. But your kinsmen, all the house of *Yisrael*, shall bewail the burning that *Hashem* has wrought.

ו וַיֹּ֣אמֶר מֹשֶׁ֣ה אֶֽל־אַהֲרֹ֡ן וּלְאֶלְעָזָר֩ וּלְאִֽיתָמָ֨ר ׀ בָּנָ֜יו רָֽאשֵׁיכֶ֥ם אַל־תִּפְרָ֣עוּ ׀ וּבִגְדֵיכֶ֤ם לֹֽא־תִפְרֹ֙מוּ֙ וְלֹ֣א תָמֻ֔תוּ וְעַ֥ל כָּל־הָעֵדָ֖ה יִקְצֹ֑ף וַאֲחֵיכֶם֙ כָּל־בֵּ֣ית יִשְׂרָאֵ֔ל יִבְכּוּ֙ אֶת־הַשְּׂרֵפָ֔ה אֲשֶׁ֖ר שָׂרַ֥ף יְהֹוָֽה׃

⁷ And so do not go outside the entrance of the Tent of Meeting, lest you die, for *Hashem's* anointing oil is upon you." And they did as *Moshe* had bidden.

ז וּמִפֶּתַח֩ אֹ֨הֶל מוֹעֵ֜ד לֹ֤א תֵֽצְאוּ֙ פֶּן־תָּמֻ֔תוּ כִּי־שֶׁ֛מֶן מִשְׁחַ֥ת יְהֹוָ֖ה עֲלֵיכֶ֑ם וַיַּעֲשׂ֖וּ כִּדְבַ֥ר מֹשֶֽׁה׃

⁸ And *Hashem* spoke to *Aharon*, saying:

ח וַיְדַבֵּ֣ר יְהֹוָ֔ה אֶֽל־אַהֲרֹ֖ן לֵאמֹֽר׃

10:3 Through those near to Me I show Myself holy The death of *Aharon's* sons, *Nadav* and *Avihu*, occurs in the midst of the joyous inauguration ceremony of the *Mishkan*. The Sages explain that they are so moved by the closeness they feel to *Hashem* at this moment of revelation, that *Nadav* and *Avihu* desire to get even closer with an offering of their own which they bring in the Holy of Holies. Though their intentions are pure, the offering is unauthorized and the entry into the Holy sanctuary forbidden, so they are punished. Their desire for closeness is reflected in *Moshe's* words to *Aharon*, "Through those near to Me I show Myself holy." *Nadav* and *Avihu* are indeed close to God, but this closeness does not allow them to bend the rules. By punishing those who were closest to Him, God's name is sanctified, as He teaches the important lesson that everyone, even those who are most powerful and respected, must be held to the same standard.

Women praying in the Western Wall tunnels at the point closest to the Holy of Holies that is not under Islamic Waqf jurisdiction

9 Drink no wine or other intoxicant, you or your sons, when you enter the Tent of Meeting, that you may not die. This is a law for all time throughout the ages,

ט יַ֣יִן וְשֵׁכָ֞ר אַל־תֵּ֣שְׁתְּ אַתָּ֣ה ׀ וּבָנֶ֣יךָ אִתָּ֗ךְ בְּבֹאֲכֶ֛ם אֶל־אֹ֥הֶל מוֹעֵ֖ד וְלֹ֣א תָמֻ֑תוּ חֻקַּ֥ת עוֹלָ֖ם לְדֹרֹתֵיכֶֽם׃

10 for you must distinguish between the sacred and the profane, and between the unclean and the clean;

י וּֽלֲהַבְדִּ֔יל בֵּ֥ין הַקֹּ֖דֶשׁ וּבֵ֣ין הַחֹ֑ל וּבֵ֥ין הַטָּמֵ֖א וּבֵ֥ין הַטָּהֽוֹר׃

11 and you must teach the Israelites all the laws which *Hashem* has imparted to them through *Moshe*.

יא וּלְהוֹרֹ֖ת אֶת־בְּנֵ֣י יִשְׂרָאֵ֑ל אֵ֚ת כׇּל־הַ֣חֻקִּ֔ים אֲשֶׁ֨ר דִּבֶּ֧ר יְהֹוָ֛ה אֲלֵיהֶ֖ם בְּיַד־מֹשֶֽׁה׃

12 *Moshe* spoke to *Aharon* and to his remaining sons, *Elazar* and *Itamar*: Take the meal offering that is left over from *Hashem*'s offerings by fire and eat it unleavened beside the *Mizbayach*, for it is most holy.

יב וַיְדַבֵּ֨ר מֹשֶׁ֜ה אֶֽל־אַהֲרֹ֗ן וְאֶ֣ל אֶ֠לְעָזָ֠ר וְאֶל־אִ֨יתָמָ֥ר ׀ בָּנָיו֮ הַנּֽוֹתָרִים֒ קְח֣וּ אֶת־הַמִּנְחָ֗ה הַנּוֹתֶ֙רֶת֙ מֵאִשֵּׁ֣י יְהֹוָ֔ה וְאִכְל֥וּהָ מַצּ֖וֹת אֵ֣צֶל הַמִּזְבֵּ֑חַ כִּ֛י קֹ֥דֶשׁ קׇֽדָשִׁ֖ים הִֽוא׃

13 You shall eat it in the sacred precinct, inasmuch as it is your due, and that of your children, from *Hashem*'s offerings by fire; for so I have been commanded.

יג וַאֲכַלְתֶּ֤ם אֹתָהּ֙ בְּמָק֣וֹם קָדֹ֔שׁ כִּ֣י חׇקְךָ֤ וְחׇק־בָּנֶ֙יךָ֙ הִ֔וא מֵאִשֵּׁ֖י יְהֹוָ֑ה כִּי־כֵ֖ן צֻוֵּֽיתִי׃

14 But the breast of elevation offering and the thigh of gift offering you, and your sons and daughters with you, may eat in any clean place, for they have been assigned as a due to you and your children from the Israelites' sacrifices of well-being.

יד וְאֵת֩ חֲזֵ֨ה הַתְּנוּפָ֜ה וְאֵ֣ת ׀ שׁ֣וֹק הַתְּרוּמָ֗ה תֹּֽאכְלוּ֙ בְּמָק֣וֹם טָה֔וֹר אַתָּ֖ה וּבָנֶ֣יךָ וּבְנֹתֶ֣יךָ אִתָּ֑ךְ כִּֽי־חׇקְךָ֤ וְחׇק־בָּנֶ֙יךָ֙ נִתְּנ֔וּ מִזִּבְחֵ֖י שַׁלְמֵ֥י בְּנֵ֥י יִשְׂרָאֵֽל׃

15 Together with the fat of fire offering, they must present the thigh of gift offering and the breast of elevation offering, which are to be elevated as an elevation offering before *Hashem*, and which are to be your due and that of your children with you for all time – as *Hashem* has commanded.

טו שׁ֣וֹק הַתְּרוּמָ֞ה וַחֲזֵ֣ה הַתְּנוּפָ֗ה עַ֣ל אִשֵּׁ֤י הַחֲלָבִים֙ יָבִ֔יאוּ לְהָנִ֥יף תְּנוּפָ֖ה לִפְנֵ֣י יְהֹוָ֑ה וְהָיָ֨ה לְךָ֜ וּלְבָנֶ֤יךָ אִתְּךָ֙ לְחׇק־עוֹלָ֔ם כַּאֲשֶׁ֖ר צִוָּ֥ה יְהֹוָֽה׃

16 Then *Moshe* inquired about the goat of sin offering, and it had already been burned! He was angry with *Elazar* and *Itamar*, *Aharon*'s remaining sons, and said,

טז וְאֵ֣ת ׀ שְׂעִ֣יר הַֽחַטָּ֗את דָּרֹ֥שׁ דָּרַ֛שׁ מֹשֶׁ֖ה וְהִנֵּ֣ה שֹׂרָ֑ף וַ֠יִּקְצֹ֠ף עַל־אֶלְעָזָ֤ר וְעַל־אִֽיתָמָר֙ בְּנֵ֣י אַהֲרֹ֔ן הַנּוֹתָרִ֖ם לֵאמֹֽר׃

17 "Why did you not eat the sin offering in the sacred area? For it is most holy, and He has given it to you to remove the guilt of the community and to make expiation for them before *Hashem*.

יז מַדּ֗וּעַ לֹֽא־אֲכַלְתֶּ֤ם אֶת־הַֽחַטָּאת֙ בִּמְק֣וֹם הַקֹּ֔דֶשׁ כִּ֛י קֹ֥דֶשׁ קׇֽדָשִׁ֖ים הִ֑וא וְאֹתָ֣הּ ׀ נָתַ֣ן לָכֶ֗ם לָשֵׂאת֙ אֶת־עֲוֺ֣ן הָֽעֵדָ֔ה לְכַפֵּ֥ר עֲלֵיהֶ֖ם לִפְנֵ֥י יְהֹוָֽה׃

18 Since its blood was not brought inside the sanctuary, you should certainly have eaten it in the sanctuary, as I commanded."

יח הֵ֚ן לֹא־הוּבָ֣א אֶת־דָּמָ֔הּ אֶל־הַקֹּ֖דֶשׁ פְּנִ֑ימָה אָכ֨וֹל תֹּאכְל֥וּ אֹתָ֛הּ בַּקֹּ֖דֶשׁ כַּאֲשֶׁ֥ר צִוֵּֽיתִי׃

19 And *Aharon* spoke to *Moshe*, "See, this day they brought their sin offering and their burnt offering before *Hashem*, and such things have befallen me! Had I eaten sin offering today, would *Hashem* have approved?"

יט וַיְדַבֵּר אַהֲרֹן אֶל־מֹשֶׁה הֵן הַיּוֹם הִקְרִיבוּ אֶת־חַטָּאתָם וְאֶת־עֹלָתָם לִפְנֵי יְהֹוָה וַתִּקְרֶאנָה אֹתִי כָּאֵלֶּה וְאָכַלְתִּי חַטָּאת הַיּוֹם הַיִּיטַב בְּעֵינֵי יְהֹוָה:

20 And when *Moshe* heard this, he approved.

כ וַיִּשְׁמַע מֹשֶׁה וַיִּיטַב בְּעֵינָיו:

11 1 *Hashem* spoke to *Moshe* and *Aharon*, saying to them:

יא א וַיְדַבֵּר יְהֹוָה אֶל־מֹשֶׁה וְאֶל־אַהֲרֹן לֵאמֹר אֲלֵהֶם:

2 Speak to *B'nei Yisrael* thus: These are the creatures that you may eat from among all the land animals:

ב דַּבְּרוּ אֶל־בְּנֵי יִשְׂרָאֵל לֵאמֹר זֹאת הַחַיָּה אֲשֶׁר תֹּאכְלוּ מִכָּל־הַבְּהֵמָה אֲשֶׁר עַל־הָאָרֶץ:

3 any animal that has true hoofs, with clefts through the hoofs, and that chews the cud – such you may eat.

ג כֹּל מַפְרֶסֶת פַּרְסָה וְשֹׁסַעַת שֶׁסַע פְּרָסֹת מַעֲלַת גֵּרָה בַּבְּהֵמָה אֹתָהּ תֹּאכֵלוּ:

4 The following, however, of those that either chew the cud or have true hoofs, you shall not eat: the camel – although it chews the cud, it has no true hoofs: it is unclean for you;

ד אַךְ אֶת־זֶה לֹא תֹאכְלוּ מִמַּעֲלֵי הַגֵּרָה וּמִמַּפְרִיסֵי הַפַּרְסָה אֶת־הַגָּמָל כִּי־מַעֲלֵה גֵרָה הוּא וּפַרְסָה אֵינֶנּוּ מַפְרִיס טָמֵא הוּא לָכֶם:

5 the daman – although it chews the cud, it has no true hoofs: it is unclean for you;

ה וְאֶת־הַשָּׁפָן כִּי־מַעֲלֵה גֵרָה הוּא וּפַרְסָה לֹא יַפְרִיס טָמֵא הוּא לָכֶם:

6 the hare – although it chews the cud, it has no true hoofs: it is unclean for you;

ו וְאֶת־הָאַרְנֶבֶת כִּי־מַעֲלַת גֵּרָה הִוא וּפַרְסָה לֹא הִפְרִיסָה טְמֵאָה הִוא לָכֶם:

7 and the swine – although it has true hoofs, with the hoofs cleft through, it does not chew the cud: it is unclean for you.

ז וְאֶת־הַחֲזִיר כִּי־מַפְרִיס פַּרְסָה הוּא וְשֹׁסַע שֶׁסַע פַּרְסָה וְהוּא גֵּרָה לֹא־יִגָּר טָמֵא הוּא לָכֶם:

8 You shall not eat of their flesh or touch their carcasses; they are unclean for you.

ח מִבְּשָׂרָם לֹא תֹאכֵלוּ וּבְנִבְלָתָם לֹא תִגָּעוּ טְמֵאִים הֵם לָכֶם:

9 These you may eat of all that live in water: anything in water, whether in the seas or in the streams, that has fins and scales – these you may eat.

ט אֶת־זֶה תֹּאכְלוּ מִכֹּל אֲשֶׁר בַּמָּיִם כֹּל אֲשֶׁר־לוֹ סְנַפִּיר וְקַשְׂקֶשֶׂת בַּמַּיִם בַּיַּמִּים וּבַנְּחָלִים אֹתָם תֹּאכֵלוּ:

10 But anything in the seas or in the streams that has no fins and scales, among all the swarming things of the water and among all the other living creatures that are in the water – they are an abomination for you

י וְכֹל אֲשֶׁר אֵין־לוֹ סְנַפִּיר וְקַשְׂקֶשֶׂת בַּיַּמִּים וּבַנְּחָלִים מִכֹּל שֶׁרֶץ הַמַּיִם וּמִכֹּל נֶפֶשׁ הַחַיָּה אֲשֶׁר בַּמָּיִם שֶׁקֶץ הֵם לָכֶם:

11 and an abomination for you they shall remain: you shall not eat of their flesh and you shall abominate their carcasses.

יא וְשֶׁקֶץ יִהְיוּ לָכֶם מִבְּשָׂרָם לֹא תֹאכֵלוּ וְאֶת־נִבְלָתָם תְּשַׁקֵּצוּ:

12 Everything in water that has no fins and scales shall be an abomination for you.

יב כֹּל אֲשֶׁר אֵין־לוֹ סְנַפִּיר וְקַשְׂקֶשֶׂת בַּמָּיִם שֶׁקֶץ הוּא לָכֶם:

13 The following you shall abominate among the birds – they shall not be eaten, they are an abomination: the eagle, the vulture, and the black vulture;

יג וְאֶת־אֵלֶּה תְּשַׁקְּצוּ מִן־הָעוֹף לֹא יֵאָכְלוּ שֶׁקֶץ הֵם אֶת־הַנֶּשֶׁר וְאֶת־הַפֶּרֶס וְאֵת הָעָזְנִיָּה:

14 the kite, falcons of every variety;

יד וְאֶת־הַדָּאָה וְאֶת־הָאַיָּה לְמִינָהּ:

15 all varieties of raven;

טו אֵת כָּל־עֹרֵב לְמִינוֹ:

16 the ostrich, the nighthawk, the sea gull; hawks of every variety;

טז וְאֵת בַּת הַיַּעֲנָה וְאֶת־הַתַּחְמָס וְאֶת־הַשָּׁחַף וְאֶת־הַנֵּץ לְמִינֵהוּ:

17 the little owl, the cormorant, and the great owl;

יז וְאֶת־הַכּוֹס וְאֶת־הַשָּׁלָךְ וְאֶת־הַיַּנְשׁוּף:

18 the white owl, the pelican, and the bustard;

יח וְאֶת־הַתִּנְשֶׁמֶת וְאֶת־הַקָּאָת וְאֶת־הָרָחָם:

19 the stork; herons of every variety; the hoopoe, and the bat.

יט וְאֵת הַחֲסִידָה הָאֲנָפָה לְמִינָהּ וְאֶת־הַדּוּכִיפַת וְאֶת־הָעֲטַלֵּף:

20 All winged swarming things that walk on fours shall be an abomination for you.

כ כֹּל שֶׁרֶץ הָעוֹף הַהֹלֵךְ עַל־אַרְבַּע שֶׁקֶץ הוּא לָכֶם:

21 But these you may eat among all the winged swarming things that walk on fours: all that have, above their feet, jointed legs to leap with on the ground

כא אַךְ אֶת־זֶה תֹּאכְלוּ מִכֹּל שֶׁרֶץ הָעוֹף הַהֹלֵךְ עַל־אַרְבַּע אֲשֶׁר־לֹא [לוֹ] כְרָעַיִם מִמַּעַל לְרַגְלָיו לְנַתֵּר בָּהֵן עַל־הָאָרֶץ:

22 of these you may eat the following: locusts of every variety; all varieties of bald locust; crickets of every variety; and all varieties of grasshopper.

כב אֶת־אֵלֶּה מֵהֶם תֹּאכֵלוּ אֶת־הָאַרְבֶּה לְמִינוֹ וְאֶת־הַסָּלְעָם לְמִינֵהוּ וְאֶת־הַחַרְגֹּל לְמִינֵהוּ וְאֶת־הֶחָגָב לְמִינֵהוּ:

23 But all other winged swarming things that have four legs shall be an abomination for you.

כג וְכֹל שֶׁרֶץ הָעוֹף אֲשֶׁר־לוֹ אַרְבַּע רַגְלָיִם שֶׁקֶץ הוּא לָכֶם:

24 And the following shall make you unclean – whoever touches their carcasses shall be unclean until evening,

כד וּלְאֵלֶּה תִּטַּמָּאוּ כָּל־הַנֹּגֵעַ בְּנִבְלָתָם יִטְמָא עַד־הָעָרֶב:

25 and whoever carries the carcasses of any of them shall wash his clothes and be unclean until evening

כה וְכָל־הַנֹּשֵׂא מִנִּבְלָתָם יְכַבֵּס בְּגָדָיו וְטָמֵא עַד־הָעָרֶב:

26 every animal that has true hoofs but without clefts through the hoofs, or that does not chew the cud. They are unclean for you; whoever touches them shall be unclean.

כו לְכָל־הַבְּהֵמָה אֲשֶׁר הִוא מַפְרֶסֶת פַּרְסָה וְשֶׁסַע אֵינֶנָּה שֹׁסַעַת וְגֵרָה אֵינֶנָּה מַעֲלָה טְמֵאִים הֵם לָכֶם כָּל־הַנֹּגֵעַ בָּהֶם יִטְמָא:

27 Also all animals that walk on paws, among those that walk on fours, are unclean for you; whoever touches their carcasses shall be unclean until evening.

כז וְכֹל הוֹלֵךְ עַל־כַּפָּיו בְּכָל־הַחַיָּה הַהֹלֶכֶת עַל־אַרְבַּע טְמֵאִים הֵם לָכֶם כָּל־הַנֹּגֵעַ בְּנִבְלָתָם יִטְמָא עַד־הָעָרֶב:

28 And anyone who carries their carcasses shall wash his clothes and remain unclean until evening. They are unclean for you.

כח וְהַנֹּשֵׂא אֶת־נִבְלָתָם יְכַבֵּס בְּגָדָיו וְטָמֵא עַד־הָעָרֶב טְמֵאִים הֵמָּה לָכֶם:

²⁹ The following shall be unclean for you from among the things that swarm on the earth: the mole, the mouse, and great lizards of every variety;

כט וְזֶה לָכֶם הַטָּמֵא בַּשֶּׁרֶץ הַשֹּׁרֵץ עַל־הָאָרֶץ הַחֹלֶד וְהָעַכְבָּר וְהַצָּב לְמִינֵהוּ:

³⁰ the gecko, the land crocodile, the lizard, the sand lizard, and the Hameleon.

ל וְהָאֲנָקָה וְהַכֹּחַ וְהַלְּטָאָה וְהַחֹמֶט וְהַתִּנְשָׁמֶת:

³¹ Those are for you the unclean among all the swarming things; whoever touches them when they are dead shall be unclean until evening.

לא אֵלֶּה הַטְּמֵאִים לָכֶם בְּכָל־הַשָּׁרֶץ כָּל־הַנֹּגֵעַ בָּהֶם בְּמֹתָם יִטְמָא עַד־הָעָרֶב:

³² And anything on which one of them falls when dead shall be unclean: be it any article of wood, or a cloth, or a skin, or a sack – any such article that can be put to use shall be dipped in water, and it shall remain unclean until evening; then it shall be clean.

לב וְכֹל אֲשֶׁר־יִפֹּל־עָלָיו מֵהֶם בְּמֹתָם יִטְמָא מִכָּל־כְּלִי־עֵץ אוֹ בֶגֶד אוֹ־עוֹר אוֹ שָׂק כָּל־כְּלִי אֲשֶׁר־יֵעָשֶׂה מְלָאכָה בָּהֶם בַּמַּיִם יוּבָא וְטָמֵא עַד־הָעֶרֶב וְטָהֵר:

³³ And if any of those falls into an earthen vessel, everything inside it shall be unclean and [the vessel] itself you shall break.

לג וְכָל־כְּלִי־חֶרֶשׂ אֲשֶׁר־יִפֹּל מֵהֶם אֶל־תּוֹכוֹ כֹּל אֲשֶׁר בְּתוֹכוֹ יִטְמָא וְאֹתוֹ תִשְׁבֹּרוּ:

³⁴ As to any food that may be eaten, it shall become unclean if it came in contact with water; as to any liquid that may be drunk, it shall become unclean if it was inside any vessel.

לד מִכָּל־הָאֹכֶל אֲשֶׁר יֵאָכֵל אֲשֶׁר יָבוֹא עָלָיו מַיִם יִטְמָא וְכָל־מַשְׁקֶה אֲשֶׁר יִשָּׁתֶה בְּכָל־כְּלִי יִטְמָא:

³⁵ Everything on which the carcass of any of them falls shall be unclean: an oven or stove shall be smashed. They are unclean and unclean they shall remain for you.

לה וְכֹל אֲשֶׁר־יִפֹּל מִנִּבְלָתָם עָלָיו יִטְמָא תַּנּוּר וְכִירַיִם יֻתָּץ טְמֵאִים הֵם וּטְמֵאִים יִהְיוּ לָכֶם:

³⁶ However, a spring or cistern in which water is collected shall be clean, but whoever touches such a carcass in it shall be unclean.

לו אַךְ מַעְיָן וּבוֹר מִקְוֵה־מַיִם יִהְיֶה טָהוֹר וְנֹגֵעַ בְּנִבְלָתָם יִטְמָא:

³⁷ If such a carcass falls upon seed grain that is to be sown, it is clean;

לז וְכִי יִפֹּל מִנִּבְלָתָם עַל־כָּל־זֶרַע זֵרוּעַ אֲשֶׁר יִזָּרֵעַ טָהוֹר הוּא:

³⁸ but if water is put on the seed and any part of a carcass falls upon it, it shall be unclean for you.

לח וְכִי יֻתַּן־מַיִם עַל־זֶרַע וְנָפַל מִנִּבְלָתָם עָלָיו טָמֵא הוּא לָכֶם:

³⁹ If an animal that you may eat has died, anyone who touches its carcass shall be unclean until evening;

לט וְכִי יָמוּת מִן־הַבְּהֵמָה אֲשֶׁר־הִיא לָכֶם לְאָכְלָה הַנֹּגֵעַ בְּנִבְלָתָהּ יִטְמָא עַד־הָעָרֶב:

⁴⁰ anyone who eats of its carcass shall wash his clothes and remain unclean until evening; and anyone who carries its carcass shall wash his clothes and remain unclean until evening.

מ וְהָאֹכֵל מִנִּבְלָתָהּ יְכַבֵּס בְּגָדָיו וְטָמֵא עַד־הָעֶרֶב וְהַנֹּשֵׂא אֶת־נִבְלָתָהּ יְכַבֵּס בְּגָדָיו וְטָמֵא עַד־הָעָרֶב:

⁴¹ All the things that swarm upon the earth are an abomination; they shall not be eaten.

מא וְכָל־הַשֶּׁרֶץ הַשֹּׁרֵץ עַל־הָאָרֶץ שֶׁקֶץ הוּא לֹא יֵאָכֵל:

42 You shall not eat, among all things that swarm upon the earth, anything that crawls on its belly, or anything that walks on fours, or anything that has many legs; for they are an abomination.

מב כֹּל הוֹלֵךְ עַל־גָּחוֹן וְכֹל הוֹלֵךְ עַל־אַרְבַּע עַד כָּל־מַרְבֵּה רַגְלַיִם לְכָל־הַשֶּׁרֶץ הַשֹּׁרֵץ עַל־הָאָרֶץ לֹא תֹאכְלוּם כִּי־שֶׁקֶץ הֵם:

43 You shall not draw abomination upon yourselves through anything that swarms; you shall not make yourselves unclean therewith and thus become unclean.

מג אַל־תְּשַׁקְּצוּ אֶת־נַפְשֹׁתֵיכֶם בְּכָל־הַשֶּׁרֶץ הַשֹּׁרֵץ וְלֹא תִטַּמְּאוּ בָּהֶם וְנִטְמֵתֶם בָּם:

44 For I *Hashem* am your God: you shall sanctify yourselves and be holy, for I am holy. You shall not make yourselves unclean through any swarming thing that moves upon the earth.

מד כִּי אֲנִי יְהֹוָה אֱלֹהֵיכֶם וְהִתְקַדִּשְׁתֶּם וִהְיִיתֶם קְדֹשִׁים כִּי קָדוֹשׁ אָנִי וְלֹא תְטַמְּאוּ אֶת־נַפְשֹׁתֵיכֶם בְּכָל־הַשֶּׁרֶץ הָרֹמֵשׂ עַל־הָאָרֶץ:

45 For I *Hashem* am He who brought you up from the land of Egypt to be your God: you shall be holy, for I am holy.

מה כִּי אֲנִי יְהֹוָה הַמַּעֲלֶה אֶתְכֶם מֵאֶרֶץ מִצְרַיִם לִהְיֹת לָכֶם לֵאלֹהִים וִהְיִיתֶם קְדֹשִׁים כִּי קָדוֹשׁ אָנִי:

KEE a-NEE a-do-NAI ha-ma-a-LEH et-KHEM may-E-retz mitz-RA-yim lih-YOT la-KHEM lay-lo-HEEM vih-yee-TEM k'-do-SHEEM KEE ka-DOSH A-nee

46 These are the instructions concerning animals, birds, all living creatures that move in water, and all creatures that swarm on earth,

מו זֹאת תּוֹרַת הַבְּהֵמָה וְהָעוֹף וְכֹל נֶפֶשׁ הַחַיָּה הָרֹמֶשֶׂת בַּמָּיִם וּלְכָל־נֶפֶשׁ הַשֹּׁרֶצֶת עַל־הָאָרֶץ:

47 for distinguishing between the unclean and the clean, between the living things that may be eaten and the living things that may not be eaten.

מז לְהַבְדִּיל בֵּין הַטָּמֵא וּבֵין הַטָּהֹר וּבֵין הַחַיָּה הַנֶּאֱכֶלֶת וּבֵין הַחַיָּה אֲשֶׁר לֹא תֵאָכֵל:

12 **1** *Hashem* spoke to *Moshe*, saying:

א וַיְדַבֵּר יְהֹוָה אֶל־מֹשֶׁה לֵּאמֹר:

2 Speak to *B'nei Yisrael* thus: When a woman at childbirth bears a male, she shall be unclean seven days; she shall be unclean as at the time of her menstrual infirmity.

ב דַּבֵּר אֶל־בְּנֵי יִשְׂרָאֵל לֵאמֹר אִשָּׁה כִּי תַזְרִיעַ וְיָלְדָה זָכָר וְטָמְאָה שִׁבְעַת יָמִים כִּימֵי נִדַּת דְּוֹתָהּ תִּטְמָא:

3 On the eighth day the flesh of his foreskin shall be circumcised.

ג וּבַיּוֹם הַשְּׁמִינִי יִמּוֹל בְּשַׂר עָרְלָתוֹ:

u-va-YOM ha-sh'-mee-NEE yi-MOL b'-SAR or-la-TO

11:45 You shall be holy, for I am holy This verse appears towards the end of the description of the kosher dietary laws. God draws a clear connection between obeying the kosher laws and sustaining a status of holiness. The Bible instructs the Children of Israel to distinguish between things which may be eaten and things which are not to be eaten. In handing these requirements to the Jewish people, *Hashem* is requiring that they distinguish themselves from the other nations. They are charged with a great responsibility to live a holy life, to follow God's commandments and to come as close as possible to the holiness of *Hashem*. Through observance of the kosher dietary laws, the People of Israel are meant to have a positive influence on the rest of the world.

A cow, one of the classic kosher animals, lying among the anemones

12:3 On the eighth day the flesh of his foreskin shall be circumcised This chapter deals with the laws of purity applying to a woman after child-

⁴ She shall remain in a state of blood purification for thirty-three days: she shall not touch any consecrated thing, nor enter the sanctuary until her period of purification is completed.

ד וּשְׁלֹשִׁים יוֹם וּשְׁלֹשֶׁת יָמִים תֵּשֵׁב בִּדְמֵי טָהֳרָה בְּכָל־קֹדֶשׁ לֹא־תִגָּע וְאֶל־הַמִּקְדָּשׁ לֹא תָבֹא עַד־מְלֹאת יְמֵי טָהֳרָהּ:

⁵ If she bears a female, she shall be unclean two weeks as during her menstruation, and she shall remain in a state of blood purification for sixty-six days.

ה וְאִם־נְקֵבָה תֵלֵד וְטָמְאָה שְׁבֻעַיִם כְּנִדָּתָהּ וְשִׁשִּׁים יוֹם וְשֵׁשֶׁת יָמִים תֵּשֵׁב עַל־דְּמֵי טָהֳרָה:

⁶ On the completion of her period of purification, for either son or daughter, she shall bring to the *Kohen*, at the entrance of the Tent of Meeting, a lamb in its first year for a burnt offering, and a pigeon or a turtledove for a sin offering.

ו וּבִמְלֹאת יְמֵי טָהֳרָהּ לְבֵן אוֹ לְבַת תָּבִיא כֶּבֶשׂ בֶּן־שְׁנָתוֹ לְעֹלָה וּבֶן־יוֹנָה אוֹ־תֹר לְחַטָּאת אֶל־פֶּתַח אֹהֶל־מוֹעֵד אֶל־הַכֹּהֵן:

⁷ He shall offer it before *Hashem* and make expiation on her behalf; she shall then be clean from her flow of blood. Such are the rituals concerning her who bears a child, male or female.

ז וְהִקְרִיבוֹ לִפְנֵי יְהֹוָה וְכִפֶּר עָלֶיהָ וְטָהֲרָה מִמְּקֹר דָּמֶיהָ זֹאת תּוֹרַת הַיֹּלֶדֶת לַזָּכָר אוֹ לַנְּקֵבָה:

⁸ If, however, her means do not suffice for a sheep, she shall take two turtledoves or two pigeons, one for a burnt offering and the other for a sin offering. The *Kohen* shall make expiation on her behalf, and she shall be clean.

ח וְאִם־לֹא תִמְצָא יָדָהּ דֵּי שֶׂה וְלָקְחָה שְׁתֵּי־תֹרִים אוֹ שְׁנֵי בְּנֵי יוֹנָה אֶחָד לְעֹלָה וְאֶחָד לְחַטָּאת וְכִפֶּר עָלֶיהָ הַכֹּהֵן וְטָהֵרָה:

13 ¹ *Hashem* spoke to *Moshe* and *Aharon*, saying:

יג א וַיְדַבֵּר יְהֹוָה אֶל־מֹשֶׁה וְאֶל־אַהֲרֹן לֵאמֹר:

² When a person has on the skin of his body a swelling, a rash, or a discoloration, and it develops into a scaly affection on the skin of his body, it shall be reported to *Aharon* the *Kohen* or to one of his sons, the *Kohanim*.

ב אָדָם כִּי־יִהְיֶה בְעוֹר־בְּשָׂרוֹ שְׂאֵת אוֹ־סַפַּחַת אוֹ בַהֶרֶת וְהָיָה בְעוֹר־בְּשָׂרוֹ לְנֶגַע צָרָעַת וְהוּבָא אֶל־אַהֲרֹן הַכֹּהֵן אוֹ אֶל־אַחַד מִבָּנָיו הַכֹּהֲנִים:

³ The *Kohen* shall examine the affection on the skin of his body: if hair in the affected patch has turned white and the affection appears to be deeper than the skin of his body, it is a leprous affection; when the *Kohen* sees it, he shall pronounce him unclean.

ג וְרָאָה הַכֹּהֵן אֶת־הַנֶּגַע בְּעוֹר־הַבָּשָׂר וְשֵׂעָר בַּנֶּגַע הָפַךְ ׀ לָבָן וּמַרְאֵה הַנֶּגַע עָמֹק מֵעוֹר בְּשָׂרוֹ נֶגַע צָרַעַת הוּא וְרָאָהוּ הַכֹּהֵן וְטִמֵּא אֹתוֹ:

birth. In this context, the Bible also mentions the law of circumcision, the removal of the baby boy's foreskin on the eighth day of his life. Circumcision was the first commandment given to *Avraham*, as detailed in *Sefer Bereishit* chapter 17. That chapter begins with the covenant *Hashem* makes with *Avraham*, promising that He will be an everlasting God to *Avraham* and his descendants, that *Avraham* will merit numerous offspring, and that *Hashem* will give them the Land of Israel as an eternal inheritance.

To this very day, the circumcision of a male descendant of *Avraham* draws the new child into the covenant with *Hashem*, and serves as a constant reminder of God's promise to remain with His people and give them *Eretz Yisrael*.

President Ezer Weizman (R) at a circumcision ceremony

4 But if it is a white discoloration on the skin of his body which does not appear to be deeper than the skin and the hair in it has not turned white, the *Kohen* shall isolate the affected person for seven days.

ד וְאִם־בַּהֶרֶת לְבָנָה הִוא בְּעוֹר בְּשָׂרוֹ וְעָמֹק אֵין־מַרְאֶהָ מִן־הָעוֹר וּשְׂעָרָה לֹא־הָפַךְ לָבָן וְהִסְגִּיר הַכֹּהֵן אֶת־הַנֶּגַע שִׁבְעַת יָמִים:

5 On the seventh day the *Kohen* shall examine him, and if the affection has remained unchanged in color and the disease has not spread on the skin, the *Kohen* shall isolate him for another seven days.

ה וְרָאָהוּ הַכֹּהֵן בַּיּוֹם הַשְּׁבִיעִי וְהִנֵּה הַנֶּגַע עָמַד בְּעֵינָיו לֹא־פָשָׂה הַנֶּגַע בָּעוֹר וְהִסְגִּירוֹ הַכֹּהֵן שִׁבְעַת יָמִים שֵׁנִית:

6 On the seventh day the *Kohen* shall examine him again: if the affection has faded and has not spread on the skin, the *Kohen* shall pronounce him clean. It is a rash; he shall wash his clothes, and he shall be clean.

ו וְרָאָה הַכֹּהֵן אֹתוֹ בַּיּוֹם הַשְּׁבִיעִי שֵׁנִית וְהִנֵּה כֵּהָה הַנֶּגַע וְלֹא־פָשָׂה הַנֶּגַע בָּעוֹר וְטִהֲרוֹ הַכֹּהֵן מִסְפַּחַת הִיא וְכִבֶּס בְּגָדָיו וְטָהֵר:

7 But if the rash should spread on the skin after he has presented himself to the *Kohen* and been pronounced clean, he shall present himself again to the *Kohen*.

ז וְאִם־פָּשֹׂה תִפְשֶׂה הַמִּסְפַּחַת בָּעוֹר אַחֲרֵי הֵרָאֹתוֹ אֶל־הַכֹּהֵן לְטָהֳרָתוֹ וְנִרְאָה שֵׁנִית אֶל־הַכֹּהֵן:

8 And if the *Kohen* sees that the rash has spread on the skin, the *Kohen* shall pronounce him unclean; it is leprosy.

ח וְרָאָה הַכֹּהֵן וְהִנֵּה פָּשְׂתָה הַמִּסְפַּחַת בָּעוֹר וְטִמְּאוֹ הַכֹּהֵן צָרַעַת הִוא:

9 When a person has a scaly affection, it shall be reported to the *Kohen*.

ט נֶגַע צָרַעַת כִּי תִהְיֶה בְּאָדָם וְהוּבָא אֶל־הַכֹּהֵן:

10 If the *Kohen* finds on the skin a white swelling which has turned some hair white, with a patch of undiscolored flesh in the swelling,

י וְרָאָה הַכֹּהֵן וְהִנֵּה שְׂאֵת־לְבָנָה בָּעוֹר וְהִיא הָפְכָה שֵׂעָר לָבָן וּמִחְיַת בָּשָׂר חַי בַּשְׂאֵת:

11 it is chronic leprosy on the skin of his body, and the *Kohen* shall pronounce him unclean; he need not isolate him, for he is unclean.

יא צָרַעַת נוֹשֶׁנֶת הִוא בְּעוֹר בְּשָׂרוֹ וְטִמְּאוֹ הַכֹּהֵן לֹא יַסְגִּרֶנּוּ כִּי טָמֵא הוּא:

12 If the eruption spreads out over the skin so that it covers all the skin of the affected person from head to foot, wherever the *Kohen* can see

יב וְאִם־פָּרוֹחַ תִּפְרַח הַצָּרַעַת בָּעוֹר וְכִסְּתָה הַצָּרַעַת אֵת כָּל־עוֹר הַנֶּגַע מֵרֹאשׁוֹ וְעַד־רַגְלָיו לְכָל־מַרְאֵה עֵינֵי הַכֹּהֵן:

13 if the *Kohen* sees that the eruption has covered the whole body – he shall pronounce the affected person clean; he is clean, for he has turned all white.

יג וְרָאָה הַכֹּהֵן וְהִנֵּה כִסְּתָה הַצָּרַעַת אֶת־כָּל־בְּשָׂרוֹ וְטִהַר אֶת־הַנָּגַע כֻּלּוֹ הָפַךְ לָבָן טָהוֹר הוּא:

14 But as soon as undiscolored flesh appears in it, he shall be unclean;

יד וּבְיוֹם הֵרָאוֹת בּוֹ בָּשָׂר חַי יִטְמָא:

15 when the *Kohen* sees the undiscolored flesh, he shall pronounce him unclean. The undiscolored flesh is unclean; it is leprosy.

טו וְרָאָה הַכֹּהֵן אֶת־הַבָּשָׂר הַחַי וְטִמְּאוֹ הַבָּשָׂר הַחַי טָמֵא הוּא צָרַעַת הוּא:

16 But if the undiscolored flesh again turns white, he shall come to the *Kohen*,

טז אוֹ כִי יָשׁוּב הַבָּשָׂר הַחַי וְנֶהְפַּךְ לְלָבָן וּבָא אֶל־הַכֹּהֵן:

17 and the *Kohen* shall examine him: if the affection has turned white, the *Kohen* shall pronounce the affected person clean; he is clean.

18 When an inflammation appears on the skin of one's body and it heals,

19 and a white swelling or a white discoloration streaked with red develops where the inflammation was, he shall present himself to the *Kohen*.

20 If the *Kohen* finds that it appears lower than the rest of the skin and that the hair in it has turned white, the *Kohen* shall pronounce him unclean; it is a leprous affection that has broken out in the inflammation.

21 But if the *Kohen* finds that there is no white hair in it and it is not lower than the rest of the skin, and it is faded, the *Kohen* shall isolate him for seven days.

22 If it should spread in the skin, the *Kohen* shall pronounce him unclean; it is an affection.

23 But if the discoloration remains stationary, not having spread, it is the scar of the inflammation; the *Kohen* shall pronounce him clean.

24 When the skin of one's body sustains a burn by fire, and the patch from the burn is a discoloration, either white streaked with red, or white,

25 the *Kohen* shall examine it. If some hair has turned white in the discoloration, which itself appears to go deeper than the skin, it is leprosy that has broken out in the burn. The *Kohen* shall pronounce him unclean; it is a leprous affection.

26 But if the *Kohen* finds that there is no white hair in the discoloration, and that it is not lower than the rest of the skin, and it is faded, the *Kohen* shall isolate him for seven days.

27 On the seventh day the *Kohen* shall examine him: if it has spread in the skin, the *Kohen* shall pronounce him unclean; it is a leprous affection.

28 But if the discoloration has remained stationary, not having spread on the skin, and it is faded, it is the swelling from the burn. The *Kohen* shall pronounce him clean, for it is the scar of the burn.

29 If a man or a woman has an affection on the head or in the beard,

יז וְרָאָהוּ הַכֹּהֵן וְהִנֵּה נֶהְפַּךְ הַנֶּגַע לְלָבָן וְטִהַר הַכֹּהֵן אֶת־הַנֶּגַע טָהוֹר הוּא:

יח וּבָשָׂר כִּי־יִהְיֶה בוֹ־בְעֹרוֹ שְׁחִין וְנִרְפָּא:

יט וְהָיָה בִּמְקוֹם הַשְּׁחִין שְׂאֵת לְבָנָה אוֹ בַהֶרֶת לְבָנָה אֲדַמְדָּמֶת וְנִרְאָה אֶל־הַכֹּהֵן:

כ וְרָאָה הַכֹּהֵן וְהִנֵּה מַרְאֶהָ שָׁפָל מִן־הָעוֹר וּשְׂעָרָהּ הָפַךְ לָבָן וְטִמְּאוֹ הַכֹּהֵן נֶגַע־צָרַעַת הִוא בַּשְּׁחִין פָּרָחָה:

כא וְאִם יִרְאֶנָּה הַכֹּהֵן וְהִנֵּה אֵין־בָּהּ שֵׂעָר לָבָן וּשְׁפָלָה אֵינֶנָּה מִן־הָעוֹר וְהִיא כֵהָה וְהִסְגִּירוֹ הַכֹּהֵן שִׁבְעַת יָמִים:

כב וְאִם־פָּשֹׂה תִפְשֶׂה בָּעוֹר וְטִמֵּא הַכֹּהֵן אֹתוֹ נֶגַע הִוא:

כג וְאִם־תַּחְתֶּיהָ תַּעֲמֹד הַבַּהֶרֶת לֹא פָשָׂתָה צָרֶבֶת הַשְּׁחִין הִוא וְטִהֲרוֹ הַכֹּהֵן:

כד אוֹ בָשָׂר כִּי־יִהְיֶה בְעֹרוֹ מִכְוַת־אֵשׁ וְהָיְתָה מִחְיַת הַמִּכְוָה בַּהֶרֶת לְבָנָה אֲדַמְדֶּמֶת אוֹ לְבָנָה:

כה וְרָאָה אֹתָהּ הַכֹּהֵן וְהִנֵּה נֶהְפַּךְ שֵׂעָר לָבָן בַּבַּהֶרֶת וּמַרְאֶהָ עָמֹק מִן־הָעוֹר צָרַעַת הִוא בַּמִּכְוָה פָּרָחָה וְטִמֵּא אֹתוֹ הַכֹּהֵן נֶגַע צָרַעַת הִוא:

כו וְאִם יִרְאֶנָּה הַכֹּהֵן וְהִנֵּה אֵין־בַּבַּהֶרֶת שֵׂעָר לָבָן וּשְׁפָלָה אֵינֶנָּה מִן־הָעוֹר וְהִוא כֵהָה וְהִסְגִּירוֹ הַכֹּהֵן שִׁבְעַת יָמִים:

כז וְרָאָהוּ הַכֹּהֵן בַּיּוֹם הַשְּׁבִיעִי אִם־פָּשֹׂה תִפְשֶׂה בָּעוֹר וְטִמֵּא הַכֹּהֵן אֹתוֹ נֶגַע צָרַעַת הִוא:

כח וְאִם־תַּחְתֶּיהָ תַעֲמֹד הַבַּהֶרֶת לֹא־פָשְׂתָה בָעוֹר וְהִוא כֵהָה שְׂאֵת הַמִּכְוָה הִוא וְטִהֲרוֹ הַכֹּהֵן כִּי־צָרֶבֶת הַמִּכְוָה הִוא:

כט וְאִישׁ אוֹ אִשָּׁה כִּי־יִהְיֶה בוֹ נָגַע בְּרֹאשׁ אוֹ בְזָקָן:

30 the *Kohen* shall examine the affection. If it appears to go deeper than the skin and there is thin yellow hair in it, the *Kohen* shall pronounce him unclean; it is a scall, a scaly eruption in the hair or beard.

ל וְרָאָה הַכֹּהֵן אֶת־הַנֶּגַע וְהִנֵּה מַרְאֵהוּ עָמֹק מִן־הָעוֹר וּבוֹ שֵׂעָר צָהֹב דָּק וְטִמֵּא אֹתוֹ הַכֹּהֵן נֶתֶק הוּא צָרַעַת הָרֹאשׁ אוֹ הַזָּקָן הוּא׃

31 But if the *Kohen* finds that the scall affection does not appear to go deeper than the skin, yet there is no black hair in it, the *Kohen* shall isolate the person with the scall affection for seven days.

לא וְכִי־יִרְאֶה הַכֹּהֵן אֶת־נֶגַע הַנֶּתֶק וְהִנֵּה אֵין־מַרְאֵהוּ עָמֹק מִן־הָעוֹר וְשֵׂעָר שָׁחֹר אֵין בּוֹ וְהִסְגִּיר הַכֹּהֵן אֶת־נֶגַע הַנֶּתֶק שִׁבְעַת יָמִים׃

32 On the seventh day the *Kohen* shall examine the affection. If the scall has not spread and no yellow hair has appeared in it, and the scall does not appear to go deeper than the skin,

לב וְרָאָה הַכֹּהֵן אֶת־הַנֶּגַע בַּיּוֹם הַשְּׁבִיעִי וְהִנֵּה לֹא־פָשָׂה הַנֶּתֶק וְלֹא־הָיָה בוֹ שֵׂעָר צָהֹב וּמַרְאֵה הַנֶּתֶק אֵין עָמֹק מִן־הָעוֹר׃

33 the person with the scall shall shave himself, but without shaving the scall; the *Kohen* shall isolate him for another seven days.

לג וְהִתְגַּלָּח וְאֶת־הַנֶּתֶק לֹא יְגַלֵּחַ וְהִסְגִּיר הַכֹּהֵן אֶת־הַנֶּתֶק שִׁבְעַת יָמִים שֵׁנִית׃

34 On the seventh day the *Kohen* shall examine the scall. If the scall has not spread on the skin, and does not appear to go deeper than the skin, the *Kohen* shall pronounce him clean; he shall wash his clothes, and he shall be clean.

לד וְרָאָה הַכֹּהֵן אֶת־הַנֶּתֶק בַּיּוֹם הַשְּׁבִיעִי וְהִנֵּה לֹא־פָשָׂה הַנֶּתֶק בָּעוֹר וּמַרְאֵהוּ אֵינֶנּוּ עָמֹק מִן־הָעוֹר וְטִהַר אֹתוֹ הַכֹּהֵן וְכִבֶּס בְּגָדָיו וְטָהֵר׃

35 If, however, the scall should spread on the skin after he has been pronounced clean,

לה וְאִם־פָּשֹׂה יִפְשֶׂה הַנֶּתֶק בָּעוֹר אַחֲרֵי טָהֳרָתוֹ׃

36 the *Kohen* shall examine him. If the scall has spread on the skin, the *Kohen* need not look for yellow hair: he is unclean.

לו וְרָאָהוּ הַכֹּהֵן וְהִנֵּה פָּשָׂה הַנֶּתֶק בָּעוֹר לֹא־יְבַקֵּר הַכֹּהֵן לַשֵּׂעָר הַצָּהֹב טָמֵא הוּא׃

37 But if the scall has remained unchanged in color, and black hair has grown in it, the scall is healed; he is clean. The *Kohen* shall pronounce him clean.

לז וְאִם־בְּעֵינָיו עָמַד הַנֶּתֶק וְשֵׂעָר שָׁחֹר צָמַח־בּוֹ נִרְפָּא הַנֶּתֶק טָהוֹר הוּא וְטִהֲרוֹ הַכֹּהֵן׃

38 If a man or a woman has the skin of the body streaked with white discolorations,

לח וְאִישׁ אוֹ־אִשָּׁה כִּי־יִהְיֶה בְעוֹר־בְּשָׂרָם בֶּהָרֹת בֶּהָרֹת לְבָנֹת׃

39 and the *Kohen* sees that the discolorations on the skin of the body are of a dull white, it is a tetter broken out on the skin; he is clean.

לט וְרָאָה הַכֹּהֵן וְהִנֵּה בְעוֹר־בְּשָׂרָם בֶּהָרֹת כֵּהוֹת לְבָנֹת בֹּהַק הוּא פָּרַח בָּעוֹר טָהוֹר הוּא׃

40 If a man loses the hair of his head and becomes bald, he is clean.

מ וְאִישׁ כִּי יִמָּרֵט רֹאשׁוֹ קֵרֵחַ הוּא טָהוֹר הוּא׃

41 If he loses the hair on the front part of his head and becomes bald at the forehead, he is clean.

מא וְאִם מִפְּאַת פָּנָיו יִמָּרֵט רֹאשׁוֹ גִּבֵּחַ הוּא טָהוֹר הוּא׃

42 But if a white affection streaked with red appears on the bald part in the front or at the back of the head, it is a scaly eruption that is spreading over the bald part in the front or at the back of the head.

מב וְכִי־יִהְיֶה בַקָּרַחַת אוֹ בַגַּבַּחַת נֶגַע לָבָן אֲדַמְדָּם צָרַעַת פֹּרַחַת הִוא בְּקָרַחְתּוֹ אוֹ בְגַבַּחְתּוֹ׃

43 The *Kohen* shall examine him: if the swollen affection on the bald part in the front or at the back of his head is white streaked with red, like the leprosy of body skin in appearance,

מג וְרָאָה אֹתוֹ הַכֹּהֵן וְהִנֵּה שְׂאֵת־הַנֶּגַע לְבָנָה אֲדַמְדֶּמֶת בְּקָרַחְתּוֹ אוֹ בְגַבַּחְתּוֹ כְּמַרְאֵה צָרַעַת עוֹר בָּשָׂר:

44 the man is leprous; he is unclean. The *Kohen* shall pronounce him unclean; he has the affection on his head.

מד אִישׁ־צָרוּעַ הוּא טָמֵא הוּא טַמֵּא יְטַמְּאֶנּוּ הַכֹּהֵן בְּרֹאשׁוֹ נִגְעוֹ:

45 As for the person with a leprous affection, his clothes shall be rent, his head shall be left bare, and he shall cover over his upper lip; and he shall call out, "Unclean! Unclean!"

מה וְהַצָּרוּעַ אֲשֶׁר־בּוֹ הַנֶּגַע בְּגָדָיו יִהְיוּ פְרֻמִים וְרֹאשׁוֹ יִהְיֶה פָרוּעַ וְעַל־שָׂפָם יַעְטֶה וְטָמֵא טָמֵא יִקְרָא:

46 He shall be unclean as long as the disease is on him. Being unclean, he shall dwell apart; his dwelling shall be outside the camp.

מו כָּל־יְמֵי אֲשֶׁר הַנֶּגַע בּוֹ יִטְמָא טָמֵא הוּא בָּדָד יֵשֵׁב מִחוּץ לַמַּחֲנֶה מוֹשָׁבוֹ:

47 When an eruptive affection occurs in a cloth of wool or linen fabric,

מז וְהַבֶּגֶד כִּי־יִהְיֶה בוֹ נֶגַע צָרָעַת בְּבֶגֶד צֶמֶר אוֹ בְּבֶגֶד פִּשְׁתִּים:

48 in the warp or in the woof of the linen or the wool, or in a skin or in anything made of skin;

מח אוֹ בִשְׁתִי אוֹ בְעֵרֶב לַפִּשְׁתִּים וְלַצָּמֶר אוֹ בְעוֹר אוֹ בְּכָל־מְלֶאכֶת עוֹר:

49 if the affection in the cloth or the skin, in the warp or the woof, or in any article of skin, is streaky green or red, it is an eruptive affection. It shall be shown to the *Kohen*;

מט וְהָיָה הַנֶּגַע יְרַקְרַק אוֹ אֲדַמְדָּם בַּבֶּגֶד אוֹ בָעוֹר אוֹ־בַשְּׁתִי אוֹ־בָעֵרֶב אוֹ בְכָל־כְּלִי־עוֹר נֶגַע צָרַעַת הוּא וְהָרְאָה אֶת־הַכֹּהֵן:

50 and the *Kohen*, after examining the affection, shall isolate the affected article for seven days.

נ וְרָאָה הַכֹּהֵן אֶת־הַנָּגַע וְהִסְגִּיר אֶת־הַנֶּגַע שִׁבְעַת יָמִים:

51 On the seventh day he shall examine the affection: if the affection has spread in the cloth – whether in the warp or the woof, or in the skin, for whatever purpose the skin may be used – the affection is a malignant eruption; it is unclean.

נא וְרָאָה אֶת־הַנֶּגַע בַּיּוֹם הַשְּׁבִיעִי כִּי־פָשָׂה הַנֶּגַע בַּבֶּגֶד אוֹ־בַשְּׁתִי אוֹ־בָעֵרֶב אוֹ בָעוֹר לְכֹל אֲשֶׁר־יֵעָשֶׂה הָעוֹר לִמְלָאכָה צָרַעַת מַמְאֶרֶת הַנֶּגַע טָמֵא הוּא:

52 The cloth – whether warp or woof in wool or linen, or any article of skin – in which the affection is found, shall be burned, for it is a malignant eruption; it shall be consumed in fire.

נב וְשָׂרַף אֶת־הַבֶּגֶד אוֹ אֶת־הַשְּׁתִי אוֹ אֶת־הָעֵרֶב בַּצֶּמֶר אוֹ בַפִּשְׁתִּים אוֹ אֶת־כָּל־כְּלִי הָעוֹר אֲשֶׁר־יִהְיֶה בוֹ הַנֶּגַע כִּי־צָרַעַת מַמְאֶרֶת הִוא בָּאֵשׁ תִּשָּׂרֵף:

53 But if the *Kohen* sees that the affection in the cloth – whether in warp or in woof, or in any article of skin – has not spread,

נג וְאִם יִרְאֶה הַכֹּהֵן וְהִנֵּה לֹא־פָשָׂה הַנֶּגַע בַּבֶּגֶד אוֹ בַשְּׁתִי אוֹ בָעֵרֶב אוֹ בְּכָל־כְּלִי־עוֹר:

54 the *Kohen* shall order the affected article washed, and he shall isolate it for another seven days.

נד וְצִוָּה הַכֹּהֵן וְכִבְּסוּ אֵת אֲשֶׁר־בּוֹ הַנָּגַע וְהִסְגִּירוֹ שִׁבְעַת־יָמִים שֵׁנִית:

55 And if, after the affected article has been washed, the *Kohen* sees that the affection has not changed color and that it has not spread, it is unclean. It shall be consumed in fire; it is a fret, whether on its inner side or on its outer side.

נה וְרָאָה הַכֹּהֵן אַחֲרֵי הֻכַּבֵּס אֶת־הַנֶּגַע וְהִנֵּה לֹא־הָפַךְ הַנֶּגַע אֶת־עֵינוֹ וְהַנֶּגַע לֹא־פָשָׂה טָמֵא הוּא בָּאֵשׁ תִּשְׂרְפֶנּוּ פְּחֶתֶת הִוא בְּקָרַחְתּוֹ אוֹ בְגַבַּחְתּוֹ:

56 But if the *Kohen* sees that the affected part, after it has been washed, is faded, he shall tear it out from the cloth or skin, whether in the warp or in the woof;

נו וְאִם רָאָה הַכֹּהֵן וְהִנֵּה כֵּהָה הַנֶּגַע אַחֲרֵי הֻכַּבֵּס אֹתוֹ וְקָרַע אֹתוֹ מִן־הַבֶּגֶד אוֹ מִן־הָעוֹר אוֹ מִן־הַשְּׁתִי אוֹ מִן־הָעֵרֶב:

57 and if it occurs again in the cloth – whether in warp or in woof – or in any article of skin, it is a wild growth; the affected article shall be consumed in fire.

נז וְאִם־תֵּרָאֶה עוֹד בַּבֶּגֶד אוֹ־בַשְּׁתִי אוֹ־בָעֵרֶב אוֹ בְכָל־כְּלִי־עוֹר פֹּרַחַת הִוא בָּאֵשׁ תִּשְׂרְפֶנּוּ אֵת אֲשֶׁר־בּוֹ הַנָּגַע:

58 If, however, the affection disappears from the cloth – warp or woof – or from any article of skin that has been washed, it shall be washed again, and it shall be clean.

נח וְהַבֶּגֶד אוֹ־הַשְּׁתִי אוֹ־הָעֵרֶב אוֹ־כָל־כְּלִי הָעוֹר אֲשֶׁר תְּכַבֵּס וְסָר מֵהֶם הַנָּגַע וְכֻבַּס שֵׁנִית וְטָהֵר:

59 Such is the procedure for eruptive affections of cloth, woolen or linen, in warp or in woof, or of any article of skin, for pronouncing it clean or unclean.

נט זֹאת תּוֹרַת נֶגַע־צָרַעַת בֶּגֶד הַצֶּמֶר אוֹ הַפִּשְׁתִּים אוֹ הַשְּׁתִי אוֹ הָעֵרֶב אוֹ כָּל־כְּלִי־עוֹר לְטַהֲרוֹ אוֹ לְטַמְּאוֹ:

ZOT to-RAT ne-ga tza-RA-at BE-ged ha-TZE-mer O ha-pish-TEEM O ha-sh'-TEE O ha-AY-rev O kol k'-lee OR l'-ta-ha-RO O l'-ta-m'-O

14 1 *Hashem* spoke to *Moshe*, saying:

א וַיְדַבֵּר יְהוָֹה אֶל־מֹשֶׁה לֵּאמֹר:

2 This shall be the ritual for a leper at the time that he is to be cleansed. When it has been reported to the *Kohen*,

ב זֹאת תִּהְיֶה תּוֹרַת הַמְּצֹרָע בְּיוֹם טָהֳרָתוֹ וְהוּבָא אֶל־הַכֹּהֵן:

3 the *Kohen* shall go outside the camp. If the *Kohen* sees that the leper has been healed of his scaly affection,

ג וְיָצָא הַכֹּהֵן אֶל־מִחוּץ לַמַּחֲנֶה וְרָאָה הַכֹּהֵן וְהִנֵּה נִרְפָּא נֶגַע־הַצָּרַעַת מִן־הַצָּרוּעַ:

4 the *Kohen* shall order two live clean birds, cedar wood, crimson stuff, and hyssop to be brought for him who is to be cleansed.

ד וְצִוָּה הַכֹּהֵן וְלָקַח לַמִּטַּהֵר שְׁתֵּי־צִפֳּרִים חַיּוֹת טְהֹרוֹת וְעֵץ אֶרֶז וּשְׁנִי תוֹלַעַת וְאֵזֹב:

5 The *Kohen* shall order one of the birds slaughtered over fresh water in an earthen vessel;

ה וְצִוָּה הַכֹּהֵן וְשָׁחַט אֶת־הַצִּפּוֹר הָאֶחָת אֶל־כְּלִי־חֶרֶשׂ עַל־מַיִם חַיִּים:

6 and he shall take the live bird, along with the cedar wood, the crimson stuff, and the hyssop, and dip them together with the live bird in the blood of the bird that was slaughtered over the fresh water.

ו אֶת־הַצִּפֹּר הַחַיָּה יִקַּח אֹתָהּ וְאֶת־עֵץ הָאֶרֶז וְאֶת־שְׁנִי הַתּוֹלַעַת וְאֶת־הָאֵזֹב וְטָבַל אוֹתָם וְאֵת הַצִּפֹּר הַחַיָּה בְּדַם הַצִּפֹּר הַשְּׁחֻטָה עַל הַמַּיִם הַחַיִּים:

13:59 Such is the procedure for eruptive affections This chapter details with the spiritual disease known as *tzaraat* (צרעת), similar in presentation to leprosy, and the subsequent process of purification from this ailment. *Tzaraat* is understood to be a punishment for a number of sins, most famously the sin of *lashon hara* (לשון הרע), or 'slander.' *Tzaraat* could appear on a person's skin, clothing or home. *Ramban* emphasizes that it is absolutely supernatural for inanimate objects to display signs of illness. Although *lashon hara* is a sin not restricted to the Land of Israel, the miraculous spiritual malady of *tzaraat* could occur only in the land where God's presence is manifest so clearly. This demonstrates that the spiritual stakes are higher for those who live in the Holy Land. We must always remember that one is held more accountable, and one's actions have greater significance, in *Eretz Yisrael*.

Yerushalayim at night

7 He shall then sprinkle it seven times on him who is to be cleansed of the eruption and cleanse him; and he shall set the live bird free in the open country.

ז וְהִזָּה עַל הַמִּטַּהֵר מִן הַצָּרַעַת שֶׁבַע פְּעָמִים וְטִהֲרוֹ וְשִׁלַּח אֶת הַצִּפֹּר הַחַיָּה עַל פְּנֵי הַשָּׂדֶה:

8 The one to be cleansed shall wash his clothes, shave off all his hair, and bathe in water; then he shall be clean. After that he may enter the camp, but he must remain outside his tent seven days.

ח וְכִבֶּס הַמִּטַּהֵר אֶת בְּגָדָיו וְגִלַּח אֶת כָּל שְׂעָרוֹ וְרָחַץ בַּמַּיִם וְטָהֵר וְאַחַר יָבוֹא אֶל הַמַּחֲנֶה וְיָשַׁב מִחוּץ לְאָהֳלוֹ שִׁבְעַת יָמִים:

9 On the seventh day he shall shave off all his hair – of head, beard, and eyebrows. When he has shaved off all his hair, he shall wash his clothes and bathe his body in water; then he shall be clean.

ט וְהָיָה בַיּוֹם הַשְּׁבִיעִי יְגַלַּח אֶת כָּל שְׂעָרוֹ אֶת רֹאשׁוֹ וְאֶת זְקָנוֹ וְאֵת גַּבֹּת עֵינָיו וְאֶת כָּל שְׂעָרוֹ יְגַלֵּחַ וְכִבֶּס אֶת בְּגָדָיו וְרָחַץ אֶת בְּשָׂרוֹ בַּמַּיִם וְטָהֵר:

10 On the eighth day he shall take two male lambs without blemish, one ewe lamb in its first year without blemish, three-tenths of a measure of choice flour with oil mixed in for a meal offering, and one *log* of oil.

י וּבַיּוֹם הַשְּׁמִינִי יִקַּח שְׁנֵי כְבָשִׂים תְּמִימִם וְכַבְשָׂה אַחַת בַּת שְׁנָתָהּ תְּמִימָה וּשְׁלֹשָׁה עֶשְׂרֹנִים סֹלֶת מִנְחָה בְּלוּלָה בַשֶּׁמֶן וְלֹג אֶחָד שָׁמֶן:

11 These shall be presented before *Hashem*, with the man to be cleansed, at the entrance of the Tent of Meeting, by the *Kohen* who performs the cleansing.

יא וְהֶעֱמִיד הַכֹּהֵן הַמְטַהֵר אֵת הָאִישׁ הַמִּטַּהֵר וְאֹתָם לִפְנֵי יְהוָה פֶּתַח אֹהֶל מוֹעֵד:

12 The *Kohen* shall take one of the male lambs and offer it with the *log* of oil as a guilt offering, and he shall elevate them as an elevation offering before *Hashem*.

יב וְלָקַח הַכֹּהֵן אֶת הַכֶּבֶשׂ הָאֶחָד וְהִקְרִיב אֹתוֹ לְאָשָׁם וְאֶת לֹג הַשָּׁמֶן וְהֵנִיף אֹתָם תְּנוּפָה לִפְנֵי יְהוָה:

13 The lamb shall be slaughtered at the spot in the sacred area where the sin offering and the burnt offering are slaughtered. For the guilt offering, like the sin offering, goes to the *Kohen*; it is most holy.

יג וְשָׁחַט אֶת הַכֶּבֶשׂ בִּמְקוֹם אֲשֶׁר יִשְׁחַט אֶת הַחַטָּאת וְאֶת הָעֹלָה בִּמְקוֹם הַקֹּדֶשׁ כִּי כַּחַטָּאת הָאָשָׁם הוּא לַכֹּהֵן קֹדֶשׁ קָדָשִׁים הוּא:

14 The *Kohen* shall take some of the blood of the guilt offering, and the *Kohen* shall put it on the ridge of the right ear of him who is being cleansed, and on the thumb of his right hand, and on the big toe of his right foot.

יד וְלָקַח הַכֹּהֵן מִדַּם הָאָשָׁם וְנָתַן הַכֹּהֵן עַל תְּנוּךְ אֹזֶן הַמִּטַּהֵר הַיְמָנִית וְעַל בֹּהֶן יָדוֹ הַיְמָנִית וְעַל בֹּהֶן רַגְלוֹ הַיְמָנִית:

15 The *Kohen* shall then take some of the *log* of oil and pour it into the palm of his own left hand.

טו וְלָקַח הַכֹּהֵן מִלֹּג הַשָּׁמֶן וְיָצַק עַל כַּף הַכֹּהֵן הַשְּׂמָאלִית:

16 And the *Kohen* shall dip his right finger in the oil that is in the palm of his left hand and sprinkle some of the oil with his finger seven times before *Hashem*.

טז וְטָבַל הַכֹּהֵן אֶת אֶצְבָּעוֹ הַיְמָנִית מִן הַשֶּׁמֶן אֲשֶׁר עַל כַּפּוֹ הַשְּׂמָאלִית וְהִזָּה מִן הַשֶּׁמֶן בְּאֶצְבָּעוֹ שֶׁבַע פְּעָמִים לִפְנֵי יְהוָה:

17 Some of the oil left in his palm shall be put by the *Kohen* on the ridge of the right ear of the one being cleansed, on the thumb of his right hand, and on the big toe of his right foot – over the blood of the guilt offering.

יז וּמִיֶּתֶר הַשֶּׁמֶן אֲשֶׁר עַל כַּפּוֹ יִתֵּן הַכֹּהֵן עַל תְּנוּךְ אֹזֶן הַמִּטַּהֵר הַיְמָנִית וְעַל בֹּהֶן יָדוֹ הַיְמָנִית וְעַל בֹּהֶן רַגְלוֹ הַיְמָנִית עַל דַּם הָאָשָׁם:

18 The rest of the oil in his palm the *Kohen* shall put on the head of the one being cleansed. Thus the *Kohen* shall make expiation for him before *Hashem*.

יח וְהַנּוֹתָר בַּשֶּׁמֶן אֲשֶׁר עַל־כַּף הַכֹּהֵן יִתֵּן עַל־רֹאשׁ הַמִּטַּהֵר וְכִפֶּר עָלָיו הַכֹּהֵן לִפְנֵי יְהֹוָה:

19 The *Kohen* shall then offer the sin offering and make expiation for the one being cleansed of his uncleanness. Last, the burnt offering shall be slaughtered,

יט וְעָשָׂה הַכֹּהֵן אֶת־הַחַטָּאת וְכִפֶּר עַל־הַמִּטַּהֵר מִטֻּמְאָתוֹ וְאַחַר יִשְׁחַט אֶת־הָעֹלָה:

20 and the *Kohen* shall offer the burnt offering and the meal offering on the *Mizbayach*, and the *Kohen* shall make expiation for him. Then he shall be clean.

כ וְהֶעֱלָה הַכֹּהֵן אֶת־הָעֹלָה וְאֶת־הַמִּנְחָה הַמִּזְבֵּחָה וְכִפֶּר עָלָיו הַכֹּהֵן וְטָהֵר:

21 If, however, he is poor and his means are insufficient, he shall take one male lamb for a guilt offering, to be elevated in expiation for him, one-tenth of a measure of choice flour with oil mixed in for a meal offering, and a *log* of oil;

כא וְאִם־דַּל הוּא וְאֵין יָדוֹ מַשֶּׂגֶת וְלָקַח כֶּבֶשׂ אֶחָד אָשָׁם לִתְנוּפָה לְכַפֵּר עָלָיו וְעִשָּׂרוֹן סֹלֶת אֶחָד בָּלוּל בַּשֶּׁמֶן לְמִנְחָה וְלֹג שָׁמֶן:

22 and two turtledoves or two pigeons, depending on his means, the one to be the sin offering and the other the burnt offering.

כב וּשְׁתֵּי תֹרִים אוֹ שְׁנֵי בְּנֵי יוֹנָה אֲשֶׁר תַּשִּׂיג יָדוֹ וְהָיָה אֶחָד חַטָּאת וְהָאֶחָד עֹלָה:

23 On the eighth day of his cleansing he shall bring them to the *Kohen* at the entrance of the Tent of Meeting, before *Hashem*.

כג וְהֵבִיא אֹתָם בַּיּוֹם הַשְּׁמִינִי לְטָהֳרָתוֹ אֶל־הַכֹּהֵן אֶל־פֶּתַח אֹהֶל־מוֹעֵד לִפְנֵי יְהֹוָה:

24 The *Kohen* shall take the lamb of guilt offering and the *log* of oil, and elevate them as an elevation offering before *Hashem*.

כד וְלָקַח הַכֹּהֵן אֶת־כֶּבֶשׂ הָאָשָׁם וְאֶת־לֹג הַשֶּׁמֶן וְהֵנִיף אֹתָם הַכֹּהֵן תְּנוּפָה לִפְנֵי יְהֹוָה:

25 When the lamb of guilt offering has been slaughtered, the *Kohen* shall take some of the blood of the guilt offering and put it on the ridge of the right ear of the one being cleansed, on the thumb of his right hand, and on the big toe of his right foot.

כה וְשָׁחַט אֶת־כֶּבֶשׂ הָאָשָׁם וְלָקַח הַכֹּהֵן מִדַּם הָאָשָׁם וְנָתַן עַל־תְּנוּךְ אֹזֶן־הַמִּטַּהֵר הַיְמָנִית וְעַל־בֹּהֶן יָדוֹ הַיְמָנִית וְעַל־בֹּהֶן רַגְלוֹ הַיְמָנִית:

26 The *Kohen* shall then pour some of the oil into the palm of his own left hand,

כו וּמִן־הַשֶּׁמֶן יִצֹק הַכֹּהֵן עַל־כַּף הַכֹּהֵן הַשְּׂמָאלִית:

27 and with the finger of his right hand the *Kohen* shall sprinkle some of the oil that is in the palm of his left hand seven times before *Hashem*.

כז וְהִזָּה הַכֹּהֵן בְּאֶצְבָּעוֹ הַיְמָנִית מִן־הַשֶּׁמֶן אֲשֶׁר עַל־כַּפּוֹ הַשְּׂמָאלִית שֶׁבַע פְּעָמִים לִפְנֵי יְהֹוָה:

28 Some of the oil in his palm shall be put by the *Kohen* on the ridge of the right ear of the one being cleansed, on the thumb of his right hand, and on the big toe of his right foot, over the same places as the blood of the guilt offering;

כח וְנָתַן הַכֹּהֵן מִן־הַשֶּׁמֶן אֲשֶׁר עַל־כַּפּוֹ עַל־תְּנוּךְ אֹזֶן הַמִּטַּהֵר הַיְמָנִית וְעַל־בֹּהֶן יָדוֹ הַיְמָנִית וְעַל־בֹּהֶן רַגְלוֹ הַיְמָנִית עַל־מְקוֹם דַּם הָאָשָׁם:

29 and what is left of the oil in his palm the *Kohen* shall put on the head of the one being cleansed, to make expiation for him before *Hashem*.

כט וְהַנּוֹתָר מִן־הַשֶּׁמֶן אֲשֶׁר עַל־כַּף הַכֹּהֵן יִתֵּן עַל־רֹאשׁ הַמִּטַּהֵר לְכַפֵּר עָלָיו לִפְנֵי יְהֹוָה:

30 He shall then offer one of the turtledoves or pigeons, depending on his means

ל וְעָשָׂה אֶת־הָאֶחָד מִן־הַתֹּרִים אוֹ מִן־
בְּנֵי הַיּוֹנָה מֵאֲשֶׁר תַּשִּׂיג יָדוֹ:

31 whichever he can afford – the one as a sin offering and the other as a burnt offering, together with the meal offering. Thus the *Kohen* shall make expiation before *Hashem* for the one being cleansed.

לא אֵת אֲשֶׁר־תַּשִּׂיג יָדוֹ אֶת־הָאֶחָד חַטָּאת
וְאֶת־הָאֶחָד עֹלָה עַל־הַמִּנְחָה וְכִפֶּר
הַכֹּהֵן עַל הַמִּטַּהֵר לִפְנֵי יְהוָה:

32 Such is the ritual for him who has a scaly affection and whose means for his cleansing are limited.

לב זֹאת תּוֹרַת אֲשֶׁר־בּוֹ נֶגַע צָרָעַת אֲשֶׁר
לֹא־תַשִּׂיג יָדוֹ בְּטָהֳרָתוֹ:

33 *Hashem* spoke to *Moshe* and *Aharon*, saying:

לג וַיְדַבֵּר יְהוָה אֶל־מֹשֶׁה וְאֶל־אַהֲרֹן
לֵאמֹר:

34 When you enter the land of Canaan that I give you as a possession, and I inflict an eruptive plague upon a house in the land you possess,

לד כִּי תָבֹאוּ אֶל־אֶרֶץ כְּנַעַן אֲשֶׁר אֲנִי נֹתֵן
לָכֶם לַאֲחֻזָּה וְנָתַתִּי נֶגַע צָרַעַת בְּבֵית
אֶרֶץ אֲחֻזַּתְכֶם:

*KEE ta-VO-u el E-retz k'-NA-an a-SHER a-NEE no-TAYN la-KHEM
la-a-khu-ZAH v'-na-ta-TEE NE-ga tza-RA-at b'VAYT E-retz a-khu-zat-KHEM*

35 the owner of the house shall come and tell the *Kohen*, saying, "Something like a plague has appeared upon my house."

לה וּבָא אֲשֶׁר־לוֹ הַבַּיִת וְהִגִּיד לַכֹּהֵן לֵאמֹר
כְּנֶגַע נִרְאָה לִי בַּבָּיִת:

36 The *Kohen* shall order the house cleared before the *Kohen* enters to examine the plague, so that nothing in the house may become unclean; after that the *Kohen* shall enter to examine the house.

לו וְצִוָּה הַכֹּהֵן וּפִנּוּ אֶת־הַבַּיִת בְּטֶרֶם יָבֹא
הַכֹּהֵן לִרְאוֹת אֶת־הַנֶּגַע וְלֹא יִטְמָא כָּל־
אֲשֶׁר בַּבָּיִת וְאַחַר כֵּן יָבֹא הַכֹּהֵן לִרְאוֹת
אֶת־הַבָּיִת:

37 If, when he examines the plague, the plague in the walls of the house is found to consist of greenish or reddish streaks that appear to go deep into the wall,

לז וְרָאָה אֶת־הַנֶּגַע וְהִנֵּה הַנֶּגַע בְּקִירֹת
הַבַּיִת שְׁקַעֲרוּרֹת יְרַקְרַקֹּת אוֹ
אֲדַמְדַּמֹּת וּמַרְאֵיהֶן שָׁפָל מִן־הַקִּיר:

38 the *Kohen* shall come out of the house to the entrance of the house, and close up the house for seven days.

לח וְיָצָא הַכֹּהֵן מִן־הַבַּיִת אֶל־פֶּתַח הַבָּיִת
וְהִסְגִּיר אֶת־הַבַּיִת שִׁבְעַת יָמִים:

14:34 When you enter the land of *Canaan* that I give you as a possession In addition to the sin of *lashon hara*, speaking negatively about others, lacking generosity and being unwilling to give to other could also cause *tzaraat* to appear on one's home. The *Kli Yakar* points out that once they took possession of the land, the Israelites found many homes filled with riches. If they failed to share what they had, *Hashem* would afflict those homes. *Hashem* bequeathed the Jewish people the Land of Israel with the expectation that they would share its bounty with others. From its inception, the contemporary State of Israel internalized this message; it is often the first to volunteer its resources and knowledge to help countries in need. In his book *Altneuland*, Theodor Herzl wrote that following the establishment of a Jewish national home, Jews would come to the aid of the suffering people in Africa, whose "problem, in all its horror, only a Jew can fathom." Israel's founding leaders took this admonition to heart and, in 1958, Golda Meir, then Israel's Foreign Minister, created a department whose mission was to help Africa overcome problems of water, irrigation, agriculture and education.

Theodor Herzl
(1860–1904)

39 On the seventh day the *Kohen* shall return. If he sees that the plague has spread on the walls of the house,

לט וְשָׁב הַכֹּהֵן בַּיּוֹם הַשְּׁבִיעִי וְרָאָה וְהִנֵּה פָּשָׂה הַנֶּגַע בְּקִירֹת הַבָּיִת:

40 the *Kohen* shall order the stones with the plague in them to be pulled out and cast outside the city into an unclean place.

מ וְצִוָּה הַכֹּהֵן וְחִלְּצוּ אֶת־הָאֲבָנִים אֲשֶׁר בָּהֵן הַנֶּגַע וְהִשְׁלִיכוּ אֶתְהֶן אֶל־מִחוּץ לָעִיר אֶל־מָקוֹם טָמֵא:

41 The house shall be scraped inside all around, and the coating that is scraped off shall be dumped outside the city in an unclean place.

מא וְאֶת־הַבַּיִת יַקְצִעַ מִבַּיִת סָבִיב וְשָׁפְכוּ אֶת־הֶעָפָר אֲשֶׁר הִקְצוּ אֶל־מִחוּץ לָעִיר אֶל־מָקוֹם טָמֵא:

42 They shall take other stones and replace those stones with them, and take other coating and plaster the house.

מב וְלָקְחוּ אֲבָנִים אֲחֵרוֹת וְהֵבִיאוּ אֶל־ תַּחַת הָאֲבָנִים וְעָפָר אַחֵר יִקַּח וְטָח אֶת־הַבָּיִת:

43 If the plague again breaks out in the house, after the stones have been pulled out and after the house has been scraped and replastered,

מג וְאִם־יָשׁוּב הַנֶּגַע וּפָרַח בַּבַּיִת אַחַר חִלֵּץ אֶת־הָאֲבָנִים וְאַחֲרֵי הִקְצוֹת אֶת־הַבַּיִת וְאַחֲרֵי הִטּוֹחַ:

44 the *Kohen* shall come to examine: if the plague has spread in the house, it is a malignant eruption in the house; it is unclean.

מד וּבָא הַכֹּהֵן וְרָאָה וְהִנֵּה פָּשָׂה הַנֶּגַע בַּבָּיִת צָרַעַת מַמְאֶרֶת הִוא בַּבַּיִת טָמֵא הוּא:

45 The house shall be torn down – its stones and timber and all the coating on the house – and taken to an unclean place outside the city.

מה וְנָתַץ אֶת־הַבַּיִת אֶת־אֲבָנָיו וְאֶת־עֵצָיו וְאֵת כָּל־עֲפַר הַבָּיִת וְהוֹצִיא אֶל־מִחוּץ לָעִיר אֶל־מָקוֹם טָמֵא:

46 Whoever enters the house while it is closed up shall be unclean until evening.

מו וְהַבָּא אֶל־הַבַּיִת כָּל־יְמֵי הִסְגִּיר אֹתוֹ יִטְמָא עַד־הָעָרֶב:

47 Whoever sleeps in the house must wash his clothes, and whoever eats in the house must wash his clothes.

מז וְהַשֹּׁכֵב בַּבַּיִת יְכַבֵּס אֶת־בְּגָדָיו וְהָאֹכֵל בַּבַּיִת יְכַבֵּס אֶת־בְּגָדָיו:

48 If, however, the *Kohen* comes and sees that the plague has not spread in the house after the house was replastered, the *Kohen* shall pronounce the house clean, for the plague has healed.

מח וְאִם־בֹּא יָבֹא הַכֹּהֵן וְרָאָה וְהִנֵּה לֹא־ פָשָׂה הַנֶּגַע בַּבַּיִת אַחֲרֵי הִטֹּחַ אֶת־ הַבָּיִת וְטִהַר הַכֹּהֵן אֶת־הַבַּיִת כִּי נִרְפָּא הַנָּגַע:

49 To purge the house, he shall take two birds, cedar wood, crimson stuff, and hyssop.

מט וְלָקַח לְחַטֵּא אֶת־הַבַּיִת שְׁתֵּי צִפֳּרִים וְעֵץ אֶרֶז וּשְׁנִי תוֹלַעַת וְאֵזֹב:

50 He shall slaughter the one bird over fresh water in an earthen vessel.

נ וְשָׁחַט אֶת־הַצִּפֹּר הָאֶחָת אֶל־כְּלִי־חֶרֶשׂ עַל־מַיִם חַיִּים:

51 He shall take the cedar wood, the hyssop, the crimson stuff, and the live bird, and dip them in the blood of the slaughtered bird and the fresh water, and sprinkle on the house seven times.

נא וְלָקַח אֶת־עֵץ־הָאֶרֶז וְאֶת־הָאֵזֹב וְאֵת שְׁנִי הַתּוֹלַעַת וְאֵת הַצִּפֹּר הַחַיָּה וְטָבַל אֹתָם בְּדַם הַצִּפֹּר הַשְּׁחוּטָה וּבַמַּיִם הַחַיִּים וְהִזָּה אֶל־הַבַּיִת שֶׁבַע פְּעָמִים:

52 Having purged the house with the blood of the bird, the fresh water, the live bird, the cedar wood, the hyssop, and the crimson stuff,

נב וְחִטֵּא אֶת־הַבַּיִת בְּדַם הַצִּפּוֹר וּבַמַּיִם הַחַיִּים וּבַצִּפֹּר הַחַיָּה וּבְעֵץ הָאֶרֶז וּבָאֵזֹב וּבִשְׁנִי הַתּוֹלָעַת:

53 he shall set the live bird free outside the city in the open country. Thus he shall make expiation for the house, and it shall be clean.

נג וְשִׁלַּח אֶת־הַצִּפֹּר הַחַיָּה אֶל־מִחוּץ לָעִיר אֶל־פְּנֵי הַשָּׂדֶה וְכִפֶּר עַל־הַבַּיִת וְטָהֵר:

54 Such is the ritual for every eruptive affection – for scalls,

נד זֹאת הַתּוֹרָה לְכָל־נֶגַע הַצָּרַעַת וְלַנָּתֶק:

55 for an eruption on a cloth or a house,

נה וּלְצָרַעַת הַבֶּגֶד וְלַבָּיִת:

56 for swellings, for rashes, or for discolorations

נו וְלַשְׂאֵת וְלַסַּפַּחַת וְלַבֶּהָרֶת:

57 to determine when they are unclean and when they are clean. Such is the ritual concerning eruptions.

נז לְהוֹרֹת בְּיוֹם הַטָּמֵא וּבְיוֹם הַטָּהֹר זֹאת תּוֹרַת הַצָּרָעַת:

15 ¹ *Hashem* spoke to *Moshe* and *Aharon*, saying:

טו א וַיְדַבֵּר יְהוָה אֶל־מֹשֶׁה וְאֶל־אַהֲרֹן לֵאמֹר:

² Speak to *B'nei Yisrael* and say to them: When any man has a discharge issuing from his member, he is unclean.

ב דַּבְּרוּ אֶל־בְּנֵי יִשְׂרָאֵל וַאֲמַרְתֶּם אֲלֵהֶם אִישׁ אִישׁ כִּי יִהְיֶה זָב מִבְּשָׂרוֹ זוֹבוֹ טָמֵא הוּא:

³ The uncleanness from his discharge shall mean the following – whether his member runs with the discharge or is stopped up so that there is no discharge, his uncleanness means this:

ג וְזֹאת תִּהְיֶה טֻמְאָתוֹ בְּזוֹבוֹ רָר בְּשָׂרוֹ אֶת־זוֹבוֹ אוֹ־הֶחְתִּים בְּשָׂרוֹ מִזּוֹבוֹ טֻמְאָתוֹ הִוא:

⁴ Any bedding on which the one with the discharge lies shall be unclean, and every object on which he sits shall be unclean.

ד כָּל־הַמִּשְׁכָּב אֲשֶׁר יִשְׁכַּב עָלָיו הַזָּב יִטְמָא וְכָל־הַכְּלִי אֲשֶׁר־יֵשֵׁב עָלָיו יִטְמָא:

⁵ Anyone who touches his bedding shall wash his clothes, bathe in water, and remain unclean until evening.

ה וְאִישׁ אֲשֶׁר יִגַּע בְּמִשְׁכָּבוֹ יְכַבֵּס בְּגָדָיו וְרָחַץ בַּמַּיִם וְטָמֵא עַד־הָעָרֶב:

⁶ Whoever sits on an object on which the one with the discharge has sat shall wash his clothes, bathe in water, and remain unclean until evening.

ו וְהַיֹּשֵׁב עַל־הַכְּלִי אֲשֶׁר־יֵשֵׁב עָלָיו הַזָּב יְכַבֵּס בְּגָדָיו וְרָחַץ בַּמַּיִם וְטָמֵא עַד־הָעָרֶב:

⁷ Whoever touches the body of the one with the discharge shall wash his clothes, bathe in water, and remain unclean until evening.

ז וְהַנֹּגֵעַ בִּבְשַׂר הַזָּב יְכַבֵּס בְּגָדָיו וְרָחַץ בַּמַּיִם וְטָמֵא עַד־הָעָרֶב:

⁸ If one with a discharge spits on one who is clean, the latter shall wash his clothes, bathe in water, and remain unclean until evening.

ח וְכִי־יָרֹק הַזָּב בַּטָּהוֹר וְכִבֶּס בְּגָדָיו וְרָחַץ בַּמַּיִם וְטָמֵא עַד־הָעָרֶב:

⁹ Any means for riding that one with a discharge has mounted shall be unclean;

ט וְכָל־הַמֶּרְכָּב אֲשֶׁר יִרְכַּב עָלָיו הַזָּב יִטְמָא:

¹⁰ whoever touches anything that was under him shall be unclean until evening; and whoever carries such things shall wash his clothes, bathe in water, and remain unclean until evening.

י וְכָל־הַנֹּגֵעַ בְּכֹל אֲשֶׁר יִהְיֶה תַחְתָּיו יִטְמָא עַד־הָעָרֶב וְהַנּוֹשֵׂא אוֹתָם יְכַבֵּס בְּגָדָיו וְרָחַץ בַּמַּיִם וְטָמֵא עַד־הָעָרֶב:

11 If one with a discharge, without having rinsed his hands in water, touches another person, that person shall wash his clothes, bathe in water, and remain unclean until evening.

יא וְכֹל אֲשֶׁר יִגַּע־בּוֹ הַזָּב וְיָדָיו לֹא־שָׁטַף בַּמָּיִם וְכִבֶּס בְּגָדָיו וְרָחַץ בַּמַּיִם וְטָמֵא עַד־הָעָרֶב:

12 An earthen vessel that one with a discharge touches shall be broken; and any wooden implement shall be rinsed with water.

יב וּכְלִי־חֶרֶשׂ אֲשֶׁר־יִגַּע־בּוֹ הַזָּב יִשָּׁבֵר וְכָל־כְּלִי־עֵץ יִשָּׁטֵף בַּמָּיִם:

13 When one with a discharge becomes clean of his discharge, he shall count off seven days for his cleansing, wash his clothes, and bathe his body in fresh water; then he shall be clean.

יג וְכִי־יִטְהַר הַזָּב מִזּוֹבוֹ וְסָפַר לוֹ שִׁבְעַת יָמִים לְטָהֳרָתוֹ וְכִבֶּס בְּגָדָיו וְרָחַץ בְּשָׂרוֹ בְּמַיִם חַיִּים וְטָהֵר:

v'-khee yit-HAR ha-ZAV mi-zo-VO v'-SA-far LO shiv-AT ya-MEEM l'-ta-ho-ra-TO v'-khi-BES b'-ga-DAV v'-ra-KHATZ b'-sa-RO b'-MA-yim kha-YEEM v'-ta-HAYR

14 On the eighth day he shall take two turtledoves or two pigeons and come before *Hashem* at the entrance of the Tent of Meeting and give them to the *Kohen*.

יד וּבַיּוֹם הַשְּׁמִינִי יִקַּח־לוֹ שְׁתֵּי תֹרִים אוֹ שְׁנֵי בְּנֵי יוֹנָה וּבָא לִפְנֵי יְהוָה אֶל־פֶּתַח אֹהֶל מוֹעֵד וּנְתָנָם אֶל־הַכֹּהֵן:

15 The *Kohen* shall offer them, the one as a sin offering and the other as a burnt offering. Thus the *Kohen* shall make expiation on his behalf, for his discharge, before *Hashem*.

טו וְעָשָׂה אֹתָם הַכֹּהֵן אֶחָד חַטָּאת וְהָאֶחָד עֹלָה וְכִפֶּר עָלָיו הַכֹּהֵן לִפְנֵי יְהוָה מִזּוֹבוֹ:

16 When a man has an emission of semen, he shall bathe his whole body in water and remain unclean until evening.

טז וְאִישׁ כִּי־תֵצֵא מִמֶּנּוּ שִׁכְבַת־זָרַע וְרָחַץ בַּמַּיִם אֶת־כָּל־בְּשָׂרוֹ וְטָמֵא עַד־הָעָרֶב:

17 All cloth or leather on which semen falls shall be washed in water and remain unclean until evening.

יז וְכָל־בֶּגֶד וְכָל־עוֹר אֲשֶׁר־יִהְיֶה עָלָיו שִׁכְבַת־זָרַע וְכֻבַּס בַּמַּיִם וְטָמֵא עַד־הָעָרֶב:

18 And if a man has carnal relations with a woman, they shall bathe in water and remain unclean until evening.

יח וְאִשָּׁה אֲשֶׁר יִשְׁכַּב אִישׁ אֹתָהּ שִׁכְבַת־זָרַע וְרָחֲצוּ בַמַּיִם וְטָמְאוּ עַד־הָעָרֶב:

19 When a woman has a discharge, her discharge being blood from her body, she shall remain in her impurity seven days; whoever touches her shall be unclean until evening.

יט וְאִשָּׁה כִּי־תִהְיֶה זָבָה דָּם יִהְיֶה זֹבָהּ בִּבְשָׂרָהּ שִׁבְעַת יָמִים תִּהְיֶה בְנִדָּתָהּ וְכָל־הַנֹּגֵעַ בָּהּ יִטְמָא עַד־הָעָרֶב:

15:13 And bathe his body in fresh water Chapter 15 discusses the different kinds of impurity that occur as a result of certain types of bodily discharges. As part of the purification process, the person who has become impure must immerse in a ritual bath. This immersion signifies an elevation in spiritual status, and it is no coincidence that water is the means through which this elevation occurs. Water is the source of life, and so it is appropriate to immerse in it during the process of spiritual rebirth and renewal. In addition, the fluid nature of water symbolizes that as spiritual beings, we are never fixed in one place. In life we have ups and downs, but there is always the potential for further growth.

Ancient ritual bath found in Qumran

20 Anything that she lies on during her impurity shall be unclean; and anything that she sits on shall be unclean.

כ וְכֹל אֲשֶׁר תִּשְׁכַּב עָלָיו בְּנִדָּתָהּ יִטְמָא וְכֹל אֲשֶׁר־תֵּשֵׁב עָלָיו יִטְמָא:

21 Anyone who touches her bedding shall wash his clothes, bathe in water, and remain unclean until evening;

כא וְכָל־הַנֹּגֵעַ בְּמִשְׁכָּבָהּ יְכַבֵּס בְּגָדָיו וְרָחַץ בַּמַּיִם וְטָמֵא עַד־הָעָרֶב:

22 and anyone who touches any object on which she has sat shall wash his clothes, bathe in water, and remain unclean until evening.

כב וְכָל־הַנֹּגֵעַ בְּכָל־כְּלִי אֲשֶׁר־תֵּשֵׁב עָלָיו יְכַבֵּס בְּגָדָיו וְרָחַץ בַּמַּיִם וְטָמֵא עַד־הָעָרֶב:

23 Be it the bedding or be it the object on which she has sat, on touching it he shall be unclean until evening.

כג וְאִם עַל־הַמִּשְׁכָּב הוּא אוֹ עַל־הַכְּלִי אֲשֶׁר־הִוא יֹשֶׁבֶת־עָלָיו בְּנָגְעוֹ־בוֹ יִטְמָא עַד־הָעָרֶב:

24 And if a man lies with her, her impurity is communicated to him; he shall be unclean seven days, and any bedding on which he lies shall become unclean.

כד וְאִם שָׁכֹב יִשְׁכַּב אִישׁ אֹתָהּ וּתְהִי נִדָּתָהּ עָלָיו וְטָמֵא שִׁבְעַת יָמִים וְכָל־הַמִּשְׁכָּב אֲשֶׁר־יִשְׁכַּב עָלָיו יִטְמָא:

25 When a woman has had a discharge of blood for many days, not at the time of her impurity, or when she has a discharge beyond her period of impurity, she shall be unclean, as though at the time of her impurity, as long as her discharge lasts.

כה וְאִשָּׁה כִּי־יָזוּב זוֹב דָּמָהּ יָמִים רַבִּים בְּלֹא עֶת־נִדָּתָהּ אוֹ כִי־תָזוּב עַל־נִדָּתָהּ כָּל־יְמֵי זוֹב טֻמְאָתָהּ כִּימֵי נִדָּתָהּ תִּהְיֶה טְמֵאָה הִוא:

26 Any bedding on which she lies while her discharge lasts shall be for her like bedding during her impurity; and any object on which she sits shall become unclean, as it does during her impurity:

כו כָּל־הַמִּשְׁכָּב אֲשֶׁר־תִּשְׁכַּב עָלָיו כָּל־יְמֵי זוֹבָהּ כְּמִשְׁכַּב נִדָּתָהּ יִהְיֶה־לָּהּ וְכָל־הַכְּלִי אֲשֶׁר תֵּשֵׁב עָלָיו טָמֵא יִהְיֶה כְּטֻמְאַת נִדָּתָהּ:

27 whoever touches them shall be unclean; he shall wash his clothes, bathe in water, and remain unclean until evening.

כז וְכָל־הַנֹּגֵעַ בָּם יִטְמָא וְכִבֶּס בְּגָדָיו וְרָחַץ בַּמַּיִם וְטָמֵא עַד־הָעָרֶב:

28 When she becomes clean of her discharge, she shall count off seven days, and after that she shall be clean.

כח וְאִם־טָהֲרָה מִזּוֹבָהּ וְסָפְרָה לָּהּ שִׁבְעַת יָמִים וְאַחַר תִּטְהָר:

29 On the eighth day she shall take two turtledoves or two pigeons, and bring them to the *Kohen* at the entrance of the Tent of Meeting.

כט וּבַיּוֹם הַשְּׁמִינִי תִּקַּח־לָהּ שְׁתֵּי תֹרִים אוֹ שְׁנֵי בְּנֵי יוֹנָה וְהֵבִיאָה אוֹתָם אֶל־הַכֹּהֵן אֶל־פֶּתַח אֹהֶל מוֹעֵד:

30 The *Kohen* shall offer the one as a sin offering and the other as a burnt offering; and the *Kohen* shall make expiation on her behalf, for her unclean discharge, before *Hashem*.

ל וְעָשָׂה הַכֹּהֵן אֶת־הָאֶחָד חַטָּאת וְאֶת־הָאֶחָד עֹלָה וְכִפֶּר עָלֶיהָ הַכֹּהֵן לִפְנֵי יְהֹוָה מִזּוֹב טֻמְאָתָהּ:

31 You shall put the Israelites on guard against their uncleanness, lest they die through their uncleanness by defiling My *Mishkan* which is among them.

לא וְהִזַּרְתֶּם אֶת־בְּנֵי־יִשְׂרָאֵל מִטֻּמְאָתָם וְלֹא יָמֻתוּ בְּטֻמְאָתָם בְּטַמְּאָם אֶת־מִשְׁכָּנִי אֲשֶׁר בְּתוֹכָם:

v'-hiz-har-TEM et b'-nay yis-ra-AYL mi-tum-a-TAM v'-LO ya-MU-tu b'-tum-a-TAM b'-ta-m'-AM et mish-ka-NEE a-SHER b'-to-KHAM

³² Such is the ritual concerning him who has a discharge: concerning him who has an emission of semen and becomes unclean thereby,

לב זֹאת תּוֹרַת הַזָּב וַאֲשֶׁר תֵּצֵא מִמֶּנּוּ שִׁכְבַת־זֶרַע לְטָמְאָה־בָהּ:

³³ and concerning her who is in menstrual infirmity, and concerning anyone, male or female, who has a discharge, and concerning a man who lies with an unclean woman.

לג וְהַדָּוָה בְּנִדָּתָהּ וְהַזָּב אֶת־זוֹבוֹ לַזָּכָר וְלַנְּקֵבָה וּלְאִישׁ אֲשֶׁר יִשְׁכַּב עִם־טְמֵאָה:

16

¹ *Hashem* spoke to *Moshe* after the death of the two sons of *Aharon* who died when they drew too close to the presence of *Hashem*.

טז א וַיְדַבֵּר יְהֹוָה אֶל־מֹשֶׁה אַחֲרֵי מוֹת שְׁנֵי בְּנֵי אַהֲרֹן בְּקָרְבָתָם לִפְנֵי־יְהֹוָה וַיָּמֻתוּ:

² *Hashem* said to *Moshe*: Tell your brother *Aharon* that he is not to come at will into the Shrine behind the curtain, in front of the cover that is upon the ark, lest he die; for I appear in the cloud over the cover.

ב וַיֹּאמֶר יְהֹוָה אֶל־מֹשֶׁה דַּבֵּר אֶל־אַהֲרֹן אָחִיךָ וְאַל־יָבֹא בְכָל־עֵת אֶל־הַקֹּדֶשׁ מִבֵּית לַפָּרֹכֶת אֶל־פְּנֵי הַכַּפֹּרֶת אֲשֶׁר עַל־הָאָרֹן וְלֹא יָמוּת כִּי בֶּעָנָן אֵרָאֶה עַל־הַכַּפֹּרֶת:

va-YO-mer a-do-NAI el mo-SHEH da-BAYR el a-ha-RON a-KHEE-kha v'-al ya-VO v-khol AYT el ha-KO-desh mi-BAYT la-pa-RO-khet el p'-NAY ha-ka-PO-ret a-SHER al ha-a-RON v'-LO ya-MUT kee be-a-NAN ay-ra-EH al ha-ka-PO-ret

³ Thus only shall *Aharon* enter the Shrine: with a bull of the herd for a sin offering and a ram for a burnt offering.

ג בְּזֹאת יָבֹא אַהֲרֹן אֶל־הַקֹּדֶשׁ בְּפַר בֶּן־בָּקָר לְחַטָּאת וְאַיִל לְעֹלָה:

⁴ He shall be dressed in a sacral linen tunic, with linen breeches next to his flesh, and be girt with a linen sash, and he shall wear a linen turban. They are sacral vestments; he shall bathe his body in water and then put them on.

ד כְּתֹנֶת־בַּד קֹדֶשׁ יִלְבָּשׁ וּמִכְנְסֵי־בַד יִהְיוּ עַל־בְּשָׂרוֹ וּבְאַבְנֵט בַּד יַחְגֹּר וּבְמִצְנֶפֶת בַּד יִצְנֹף בִּגְדֵי־קֹדֶשׁ הֵם וְרָחַץ בַּמַּיִם אֶת־בְּשָׂרוֹ וּלְבֵשָׁם:

k'-to-net BAD KO-desh yil-BASH u-mikh-n'-say VAD yih-YU al b'-sa-RO uv-av-NAYT BAD yakh-GOR u-v'-mitz-NE-fet BAD yitz-NOF big-day KO-desh HAYM v'-ra-KHATZ ba-MA-yim et b'-sa-RO ul-vay-SHAM

16:2 He is not to come at will into the Shrine behind the curtain The service detailed in this chapter is performed by the *Kohen Gadol,* 'high priest,' in the Holy of Holies on *Yom Kippur,* the 'Day of Atonement.' This unique service represents a pinnacle of holiness, as it brings the holiest person to the holiest place on the holiest day of the year. Tradition tells us that the world was created from the stone that stands at the location of the Holy of Holies on the Temple Mount. When the *Kohen Gadol* enters this same spot, he atones for the sins of mankind beginning with the time of *Adam* and the creation of the world. *Adam* himself was formed from the earth at the spot of the *Mizbayach,* close to the area of the Holy of Holies. To this day, people from all over the world are drawn to the Temple Mount, the place from which all of mankind originated. Yet,

Aerial view of the Temple Mount

on account of political pressures, currently only Muslims are granted full access to the Temple Mount; Jews are not even allowed to utter words of prayer at this holy site. We pray for the day when this holy mountain is restored to its vital role as a place of prayer for all nations.

16:4 He shall be dressed in a sacral linen tunic On a regular day the *Kohen Gadol* wears eight garments, four of which are decorated with gold. However, when he enters the Holy of Holies on *Yom Kippur* he wears only four white linen garments. The simplicity of his attire portrays feelings of humility as he approaches *Hashem* on the holiest day of the year, and the white color is symbolic of forgiveness. As the *Kohen Gadol* stands before God and begs forgiveness for himself, his family, and the entire nation, his clothing reminds him that he is at the mercy of God's benevolence, yet also instills confidence that God, in His compassion, will forgive His people.

5 And from the Israelite community he shall take two he-goats for a sin offering and a ram for a burnt offering.

ה וּמֵאֵת עֲדַת בְּנֵי יִשְׂרָאֵל יִקַּח שְׁנֵי־שְׂעִירֵי עִזִּים לְחַטָּאת וְאַיִל אֶחָד לְעֹלָה:

6 *Aharon* is to offer his own bull of sin offering, to make expiation for himself and for his household.

ו וְהִקְרִיב אַהֲרֹן אֶת־פַּר הַחַטָּאת אֲשֶׁר־לוֹ וְכִפֶּר בַּעֲדוֹ וּבְעַד בֵּיתוֹ:

7 *Aharon** shall take the two he-goats and let them stand before *Hashem* at the entrance of the Tent of Meeting;

ז וְלָקַח אֶת־שְׁנֵי הַשְּׂעִירִם וְהֶעֱמִיד אֹתָם לִפְנֵי יְהֹוָה פֶּתַח אֹהֶל מוֹעֵד:

8 and he shall place lots upon the two goats, one marked for *Hashem* and the other marked for Azazel.

ח וְנָתַן אַהֲרֹן עַל־שְׁנֵי הַשְּׂעִירִם גּוֹרָלוֹת גּוֹרָל אֶחָד לַיהֹוָה וְגוֹרָל אֶחָד לַעֲזָאזֵל:

9 *Aharon* shall bring forward the goat designated by lot for *Hashem*, which he is to offer as a sin offering;

ט וְהִקְרִיב אַהֲרֹן אֶת־הַשָּׂעִיר אֲשֶׁר עָלָה עָלָיו הַגּוֹרָל לַיהֹוָה וְעָשָׂהוּ חַטָּאת:

10 while the goat designated by lot for Azazel shall be left standing alive before *Hashem*, to make expiation with it and to send it off to the wilderness for Azazel.

י וְהַשָּׂעִיר אֲשֶׁר עָלָה עָלָיו הַגּוֹרָל לַעֲזָאזֵל יָעֳמַד־חַי לִפְנֵי יְהֹוָה לְכַפֵּר עָלָיו לְשַׁלַּח אֹתוֹ לַעֲזָאזֵל הַמִּדְבָּרָה:

11 *Aharon* shall then offer his bull of sin offering, to make expiation for himself and his household. He shall slaughter his bull of sin offering,

יא וְהִקְרִיב אַהֲרֹן אֶת־פַּר הַחַטָּאת אֲשֶׁר־לוֹ וְכִפֶּר בַּעֲדוֹ וּבְעַד בֵּיתוֹ וְשָׁחַט אֶת־פַּר הַחַטָּאת אֲשֶׁר־לוֹ:

12 and he shall take a panful of glowing coals scooped from the *Mizbayach* before *Hashem*, and two handfuls of finely ground aromatic incense, and bring this behind the curtain.

יב וְלָקַח מְלֹא־הַמַּחְתָּה גַּחֲלֵי־אֵשׁ מֵעַל הַמִּזְבֵּחַ מִלִּפְנֵי יְהֹוָה וּמְלֹא חָפְנָיו קְטֹרֶת סַמִּים דַּקָּה וְהֵבִיא מִבֵּית לַפָּרֹכֶת:

13 He shall put the incense on the fire before *Hashem*, so that the cloud from the incense screens the cover that is over [the *Aron* of] the Pact, lest he die.

יג וְנָתַן אֶת־הַקְּטֹרֶת עַל־הָאֵשׁ לִפְנֵי יְהֹוָה וְכִסָּה עֲנַן הַקְּטֹרֶת אֶת־הַכַּפֹּרֶת אֲשֶׁר עַל־הָעֵדוּת וְלֹא יָמוּת:

14 He shall take some of the blood of the bull and sprinkle it with his finger over the cover on the east side; and in front of the cover he shall sprinkle some of the blood with his finger seven times.

יד וְלָקַח מִדַּם הַפָּר וְהִזָּה בְאֶצְבָּעוֹ עַל־פְּנֵי הַכַּפֹּרֶת קֵדְמָה וְלִפְנֵי הַכַּפֹּרֶת יַזֶּה שֶׁבַע־פְּעָמִים מִן־הַדָּם בְּאֶצְבָּעוֹ:

15 He shall then slaughter the people's goat of sin offering, bring its blood behind the curtain, and do with its blood as he has done with the blood of the bull: he shall sprinkle it over the cover and in front of the cover.

טו וְשָׁחַט אֶת־שְׂעִיר הַחַטָּאת אֲשֶׁר לָעָם וְהֵבִיא אֶת־דָּמוֹ אֶל־מִבֵּית לַפָּרֹכֶת וְעָשָׂה אֶת־דָּמוֹ כַּאֲשֶׁר עָשָׂה לְדַם הַפָּר וְהִזָּה אֹתוֹ עַל־הַכַּפֹּרֶת וְלִפְנֵי הַכַּפֹּרֶת:

---

* *"Aharon"* moved up from v. 8 for clarity

16 Thus he shall purge the Shrine of the uncleanness and transgression of the Israelites, whatever their sins; and he shall do the same for the Tent of Meeting, which abides with them in the midst of their uncleanness.

טז וְכִפֶּר עַל־הַקֹּדֶשׁ מִטֻּמְאֹת בְּנֵי יִשְׂרָאֵל וּמִפִּשְׁעֵיהֶם לְכָל־חַטֹּאתָם וְכֵן יַעֲשֶׂה לְאֹהֶל מוֹעֵד הַשֹּׁכֵן אִתָּם בְּתוֹךְ טֻמְאֹתָם:

17 When he goes in to make expiation in the Shrine, nobody else shall be in the Tent of Meeting until he comes out. When he has made expiation for himself and his household, and for the whole congregation of *Yisrael*,

יז וְכָל־אָדָם לֹא־יִהְיֶה בְּאֹהֶל מוֹעֵד בְּבֹאוֹ לְכַפֵּר בַּקֹּדֶשׁ עַד־צֵאתוֹ וְכִפֶּר בַּעֲדוֹ וּבְעַד בֵּיתוֹ וּבְעַד כָּל־קְהַל יִשְׂרָאֵל:

18 he shall go out to the *Mizbayach* that is before *Hashem* and purge it: he shall take some of the blood of the bull and of the goat and apply it to each of the horns of the *Mizbayach*;

יח וְיָצָא אֶל־הַמִּזְבֵּחַ אֲשֶׁר לִפְנֵי־יְהֹוָה וְכִפֶּר עָלָיו וְלָקַח מִדַּם הַפָּר וּמִדַּם הַשָּׂעִיר וְנָתַן עַל־קַרְנוֹת הַמִּזְבֵּחַ סָבִיב:

19 and the rest of the blood he shall sprinkle on it with his finger seven times. Thus he shall cleanse it of the uncleanness of the Israelites and consecrate it.

יט וְהִזָּה עָלָיו מִן־הַדָּם בְּאֶצְבָּעוֹ שֶׁבַע פְּעָמִים וְטִהֲרוֹ וְקִדְּשׁוֹ מִטֻּמְאֹת בְּנֵי יִשְׂרָאֵל:

20 When he has finished purging the Shrine, the Tent of Meeting, and the *Mizbayach*, the live goat shall be brought forward.

כ וְכִלָּה מִכַּפֵּר אֶת־הַקֹּדֶשׁ וְאֶת־אֹהֶל מוֹעֵד וְאֶת־הַמִּזְבֵּחַ וְהִקְרִיב אֶת־הַשָּׂעִיר הֶחָי:

21 *Aharon* shall lay both his hands upon the head of the live goat and confess over it all the iniquities and transgressions of the Israelites, whatever their sins, putting them on the head of the goat; and it shall be sent off to the wilderness through a designated man.

כא וְסָמַךְ אַהֲרֹן אֶת־שְׁתֵּי ידו [יָדָיו] עַל רֹאשׁ הַשָּׂעִיר הַחַי וְהִתְוַדָּה עָלָיו אֶת־כָּל־עֲוֹנֹת בְּנֵי יִשְׂרָאֵל וְאֶת־כָּל־פִּשְׁעֵיהֶם לְכָל־חַטֹּאתָם וְנָתַן אֹתָם עַל־רֹאשׁ הַשָּׂעִיר וְשִׁלַּח בְּיַד־אִישׁ עִתִּי הַמִּדְבָּרָה:

22 Thus the goat shall carry on it all their iniquities to an inaccessible region; and the goat shall be set free in the wilderness.

כב וְנָשָׂא הַשָּׂעִיר עָלָיו אֶת־כָּל־עֲוֹנֹתָם אֶל־אֶרֶץ גְּזֵרָה וְשִׁלַּח אֶת־הַשָּׂעִיר בַּמִּדְבָּר:

23 And *Aharon* shall go into the Tent of Meeting, take off the linen vestments that he put on when he entered the Shrine, and leave them there.

כג וּבָא אַהֲרֹן אֶל־אֹהֶל מוֹעֵד וּפָשַׁט אֶת־בִּגְדֵי הַבָּד אֲשֶׁר לָבַשׁ בְּבֹאוֹ אֶל־הַקֹּדֶשׁ וְהִנִּיחָם שָׁם:

24 He shall bathe his body in water in the holy precinct and put on his vestments; then he shall come out and offer his burnt offering and the burnt offering of the people, making expiation for himself and for the people.

כד וְרָחַץ אֶת־בְּשָׂרוֹ בַמַּיִם בְּמָקוֹם קָדוֹשׁ וְלָבַשׁ אֶת־בְּגָדָיו וְיָצָא וְעָשָׂה אֶת־עֹלָתוֹ וְאֶת־עֹלַת הָעָם וְכִפֶּר בַּעֲדוֹ וּבְעַד הָעָם:

25 The fat of the sin offering he shall turn into smoke on the *Mizbayach*.

כה וְאֵת חֵלֶב הַחַטָּאת יַקְטִיר הַמִּזְבֵּחָה:

26 He who set the Azazel-goat free shall wash his clothes and bathe his body in water; after that he may reenter the camp.

כו וְהַמְשַׁלֵּחַ אֶת־הַשָּׂעִיר לַעֲזָאזֵל יְכַבֵּס בְּגָדָיו וְרָחַץ אֶת־בְּשָׂרוֹ בַּמָּיִם וְאַחֲרֵי־כֵן יָבוֹא אֶל־הַמַּחֲנֶה׃

27 The bull of sin offering and the goat of sin offering whose blood was brought in to purge the Shrine shall be taken outside the camp; and their hides, flesh, and dung shall be consumed in fire.

כז וְאֵת פַּר הַחַטָּאת וְאֵת שְׂעִיר הַחַטָּאת אֲשֶׁר הוּבָא אֶת־דָּמָם לְכַפֵּר בַּקֹּדֶשׁ יוֹצִיא אֶל־מִחוּץ לַמַּחֲנֶה וְשָׂרְפוּ בָאֵשׁ אֶת־עֹרֹתָם וְאֶת־בְּשָׂרָם וְאֶת־פִּרְשָׁם׃

28 He who burned them shall wash his clothes and bathe his body in water; after that he may re-enter the camp.

כח וְהַשֹּׂרֵף אֹתָם יְכַבֵּס בְּגָדָיו וְרָחַץ אֶת־בְּשָׂרוֹ בַּמָּיִם וְאַחֲרֵי־כֵן יָבוֹא אֶל־הַמַּחֲנֶה׃

29 And this shall be to you a law for all time: In the seventh month, on the tenth day of the month, you shall practice self-denial; and you shall do no manner of work, neither the citizen nor the alien who resides among you.

כט וְהָיְתָה לָכֶם לְחֻקַּת עוֹלָם בַּחֹדֶשׁ הַשְּׁבִיעִי בֶּעָשׂוֹר לַחֹדֶשׁ תְּעַנּוּ אֶת־נַפְשֹׁתֵיכֶם וְכָל־מְלָאכָה לֹא תַעֲשׂוּ הָאֶזְרָח וְהַגֵּר הַגָּר בְּתוֹכְכֶם׃

30 For on this day atonement shall be made for you to cleanse you of all your sins; you shall be clean before *Hashem*.

ל כִּי־בַיּוֹם הַזֶּה יְכַפֵּר עֲלֵיכֶם לְטַהֵר אֶתְכֶם מִכֹּל חַטֹּאתֵיכֶם לִפְנֵי יְהוָה תִּטְהָרוּ׃

kee va-YOM ha-ZEH y'-kha-PAYR a-lay-KHEM l'-ta-HAYR et-KHEM mi-KOL kha-TO-tay-KHEM lif-NAY a-do-NAI tit-HA-ru

31 It shall be a *Shabbat* of complete rest for you, and you shall practice self-denial; it is a law for all time.

לא שַׁבַּת שַׁבָּתוֹן הִיא לָכֶם וְעִנִּיתֶם אֶת־נַפְשֹׁתֵיכֶם חֻקַּת עוֹלָם׃

32 The *Kohen* who has been anointed and ordained to serve as *Kohen* in place of his father shall make expiation. He shall put on the linen vestments, the sacral vestments.

לב וְכִפֶּר הַכֹּהֵן אֲשֶׁר־יִמְשַׁח אֹתוֹ וַאֲשֶׁר יְמַלֵּא אֶת־יָדוֹ לְכַהֵן תַּחַת אָבִיו וְלָבַשׁ אֶת־בִּגְדֵי הַבָּד בִּגְדֵי הַקֹּדֶשׁ׃

33 He shall purge the innermost Shrine; he shall purge the Tent of Meeting and the *Mizbayach*; and he shall make expiation for the *Kohanim* and for all the people of the congregation.

לג וְכִפֶּר אֶת־מִקְדַּשׁ הַקֹּדֶשׁ וְאֶת־אֹהֶל מוֹעֵד וְאֶת־הַמִּזְבֵּחַ יְכַפֵּר וְעַל הַכֹּהֲנִים וְעַל־כָּל־עַם הַקָּהָל יְכַפֵּר׃

34 This shall be to you a law for all time: to make atonement for the Israelites for all their sins once a year. And *Moshe* did as *Hashem* had commanded him.

לד וְהָיְתָה־זֹּאת לָכֶם לְחֻקַּת עוֹלָם לְכַפֵּר עַל־בְּנֵי יִשְׂרָאֵל מִכָּל־חַטֹּאתָם אַחַת בַּשָּׁנָה וַיַּעַשׂ כַּאֲשֶׁר צִוָּה יְהוָה אֶת־מֹשֶׁה׃

17 1 *Hashem* spoke to *Moshe*, saying:

יז א וַיְדַבֵּר יְהוָה אֶל־מֹשֶׁה לֵּאמֹר׃

2 Speak to *Aharon* and his sons and to all *B'nei Yisrael* and say to them: This is what *Hashem* has commanded:

ב דַּבֵּר אֶל־אַהֲרֹן וְאֶל־בָּנָיו וְאֶל כָּל־בְּנֵי יִשְׂרָאֵל וְאָמַרְתָּ אֲלֵיהֶם זֶה הַדָּבָר אֲשֶׁר־צִוָּה יְהוָה לֵאמֹר׃

3 if anyone of the house of *Yisrael* slaughters an ox or sheep or goat in the camp, or does so outside the camp,

ג אִישׁ אִישׁ מִבֵּית יִשְׂרָאֵל אֲשֶׁר יִשְׁחַט שׁוֹר אוֹ־כֶשֶׂב אוֹ־עֵז בַּמַּחֲנֶה אוֹ אֲשֶׁר יִשְׁחַט מִחוּץ לַמַּחֲנֶה׃

Leviticus

4 and does not bring it to the entrance of the Tent of Meeting to present it as an offering to *Hashem*, before *Hashem*'s *Mishkan*, bloodguilt shall be imputed to that man: he has shed blood; that man shall be cut off from among his people.

ד וְאֶל־פֶּתַח אֹהֶל מוֹעֵד לֹא הֱבִיאוֹ לְהַקְרִיב קָרְבָּן לַיהוָה לִפְנֵי מִשְׁכַּן יהוָה דָּם יֵחָשֵׁב לָאִישׁ הַהוּא דָּם שָׁפָךְ וְנִכְרַת הָאִישׁ הַהוּא מִקֶּרֶב עַמּוֹ:

v'-el PE-takh O-hel mo-AYD LO he-vee-O l'-hak-REEV kor-BAN la-do-NAI lif-NAY mish-KAN a-do-NAI DAM yay-kha-SHAYV la-EESH ha-HU DAM sha-FAKH v'-nikh-RAT ha-EESH ha-HU mi-KE-rev a-MO

5 This is in order that the Israelites may bring the sacrifices which they have been making in the open – that they may bring them before *Hashem*, to the *Kohen*, at the entrance of the Tent of Meeting, and offer them as sacrifices of well-being to *Hashem*;

ה לְמַעַן אֲשֶׁר יָבִיאוּ בְּנֵי יִשְׂרָאֵל אֶת־זִבְחֵיהֶם אֲשֶׁר הֵם זֹבְחִים עַל־פְּנֵי הַשָּׂדֶה וֶהֱבִיאָם לַיהוָה אֶל־פֶּתַח אֹהֶל מוֹעֵד אֶל־הַכֹּהֵן וְזָבְחוּ זִבְחֵי שְׁלָמִים לַיהוָה אוֹתָם:

6 that the *Kohen* may dash the blood against the *Mizbayach* of *Hashem* at the entrance of the Tent of Meeting, and turn the fat into smoke as a pleasing odor to *Hashem*;

ו וְזָרַק הַכֹּהֵן אֶת־הַדָּם עַל־מִזְבַּח יהוָה פֶּתַח אֹהֶל מוֹעֵד וְהִקְטִיר הַחֵלֶב לְרֵיחַ נִיחֹחַ לַיהוָה:

7 and that they may offer their sacrifices no more to the goat-demons after whom they stray. This shall be to them a law for all time, throughout the ages.

ז וְלֹא־יִזְבְּחוּ עוֹד אֶת־זִבְחֵיהֶם לַשְּׂעִירִם אֲשֶׁר הֵם זֹנִים אַחֲרֵיהֶם חֻקַּת עוֹלָם תִּהְיֶה־זֹּאת לָהֶם לְדֹרֹתָם:

8 Say to them further: If anyone of the house of *Yisrael* or of the strangers who reside among them offers a burnt offering or a sacrifice,

ח וַאֲלֵהֶם תֹּאמַר אִישׁ אִישׁ מִבֵּית יִשְׂרָאֵל וּמִן־הַגֵּר אֲשֶׁר־יָגוּר בְּתוֹכָם אֲשֶׁר־יַעֲלֶה עֹלָה אוֹ־זָבַח:

9 and does not bring it to the entrance of the Tent of Meeting to offer it to *Hashem*, that person shall be cut off from his people.

ט וְאֶל־פֶּתַח אֹהֶל מוֹעֵד לֹא יְבִיאֶנּוּ לַעֲשׂוֹת אֹתוֹ לַיהוָה וְנִכְרַת הָאִישׁ הַהוּא מֵעַמָּיו:

10 And if anyone of the house of *Yisrael* or of the strangers who reside among them partakes of any blood, I will set My face against the person who partakes of the blood, and I will cut him off from among his kin.

י וְאִישׁ אִישׁ מִבֵּית יִשְׂרָאֵל וּמִן־הַגֵּר הַגָּר בְּתוֹכָם אֲשֶׁר יֹאכַל כָּל־דָּם וְנָתַתִּי פָנַי בַּנֶּפֶשׁ הָאֹכֶלֶת אֶת־הַדָּם וְהִכְרַתִּי אֹתָהּ מִקֶּרֶב עַמָּהּ:

17:4 And does not bring it to the entrance of the Tent of Meeting Once the *Mishkan* is constructed, and again after the *Beit Hamikdash* is built in *Yerushalayim*, it becomes forbidden to offer sacrifices anywhere else. This is because *Hashem* wants the acts of worshipping Him to bring unity among the people, and is also designed to minimize the danger of changes being introduced to the manner of worship. In addition, the mandate that sacrifices be brought only in the *Beit Hamikdash* requires everyone to travel to *Yerushalayim* at least three times a year. God's system ensures that everyone will have the triannual opportunity to be uplifted by the holiness of the *Beit Hamikdash* and the holy city of *Yerushalayim*.

Model of the Second Beit Hamikdash

¹¹ For the life of the flesh is in the blood, and I have assigned it to you for making expiation for your lives upon the *Mizbayach*; it is the blood, as life, that effects expiation.

יא כִּי נֶפֶשׁ הַבָּשָׂר בַּדָּם הִוא וַאֲנִי נְתַתִּיו לָכֶם עַל־הַמִּזְבֵּחַ לְכַפֵּר עַל־נַפְשֹׁתֵיכֶם כִּי־הַדָּם הוּא בַּנֶּפֶשׁ יְכַפֵּר:

¹² Therefore I say to *B'nei Yisrael*: No person among you shall partake of blood, nor shall the stranger who resides among you partake of blood.

יב עַל־כֵּן אָמַרְתִּי לִבְנֵי יִשְׂרָאֵל כָּל־נֶפֶשׁ מִכֶּם לֹא־תֹאכַל דָּם וְהַגֵּר הַגָּר בְּתוֹכְכֶם לֹא־יֹאכַל דָּם:

¹³ And if any Israelite or any stranger who resides among them hunts down an animal or a bird that may be eaten, he shall pour out its blood and cover it with earth.

יג וְאִישׁ אִישׁ מִבְּנֵי יִשְׂרָאֵל וּמִן־הַגֵּר הַגָּר בְּתוֹכָם אֲשֶׁר יָצוּד צֵיד חַיָּה אוֹ־עוֹף אֲשֶׁר יֵאָכֵל וְשָׁפַךְ אֶת־דָּמוֹ וְכִסָּהוּ בֶּעָפָר:

¹⁴ For the life of all flesh – its blood is its life. Therefore I say to *B'nei Yisrael*: You shall not partake of the blood of any flesh, for the life of all flesh is its blood. Anyone who partakes of it shall be cut off.

יד כִּי־נֶפֶשׁ כָּל־בָּשָׂר דָּמוֹ בְנַפְשׁוֹ הוּא וָאֹמַר לִבְנֵי יִשְׂרָאֵל דַּם כָּל־בָּשָׂר לֹא תֹאכֵלוּ כִּי נֶפֶשׁ כָּל־בָּשָׂר דָּמוֹ הִוא כָּל־אֹכְלָיו יִכָּרֵת:

¹⁵ Any person, whether citizen or stranger, who eats what has died or has been torn by beasts shall wash his clothes, bathe in water, and remain unclean until evening; then he shall be clean.

טו וְכָל־נֶפֶשׁ אֲשֶׁר תֹּאכַל נְבֵלָה וּטְרֵפָה בָּאֶזְרָח וּבַגֵּר וְכִבֶּס בְּגָדָיו וְרָחַץ בַּמַּיִם וְטָמֵא עַד־הָעֶרֶב וְטָהֵר:

¹⁶ But if he does not wash [his clothes] and bathe his body, he shall bear his guilt.

טז וְאִם לֹא יְכַבֵּס וּבְשָׂרוֹ לֹא יִרְחָץ וְנָשָׂא עֲוֹנוֹ:

8 ¹ *Hashem* spoke to *Moshe*, saying:

יח א וַיְדַבֵּר יְהוָֹה אֶל־מֹשֶׁה לֵּאמֹר:

² Speak to *B'nei Yisrael* and say to them: I *Hashem* am your God.

ב דַּבֵּר אֶל־בְּנֵי יִשְׂרָאֵל וְאָמַרְתָּ אֲלֵהֶם אֲנִי יְהוָֹה אֱלֹהֵיכֶם:

³ You shall not copy the practices of the land of Egypt where you dwelt, or of the land of Canaan to which I am taking you; nor shall you follow their laws.

ג כְּמַעֲשֵׂה אֶרֶץ־מִצְרַיִם אֲשֶׁר יְשַׁבְתֶּם־בָּהּ לֹא תַעֲשׂוּ וּכְמַעֲשֵׂה אֶרֶץ־כְּנַעַן אֲשֶׁר אֲנִי מֵבִיא אֶתְכֶם שָׁמָּה לֹא תַעֲשׂוּ וּבְחֻקֹּתֵיהֶם לֹא תֵלֵכוּ:

k'-ma-a-SAY e-retz mitz-RA-yim a-SHER y'-shav-tem BA LO ta-a-SU u-kh'-ma-a-SAY e-retz k'-NA-an a-SHER a-NEE may-VEE et-KHEM SHA-ma LO ta-a-SU uv-khu-ko-tay-HEM lo tay-LAY-khu

18:3 Or of the land of Canaan This verse warns the Israelites to avoid the negative behaviors (such as incest and child sacrifices) that were prevalent in Canaan. The chapter ends with an incredible, spiritual statement. It warns that *Eretz Yisrael* itself is so pure that it cannot tolerate abominable behavior, and will therefore expel any nation that defiles itself and the land, including the Jewish people. Ultimately, the Jews were indeed expelled from the land because of their sins. In modern times, even as we are grateful that *Hashem* has returned the Children of Israel to the land, this warning must be taken to heart. The land must be kept pure, and the people's behavior must adhere to the teachings of the Bible.

Reading from the *Torah* at the Western Wall

4 My rules alone shall you observe, and faithfully follow My laws: I *Hashem* am your God.

ד אֶת־מִשְׁפָּטַי תַּעֲשׂוּ וְאֶת־חֻקֹּתַי תִּשְׁמְרוּ לָלֶכֶת בָּהֶם אֲנִי יְהוָה אֱלֹהֵיכֶם:

5 You shall keep My laws and My rules, by the pursuit of which man shall live: I am *Hashem.*

ה וּשְׁמַרְתֶּם אֶת־חֻקֹּתַי וְאֶת־מִשְׁפָּטַי אֲשֶׁר יַעֲשֶׂה אֹתָם הָאָדָם וָחַי בָּהֶם אֲנִי יְהוָה:

6 None of you shall come near anyone of his own flesh to uncover nakedness: I am *Hashem.*

ו אִישׁ אִישׁ אֶל־כָּל־שְׁאֵר בְּשָׂרוֹ לֹא תִקְרְבוּ לְגַלּוֹת עֶרְוָה אֲנִי יְהוָה:

7 Your father's nakedness, that is, the nakedness of your mother, you shall not uncover; she is your mother – you shall not uncover her nakedness.

ז עֶרְוַת אָבִיךָ וְעֶרְוַת אִמְּךָ לֹא תְגַלֵּה אִמְּךָ הִוא לֹא תְגַלֶּה עֶרְוָתָהּ:

8 Do not uncover the nakedness of your father's wife; it is the nakedness of your father.

ח עֶרְוַת אֵשֶׁת־אָבִיךָ לֹא תְגַלֵּה עֶרְוַת אָבִיךָ הִוא:

9 The nakedness of your sister – your father's daughter or your mother's, whether born into the household or outside – do not uncover their nakedness.

ט עֶרְוַת אֲחוֹתְךָ בַת־אָבִיךָ אוֹ בַת־אִמֶּךָ מוֹלֶדֶת בַּיִת אוֹ מוֹלֶדֶת חוּץ לֹא תְגַלֵּה עֶרְוָתָן:

10 The nakedness of your son's daughter, or of your daughter's daughter – do not uncover their nakedness; for their nakedness is yours.

י עֶרְוַת בַּת־בִּנְךָ אוֹ בַת־בִּתְּךָ לֹא תְגַלֶּה עֶרְוָתָן כִּי עֶרְוָתְךָ הֵנָּה:

11 The nakedness of your father's wife's daughter, who has born into your father's household – she is your sister; do not uncover her nakedness.

יא עֶרְוַת בַּת־אֵשֶׁת אָבִיךָ מוֹלֶדֶת אָבִיךָ אֲחוֹתְךָ הִוא לֹא תְגַלֶּה עֶרְוָתָהּ:

12 Do not uncover the nakedness of your father's sister; she is your father's flesh.

יב עֶרְוַת אֲחוֹת־אָבִיךָ לֹא תְגַלֵּה שְׁאֵר אָבִיךָ הִוא:

13 Do not uncover the nakedness of your mother's sister; for she is your mother's flesh.

יג עֶרְוַת אֲחוֹת־אִמְּךָ לֹא תְגַלֵּה כִּי־שְׁאֵר אִמְּךָ הִוא:

14 Do not uncover the nakedness of your father's brother: do not approach his wife; she is your aunt.

יד עֶרְוַת אֲחִי־אָבִיךָ לֹא תְגַלֵּה אֶל־אִשְׁתּוֹ לֹא תִקְרָב דֹּדָתְךָ הִוא:

15 Do not uncover the nakedness of your daughter-in-law: she is your son's wife; you shall not uncover her nakedness.

טו עֶרְוַת כַּלָּתְךָ לֹא תְגַלֵּה אֵשֶׁת בִּנְךָ הִוא לֹא תְגַלֶּה עֶרְוָתָהּ:

16 Do not uncover the nakedness of your brother's wife; it is the nakedness of your brother.

טז עֶרְוַת אֵשֶׁת־אָחִיךָ לֹא תְגַלֵּה עֶרְוַת אָחִיךָ הִוא:

17 Do not uncover the nakedness of a woman and her daughter; nor shall you marry her son's daughter or her daughter's daughter and uncover her nakedness: they are kindred; it is depravity.

יז עֶרְוַת אִשָּׁה וּבִתָּהּ לֹא תְגַלֵּה אֶת־בַּת־בְּנָהּ וְאֶת־בַּת־בִּתָּהּ לֹא תִקַּח לְגַלּוֹת עֶרְוָתָהּ שַׁאֲרָה הֵנָּה זִמָּה הִוא:

18 Do not marry a woman as a rival to her sister and uncover her nakedness in the other's lifetime.

יח וְאִשָּׁה אֶל־אֲחֹתָהּ לֹא תִקָּח לִצְרֹר לְגַלּוֹת עֶרְוָתָהּ עָלֶיהָ בְּחַיֶּיהָ:

¹⁹ Do not come near a woman during her period of uncleanness to uncover her nakedness.

יט וְאֶל־אִשָּׁה בְּנִדַּת טֻמְאָתָהּ לֹא תִקְרַב לְגַלּוֹת עֶרְוָתָהּ:

²⁰ Do not have carnal relations with your neighbor's wife and defile yourself with her.

כ וְאֶל־אֵשֶׁת עֲמִיתְךָ לֹא־תִתֵּן שְׁכָבְתְּךָ לְזָרַע לְטָמְאָה־בָהּ:

²¹ Do not allow any of your offspring to be offered up to Molech, and do not profane the name of your God: I am *Hashem*.

כא וּמִזַּרְעֲךָ לֹא־תִתֵּן לְהַעֲבִיר לַמֹּלֶךְ וְלֹא תְחַלֵּל אֶת־שֵׁם אֱלֹהֶיךָ אֲנִי יְהוָה:

²² Do not lie with a male as one lies with a woman; it is an abhorrence.

כב וְאֶת־זָכָר לֹא תִשְׁכַּב מִשְׁכְּבֵי אִשָּׁה תּוֹעֵבָה הִוא:

²³ Do not have carnal relations with any beast and defile yourself thereby; and let no woman lend herself to a beast to mate with it; it is perversion.

כג וּבְכָל־בְּהֵמָה לֹא־תִתֵּן שְׁכָבְתְּךָ לְטָמְאָה־בָהּ וְאִשָּׁה לֹא־תַעֲמֹד לִפְנֵי בְהֵמָה לְרִבְעָהּ תֶּבֶל הוּא:

²⁴ Do not defile yourselves in any of those ways, for it is by such that the nations that I am casting out before you defiled themselves.

כד אַל־תִּטַּמְּאוּ בְּכָל־אֵלֶּה כִּי בְכָל־אֵלֶּה נִטְמְאוּ הַגּוֹיִם אֲשֶׁר־אֲנִי מְשַׁלֵּחַ מִפְּנֵיכֶם:

²⁵ Thus the land became defiled; and I called it to account for its iniquity, and the land spewed out its inhabitants.

כה וַתִּטְמָא הָאָרֶץ וָאֶפְקֹד עֲוֹנָהּ עָלֶיהָ וַתָּקִא הָאָרֶץ אֶת־יֹשְׁבֶיהָ:

²⁶ But you must keep My laws and My rules, and you must not do any of those abhorrent things, neither the citizen nor the stranger who resides among you;

כו וּשְׁמַרְתֶּם אַתֶּם אֶת־חֻקֹּתַי וְאֶת־מִשְׁפָּטַי וְלֹא תַעֲשׂוּ מִכֹּל הַתּוֹעֵבֹת הָאֵלֶּה הָאֶזְרָח וְהַגֵּר הַגָּר בְּתוֹכְכֶם:

²⁷ for all those abhorrent things were done by the people who were in the land before you, and the land became defiled.

כז כִּי אֶת־כָּל־הַתּוֹעֵבֹת הָאֵל עָשׂוּ אַנְשֵׁי־הָאָרֶץ אֲשֶׁר לִפְנֵיכֶם וַתִּטְמָא הָאָרֶץ:

²⁸ So let not the land spew you out for defiling it, as it spewed out the nation that came before you.

כח וְלֹא־תָקִיא הָאָרֶץ אֶתְכֶם בְּטַמַּאֲכֶם אֹתָהּ כַּאֲשֶׁר קָאָה אֶת־הַגּוֹי אֲשֶׁר לִפְנֵיכֶם:

²⁹ All who do any of those abhorrent things – such persons shall be cut off from their people.

כט כִּי כָּל־אֲשֶׁר יַעֲשֶׂה מִכֹּל הַתּוֹעֵבֹת הָאֵלֶּה וְנִכְרְתוּ הַנְּפָשׁוֹת הָעֹשֹׂת מִקֶּרֶב עַמָּם:

³⁰ You shall keep My charge not to engage in any of the abhorrent practices that were carried on before you, and you shall not defile yourselves through them: I *Hashem* am your God.

ל וּשְׁמַרְתֶּם אֶת־מִשְׁמַרְתִּי לְבִלְתִּי עֲשׂוֹת מֵחֻקּוֹת הַתּוֹעֵבֹת אֲשֶׁר נַעֲשׂוּ לִפְנֵיכֶם וְלֹא תִטַּמְּאוּ בָּהֶם אֲנִי יְהוָה אֱלֹהֵיכֶם:

9 ¹ *Hashem* spoke to *Moshe*, saying:

יט א וַיְדַבֵּר יְהוָה אֶל־מֹשֶׁה לֵּאמֹר:

² Speak to the whole Israelite community and say to them: You shall be holy, for I, *Hashem* your God, am holy.

ב דַּבֵּר אֶל־כָּל־עֲדַת בְּנֵי־יִשְׂרָאֵל וְאָמַרְתָּ אֲלֵהֶם קְדֹשִׁים תִּהְיוּ כִּי קָדוֹשׁ אֲנִי יְהוָה אֱלֹהֵיכֶם:

³ You shall each revere his mother and his father, and keep My *Shabbatot*: I *Hashem* am your God.

ג אִישׁ אִמּוֹ וְאָבִיו תִּירָאוּ וְאֶת־שַׁבְּתֹתַי תִּשְׁמֹרוּ אֲנִי יְהוָה אֱלֹהֵיכֶם:

4 Do not turn to idols or make molten gods for
yourselves: I *Hashem* am your God.

ד אַל־תִּפְנוּ אֶל־הָאֱלִילִים וֵאלֹהֵי מַסֵּכָה
לֹא תַעֲשׂוּ לָכֶם אֲנִי יְהֹוָה אֱלֹהֵיכֶם:

5 When you sacrifice an offering of well-being to
Hashem, sacrifice it so that it may be accepted on
your behalf.

ה וְכִי תִזְבְּחוּ זֶבַח שְׁלָמִים לַיהֹוָה לִרְצֹנְכֶם
תִּזְבָּחֻהוּ:

6 It shall be eaten on the day you sacrifice it, or on the
day following; but what is left by the third day must
be consumed in fire.

ו בְּיוֹם זִבְחֲכֶם יֵאָכֵל וּמִמָּחֳרָת וְהַנּוֹתָר
עַד־יוֹם הַשְּׁלִישִׁי בָּאֵשׁ יִשָּׂרֵף:

7 If it should be eaten on the third day, it is an
offensive thing, it will not be acceptable.

ז וְאִם הֵאָכֹל יֵאָכֵל בַּיּוֹם הַשְּׁלִישִׁי פִּגּוּל
הוּא לֹא יֵרָצֶה:

8 And he who eats of it shall bear his guilt, for he has
profaned what is sacred to *Hashem*; that person
shall be cut off from his kin.

ח וְאֹכְלָיו עֲוֺנוֹ יִשָּׂא כִּי־אֶת־קֹדֶשׁ יְהֹוָה
חִלֵּל וְנִכְרְתָה הַנֶּפֶשׁ הַהִוא מֵעַמֶּיהָ:

9 When you reap the harvest of your land, you shall
not reap all the way to the edges of your field, or
gather the gleanings of your harvest.

ט וּבְקֻצְרְכֶם אֶת־קְצִיר אַרְצְכֶם לֹא
תְכַלֶּה פְּאַת שָׂדְךָ לִקְצֹר וְלֶקֶט קְצִירְךָ
לֹא תְלַקֵּט:

*uv-kutz-r'-KHEM et k'-TZEER ar-tz'-KHEM LO t'-kha-LE p'-AT
sa-d'-KHA lik-TZOR v'-LE-ket k'-tzee-r'-KHA LO t'-la-KAYT*

10 You shall not pick your vineyard bare, or gather the
fallen fruit of your vineyard; you shall leave them
for the poor and the stranger: I *Hashem* am your
God.

י וְכַרְמְךָ לֹא תְעוֹלֵל וּפֶרֶט כַּרְמְךָ לֹא
תְלַקֵּט לֶעָנִי וְלַגֵּר תַּעֲזֹב אֹתָם אֲנִי יְהֹוָה
אֱלֹהֵיכֶם:

11 You shall not steal; you shall not deal deceitfully or
falsely with one another.

יא לֹא תִּגְנֹבוּ וְלֹא־תְכַחֲשׁוּ וְלֹא־תְשַׁקְּרוּ
אִישׁ בַּעֲמִיתוֹ:

12 You shall not swear falsely by My name, profaning
the name of your God: I am *Hashem*.

יב וְלֹא־תִשָּׁבְעוּ בִשְׁמִי לַשָּׁקֶר וְחִלַּלְתָּ
אֶת־שֵׁם אֱלֹהֶיךָ אֲנִי יְהֹוָה:

13 You shall not defraud your fellow. You shall not
commit robbery. The wages of a laborer shall not
remain with you until morning.

יג לֹא־תַעֲשֹׁק אֶת־רֵעֲךָ וְלֹא תִגְזֹל לֹא־
תָלִין פְּעֻלַּת שָׂכִיר אִתְּךָ עַד־בֹּקֶר:

14 You shall not insult the deaf, or place a stumbling
block before the blind. You shall fear your God: I
am *Hashem*.

יד לֹא־תְקַלֵּל חֵרֵשׁ וְלִפְנֵי עִוֵּר לֹא תִתֵּן
מִכְשֹׁל וְיָרֵאתָ מֵּאֱלֹהֶיךָ אֲנִי יְהֹוָה:

15 You shall not render an unfair decision: do not
favor the poor or show deference to the rich; judge
your kinsman fairly.

טו לֹא־תַעֲשׂוּ עָוֶל בַּמִּשְׁפָּט לֹא־תִשָּׂא פְנֵי־
דָל וְלֹא תֶהְדַּר פְּנֵי גָדוֹל בְּצֶדֶק תִּשְׁפֹּט
עֲמִיתֶךָ:

16 Do not deal basely with your countrymen. Do not
profit by the blood of your fellow: I am *Hashem*.

טז לֹא־תֵלֵךְ רָכִיל בְּעַמֶּיךָ לֹא תַעֲמֹד עַל־
דַּם רֵעֶךָ אֲנִי יְהֹוָה:

17 You shall not hate your kinsfolk in your heart.
Reprove your kinsman but incur no guilt because
of him.

יז לֹא־תִשְׂנָא אֶת־אָחִיךָ בִּלְבָבֶךָ הוֹכֵחַ
תּוֹכִיחַ אֶת־עֲמִיתֶךָ וְלֹא־תִשָּׂא עָלָיו
חֵטְא:

18 You shall not take vengeance or bear a grudge against your countrymen. Love your fellow as yourself: I am *Hashem*.

לֹא־תִקֹּם וְלֹא־תִטֹּר אֶת־בְּנֵי עַמֶּךָ וְאָהַבְתָּ לְרֵעֲךָ כָּמוֹךָ אֲנִי יְהֹוָה:

lo ti-KOM v'-lo ti-TOR et b'-NAY a-ME-kha v'-a-hav-TA l'-ray-a-KHA ka-MO-kha a-NEE a-do-NAI

19 You shall observe My laws. You shall not let your cattle mate with a different kind; you shall not sow your field with two kinds of seed; you shall not put on cloth from a mixture of two kinds of material.

אֶת־חֻקֹּתַי תִּשְׁמֹרוּ בְּהֶמְתְּךָ לֹא־תַרְבִּיעַ כִּלְאַיִם שָׂדְךָ לֹא־תִזְרַע כִּלְאָיִם וּבֶגֶד כִּלְאַיִם שַׁעַטְנֵז לֹא יַעֲלֶה עָלֶיךָ:

20 If a man has carnal relations with a woman who is a slave and has been designated for another man, but has not been redeemed or given her freedom, there shall be an indemnity; they shall not, however, be put to death, since she has not been freed.

וְאִישׁ כִּי־יִשְׁכַּב אֶת־אִשָּׁה שִׁכְבַת־זֶרַע וְהִוא שִׁפְחָה נֶחֱרֶפֶת לְאִישׁ וְהָפְדֵּה לֹא נִפְדָּתָה אוֹ חֻפְשָׁה לֹא נִתַּן־לָהּ בִּקֹּרֶת תִּהְיֶה לֹא יוּמְתוּ כִּי־לֹא חֻפָּשָׁה:

21 But he must bring to the entrance of the Tent of Meeting, as his guilt offering to *Hashem*, a ram of guilt offering.

וְהֵבִיא אֶת־אֲשָׁמוֹ לַיהֹוָה אֶל־פֶּתַח אֹהֶל מוֹעֵד אֵיל אָשָׁם:

22 With the ram of guilt offering the *Kohen* shall make expiation for him before *Hashem* for the sin that he committed; and the sin that he committed will be forgiven him.

וְכִפֶּר עָלָיו הַכֹּהֵן בְּאֵיל הָאָשָׁם לִפְנֵי יְהֹוָה עַל־חַטָּאתוֹ אֲשֶׁר חָטָא וְנִסְלַח לוֹ מֵחַטָּאתוֹ אֲשֶׁר חָטָא:

23 When you enter the land and plant any tree for food, you shall regard its fruit as forbidden. Three years it shall be forbidden for you, not to be eaten.

וְכִי־תָבֹאוּ אֶל־הָאָרֶץ וּנְטַעְתֶּם כָּל־עֵץ מַאֲכָל וַעֲרַלְתֶּם עָרְלָתוֹ אֶת־פִּרְיוֹ שָׁלֹשׁ שָׁנִים יִהְיֶה לָכֶם עֲרֵלִים לֹא יֵאָכֵל:

v'-khee ta-VO-u el ha-A-retz u-n'-ta-TEM kol AYTZ ma-a-KHAL va-a-ral-TEM or-la-TO et pir-YO sha-LOSH sha-NEEM yih-YEH la-KHEM a-ray-LEEM LO yay-a-KHAYL

24 In the fourth year all its fruit shall be set aside for jubilation before *Hashem*;

וּבַשָּׁנָה הָרְבִיעִת יִהְיֶה כָּל־פִּרְיוֹ קֹדֶשׁ הִלּוּלִים לַיהֹוָה:

19:18 Love your fellow as yourself In a speech given in 1944 to a gathering of youth groups in Haifa, Prime Minister David Ben Gurion referred to these words as an example of how Judaism serves as a paradigm of a society built on morality, peace and love: "Ours was a tiny nation inhabiting a small country, and there have been many tiny nations and many small countries, but ours was a tiny nation possessed of a great spirit; an inspired people that believed in its pioneering mission to all men, in the mission that had been preached by the prophets of Israel. This people gave the world great and eternal moral truths and commandments. This people rose to prophetic visions of the unity of the Creator with His creation, of the dignity and infinite worth of the individual because every man is created in the divine image, of social justice, universal peace, and love: 'Thou shalt love thy neighbor as thyself.' This people was the first to prophesy about 'the end of days,' the first to see the vision of a new human society." Even though Ben Gurion was not a religious Jew, he was deeply influenced by the Bible, which had a profound impact on his outlook and his actions on behalf of the Jewish State.

Prime Minister
David Ben Gurion
(1886–1973)

Leviticus

25 and only in the fifth year may you use its fruit – that its yield to you may be increased: I *Hashem* am your God.

26 You shall not eat anything with its blood. You shall not practice divination or soothsaying.

27 You shall not round off the side-growth on your head, or destroy the side-growth of your beard.

28 You shall not make gashes in your flesh for the dead, or incise any marks on yourselves: I am *Hashem*.

29 Do not degrade your daughter and make her a harlot, lest the land fall into harlotry and the land be filled with depravity.

30 You shall keep My *Shabbatot* and venerate My sanctuary: I am *Hashem*.

31 Do not turn to ghosts and do not inquire of familiar spirits, to be defiled by them: I *Hashem* am your God.

32 You shall rise before the aged and show deference to the old; you shall fear your God: I am *Hashem*.

33 When a stranger resides with you in your land, you shall not wrong him.

34 The stranger who resides with you shall be to you as one of your citizens; you shall love him as yourself, for you were strangers in the land of Egypt: I *Hashem* am your God.

35 You shall not falsify measures of length, weight, or capacity.

36 You shall have an honest balance, honest weights, an honest *efah*, and an honest *hin*. I *Hashem* am your God who freed you from the land of Egypt.

37 You shall faithfully observe all My laws and all My rules: I am *Hashem*.

20 1 And *Hashem* spoke to *Moshe*:

2 Say further to *B'nei Yisrael*: Anyone among the Israelites, or among the strangers residing in *Yisrael*, who gives any of his offspring to Molech, shall be put to death; the people of the land shall pelt him with stones.

כה וּבַשָּׁנָה הַחֲמִישִׁת תֹּאכְלוּ אֶת־פִּרְיוֹ לְהוֹסִיף לָכֶם תְּבוּאָתוֹ אֲנִי יְהֹוָה אֱלֹהֵיכֶם:

כו לֹא תֹאכְלוּ עַל־הַדָּם לֹא תְנַחֲשׁוּ וְלֹא תְעוֹנֵנוּ:

כז לֹא תַקִּפוּ פְּאַת רֹאשְׁכֶם וְלֹא תַשְׁחִית אֵת פְּאַת זְקָנֶךָ:

כח וְשֶׂרֶט לָנֶפֶשׁ לֹא תִתְּנוּ בִּבְשַׂרְכֶם וּכְתֹבֶת קַעֲקַע לֹא תִתְּנוּ בָּכֶם אֲנִי יְהֹוָה:

כט אַל־תְּחַלֵּל אֶת־בִּתְּךָ לְהַזְנוֹתָהּ וְלֹא־תִזְנֶה הָאָרֶץ וּמָלְאָה הָאָרֶץ זִמָּה:

ל אֶת־שַׁבְּתֹתַי תִּשְׁמֹרוּ וּמִקְדָּשִׁי תִּירָאוּ אֲנִי יְהֹוָה:

לא אַל־תִּפְנוּ אֶל־הָאֹבֹת וְאֶל־הַיִּדְּעֹנִים אַל־תְּבַקְשׁוּ לְטָמְאָה בָהֶם אֲנִי יְהֹוָה אֱלֹהֵיכֶם:

לב מִפְּנֵי שֵׂיבָה תָּקוּם וְהָדַרְתָּ פְּנֵי זָקֵן וְיָרֵאתָ מֵּאֱלֹהֶיךָ אֲנִי יְהֹוָה:

לג וְכִי־יָגוּר אִתְּךָ גֵּר בְּאַרְצְכֶם לֹא תוֹנוּ אֹתוֹ:

לד כְּאֶזְרָח מִכֶּם יִהְיֶה לָכֶם הַגֵּר הַגָּר אִתְּכֶם וְאָהַבְתָּ לוֹ כָּמוֹךָ כִּי־גֵרִים הֱיִיתֶם בְּאֶרֶץ מִצְרָיִם אֲנִי יְהֹוָה אֱלֹהֵיכֶם:

לה לֹא־תַעֲשׂוּ עָוֶל בַּמִּשְׁפָּט בַּמִּדָּה בַּמִּשְׁקָל וּבַמְּשׂוּרָה:

לו מֹאזְנֵי צֶדֶק אַבְנֵי־צֶדֶק אֵיפַת צֶדֶק וְהִין צֶדֶק יִהְיֶה לָכֶם אֲנִי יְהֹוָה אֱלֹהֵיכֶם אֲשֶׁר־הוֹצֵאתִי אֶתְכֶם מֵאֶרֶץ מִצְרָיִם:

לז וּשְׁמַרְתֶּם אֶת־כָּל־חֻקֹּתַי וְאֶת־כָּל־מִשְׁפָּטַי וַעֲשִׂיתֶם אֹתָם אֲנִי יְהֹוָה:

כ א וַיְדַבֵּר יְהֹוָה אֶל־מֹשֶׁה לֵּאמֹר:

ב וְאֶל־בְּנֵי יִשְׂרָאֵל תֹּאמַר אִישׁ אִישׁ מִבְּנֵי יִשְׂרָאֵל וּמִן־הַגֵּר הַגָּר בְּיִשְׂרָאֵל אֲשֶׁר יִתֵּן מִזַּרְעוֹ לַמֹּלֶךְ מוֹת יוּמָת עַם הָאָרֶץ יִרְגְּמֻהוּ בָאָבֶן:

3 And I will set My face against that man and will cut him off from among his people, because he gave of his offspring to Molech and so defiled My sanctuary and profaned My holy name.

4 And if the people of the land should shut their eyes to that man when he gives of his offspring to Molech, and should not put him to death,

5 I Myself will set My face against that man and his kin, and will cut off from among their people both him and all who follow him in going astray after Molech.

6 And if any person turns to ghosts and familiar spirits and goes astray after them, I will set My face against that person and cut him off from among his people.

7 You shall sanctify yourselves and be holy, for I *Hashem* am your God.

8 You shall faithfully observe My laws: I *Hashem* make you holy.

9 If anyone insults his father or his mother, he shall be put to death; he has insulted his father and his mother – his bloodguilt is upon him.

10 If a man commits adultery with a married woman, committing adultery with another man's wife, the adulterer and the adulteress shall be put to death.

11 If a man lies with his father's wife, it is the nakedness of his father that he has uncovered; the two shall be put to death – their bloodguilt is upon them.

12 If a man lies with his daughter-in-law, both of them shall be put to death; they have committed incest – their bloodguilt is upon them.

13 If a man lies with a male as one lies with a woman, the two of them have done an abhorrent thing; they shall be put to death – their bloodguilt is upon them.

14 If a man marries a woman and her mother, it is depravity; both he and they shall be put to the fire, that there be no depravity among you.

15 If a man has carnal relations with a beast, he shall be put to death; and you shall kill the beast.

ג וַאֲנִי אֶתֵּן אֶת־פָּנַי בָּאִישׁ הַהוּא וְהִכְרַתִּי אֹתוֹ מִקֶּרֶב עַמּוֹ כִּי מִזַּרְעוֹ נָתַן לַמֹּלֶךְ לְמַעַן טַמֵּא אֶת־מִקְדָּשִׁי וּלְחַלֵּל אֶת־שֵׁם קָדְשִׁי:

ד וְאִם הַעְלֵם יַעְלִימוּ עַם הָאָרֶץ אֶת־עֵינֵיהֶם מִן־הָאִישׁ הַהוּא בְּתִתּוֹ מִזַּרְעוֹ לַמֹּלֶךְ לְבִלְתִּי הָמִית אֹתוֹ:

ה וְשַׂמְתִּי אֲנִי אֶת־פָּנַי בָּאִישׁ הַהוּא וּבְמִשְׁפַּחְתּוֹ וְהִכְרַתִּי אֹתוֹ וְאֵת כָּל־הַזֹּנִים אַחֲרָיו לִזְנוֹת אַחֲרֵי הַמֹּלֶךְ מִקֶּרֶב עַמָּם:

ו וְהַנֶּפֶשׁ אֲשֶׁר תִּפְנֶה אֶל־הָאֹבֹת וְאֶל־הַיִּדְּעֹנִים לִזְנוֹת אַחֲרֵיהֶם וְנָתַתִּי אֶת־פָּנַי בַּנֶּפֶשׁ הַהִוא וְהִכְרַתִּי אֹתוֹ מִקֶּרֶב עַמּוֹ:

ז וְהִתְקַדִּשְׁתֶּם וִהְיִיתֶם קְדֹשִׁים כִּי אֲנִי יְהֹוָה אֱלֹהֵיכֶם:

ח וּשְׁמַרְתֶּם אֶת־חֻקֹּתַי וַעֲשִׂיתֶם אֹתָם אֲנִי יְהֹוָה מְקַדִּשְׁכֶם:

ט כִּי־אִישׁ אִישׁ אֲשֶׁר יְקַלֵּל אֶת־אָבִיו וְאֶת־אִמּוֹ מוֹת יוּמָת אָבִיו וְאִמּוֹ קִלֵּל דָּמָיו בּוֹ:

י וְאִישׁ אֲשֶׁר יִנְאַף אֶת־אֵשֶׁת אִישׁ אֲשֶׁר יִנְאַף אֶת־אֵשֶׁת רֵעֵהוּ מוֹת־יוּמַת הַנֹּאֵף וְהַנֹּאָפֶת:

יא וְאִישׁ אֲשֶׁר יִשְׁכַּב אֶת־אֵשֶׁת אָבִיו עֶרְוַת אָבִיו גִּלָּה מוֹת־יוּמְתוּ שְׁנֵיהֶם דְּמֵיהֶם בָּם:

יב וְאִישׁ אֲשֶׁר יִשְׁכַּב אֶת־כַּלָּתוֹ מוֹת יוּמְתוּ שְׁנֵיהֶם תֶּבֶל עָשׂוּ דְּמֵיהֶם בָּם:

יג וְאִישׁ אֲשֶׁר יִשְׁכַּב אֶת־זָכָר מִשְׁכְּבֵי אִשָּׁה תּוֹעֵבָה עָשׂוּ שְׁנֵיהֶם מוֹת יוּמָתוּ דְּמֵיהֶם בָּם:

יד וְאִישׁ אֲשֶׁר יִקַּח אֶת־אִשָּׁה וְאֶת־אִמָּהּ זִמָּה הִוא בָּאֵשׁ יִשְׂרְפוּ אֹתוֹ וְאֶתְהֶן וְלֹא־תִהְיֶה זִמָּה בְּתוֹכְכֶם:

טו וְאִישׁ אֲשֶׁר יִתֵּן שְׁכָבְתּוֹ בִּבְהֵמָה מוֹת יוּמָת וְאֶת־הַבְּהֵמָה תַּהֲרֹגוּ:

16 If a woman approaches any beast to mate with it, you shall kill the woman and the beast; they shall be put to death – their bloodguilt is upon them.

טז וְאִשָּׁה אֲשֶׁר תִּקְרַב אֶל־כָּל־בְּהֵמָה לְרִבְעָה אֹתָהּ וְהָרַגְתָּ אֶת־הָאִשָּׁה וְאֶת־הַבְּהֵמָה מוֹת יוּמָתוּ דְּמֵיהֶם בָּם:

17 If a man marries his sister, the daughter of either his father or his mother, so that he sees her nakedness and she sees his nakedness, it is a disgrace; they shall be excommunicated in the sight of their kinsfolk. He has uncovered the nakedness of his sister, he shall bear his guilt.

יז וְאִישׁ אֲשֶׁר־יִקַּח אֶת־אֲחֹתוֹ בַּת־אָבִיו אוֹ בַת־אִמּוֹ וְרָאָה אֶת־עֶרְוָתָהּ וְהִיא־תִרְאֶה אֶת־עֶרְוָתוֹ חֶסֶד הוּא וְנִכְרְתוּ לְעֵינֵי בְּנֵי עַמָּם עֶרְוַת אֲחֹתוֹ גִּלָּה עֲוֹנוֹ יִשָּׂא:

18 If a man lies with a woman in her infirmity and uncovers her nakedness, he has laid bare her flow and she has exposed her blood flow; both of them shall be cut off from among their people.

יח וְאִישׁ אֲשֶׁר־יִשְׁכַּב אֶת־אִשָּׁה דָּוָה וְגִלָּה אֶת־עֶרְוָתָהּ אֶת־מְקֹרָהּ הֶעֱרָה וְהִיא גִּלְּתָה אֶת־מְקוֹר דָּמֶיהָ וְנִכְרְתוּ שְׁנֵיהֶם מִקֶּרֶב עַמָּם:

19 You shall not uncover the nakedness of your mother's sister or of your father's sister, for that is laying bare one's own flesh; they shall bear their guilt.

יט וְעֶרְוַת אֲחוֹת אִמְּךָ וַאֲחוֹת אָבִיךָ לֹא תְגַלֵּה כִּי אֶת־שְׁאֵרוֹ הֶעֱרָה עֲוֹנָם יִשָּׂאוּ:

20 If a man lies with his uncle's wife, it is his uncle's nakedness that he has uncovered. They shall bear their guilt: they shall die childless.

כ וְאִישׁ אֲשֶׁר יִשְׁכַּב אֶת־דֹּדָתוֹ עֶרְוַת דֹּדוֹ גִּלָּה חֶטְאָם יִשָּׂאוּ עֲרִירִים יָמֻתוּ:

21 If a man marries the wife of his brother, it is indecency. It is the nakedness of his brother that he has uncovered; they shall remain childless.

כא וְאִישׁ אֲשֶׁר יִקַּח אֶת־אֵשֶׁת אָחִיו נִדָּה הִוא עֶרְוַת אָחִיו גִּלָּה עֲרִירִים יִהְיוּ:

22 You shall faithfully observe all My laws and all My regulations, lest the land to which I bring you to settle in spew you out.

כב וּשְׁמַרְתֶּם אֶת־כָּל־חֻקֹּתַי וְאֶת־כָּל־מִשְׁפָּטַי וַעֲשִׂיתֶם אֹתָם וְלֹא־תָקִיא אֶתְכֶם הָאָרֶץ אֲשֶׁר אֲנִי מֵבִיא אֶתְכֶם שָׁמָּה לָשֶׁבֶת בָּהּ:

ush-mar-TEM et kol khu-ko-TAI v'-et kol mish-pa-TAI
va-a-see-TEM o-TAM v'-lo ta-KEE et-KHEM ha-A-retz a-SHER
a-NEE may-VEE et-KHEM SHA-mah la-SHE-vet BAH

23 You shall not follow the practices of the nation that I am driving out before you. For it is because they did all these things that I abhorred them

כג וְלֹא תֵלְכוּ בְּחֻקֹּת הַגּוֹי אֲשֶׁר־אֲנִי מְשַׁלֵּחַ מִפְּנֵיכֶם כִּי אֶת־כָּל־אֵלֶּה עָשׂוּ וָאָקֻץ בָּם:

20:22 Lest the land to which I bring you to settle in spew you out Following the warning in Chapter 18 against embracing the abomination of the Canaanites lest the Children of Israel be expelled from their land, Chapter 20 gives an example of such abominable behavior, containing a list of forbidden relationships that are detestable in *Hashem's* eyes. This verse then says that they must follow the commandments, "lest the land to which I bring you to settle in spew you out." This expression attributes human-like sensitivity to the Land of Israel; it cannot stomach impurity and abomination, and thus engaging in illicit relationships will result in exile from the land. This is a further example of the reality that the gift of *Eretz Yisrael* is dependent on maintaining a high level of purity and faith, since the land's sanctity cannot tolerate immorality.

A man blowing the *shofar* (ram's horn)

24 and said to you: You shall possess their land, for I will give it to you to possess, a land flowing with milk and honey. I *Hashem* am your God who has set you apart from other peoples.

כד וָאֹמַר לָכֶם אַתֶּם תִּירְשׁוּ אֶת־אַדְמָתָם וַאֲנִי אֶתְּנֶנָּה לָכֶם לָרֶשֶׁת אֹתָהּ אֶרֶץ זָבַת חָלָב וּדְבָשׁ אֲנִי יְהוָה אֱלֹהֵיכֶם אֲשֶׁר־הִבְדַּלְתִּי אֶתְכֶם מִן־הָעַמִּים:

va-o-MAR la-KHEM a-TEM tee-r'-SHU et ad-ma-TAM va-a-NEE et-NE-na la-KHEM la-RE-shet o-TAH E-retz za-VAT kha-LAV ud-VASH a-NEE a-do-NAI e-lo-hay-KHEM a-sher hiv-DAL-tee et-KHEM min ha-a-MEEM

25 So you shall set apart the clean beast from the unclean, the unclean bird from the clean. You shall not draw abomination upon yourselves through beast or bird or anything with which the ground is alive, which I have set apart for you to treat as unclean.

כה וְהִבְדַּלְתֶּם בֵּין־הַבְּהֵמָה הַטְּהֹרָה לַטְּמֵאָה וּבֵין־הָעוֹף הַטָּמֵא לַטָּהֹר וְלֹא־תְשַׁקְּצוּ אֶת־נַפְשֹׁתֵיכֶם בַּבְּהֵמָה וּבָעוֹף וּבְכֹל אֲשֶׁר תִּרְמֹשׂ הָאֲדָמָה אֲשֶׁר־הִבְדַּלְתִּי לָכֶם לְטַמֵּא:

26 You shall be holy to Me, for I *Hashem* am holy, and I have set you apart from other peoples to be Mine.

כו וִהְיִיתֶם לִי קְדֹשִׁים כִּי קָדוֹשׁ אֲנִי יְהוָה וָאַבְדִּל אֶתְכֶם מִן־הָעַמִּים לִהְיוֹת לִי:

27 A man or a woman who has a ghost or a familiar spirit shall be put to death; they shall be pelted with stones – their bloodguilt shall be upon them.

כז וְאִישׁ אוֹ־אִשָּׁה כִּי־יִהְיֶה בָהֶם אוֹב אוֹ יִדְּעֹנִי מוֹת יוּמָתוּ בָּאֶבֶן יִרְגְּמוּ אֹתָם דְּמֵיהֶם בָּם:

1 *Hashem* said to *Moshe*: Speak to the *Kohanim*, the sons of *Aharon*, and say to them: None shall defile himself for any [dead] person among his kin,

כא א וַיֹּאמֶר יְהוָה אֶל־מֹשֶׁה אֱמֹר אֶל־הַכֹּהֲנִים בְּנֵי אַהֲרֹן וְאָמַרְתָּ אֲלֵהֶם לְנֶפֶשׁ לֹא־יִטַּמָּא בְּעַמָּיו:

va-YO-mer a-do-NAI el mo-SHEH e-MOR el ha-ko-ha-NEEM b'-NAY a-ha-RON v'-a-mar-TA a-lay-HEM l'-NE-fesh lo yi-ta-MA b'-a-MAV

2 except for the relatives that are closest to him: his mother, his father, his son, his daughter, and his brother;

ב כִּי אִם־לִשְׁאֵרוֹ הַקָּרֹב אֵלָיו לְאִמּוֹ וּלְאָבִיו וְלִבְנוֹ וּלְבִתּוֹ וּלְאָחִיו:

3 also for a virgin sister, close to him because she has not married, for her he may defile himself.

ג וְלַאֲחֹתוֹ הַבְּתוּלָה הַקְּרוֹבָה אֵלָיו אֲשֶׁר לֹא־הָיְתָה לְאִישׁ לָהּ יִטַּמָּא:

4 But he shall not defile himself as a kinsman by marriage, and so profane himself.

ד לֹא יִטַּמָּא בַּעַל בְּעַמָּיו לְהֵחַלּוֹ:

21:1 None shall defile himself for any [dead] person among his kin While the entire Nation of Israel is commanded to maintain a certain level of holiness, the *Kohanim* were held to an even higher standard. For example, a priest may not become ritually impure through contact with a dead body. Therefore, he may not participate in the burial of anyone other than his immediate relatives. However, *Rashi* teaches that there is an exception to this rule. If there is no one else to bury the person, then even the *Kohen Gadol* is obligated to perform the burial, even if the deceased is not "among his kin." This is particularly striking, since under normal circumstances, unlike ordinary *Kohanim*, the *Kohen Gadol* may not participate in the burial of even his closest relatives. In this way, the Bible teaches that an elevated status must not make one oblivious to the needs of people. On the contrary, it is the obligation of those with heightened responsibility to see to it that everyone is taken care of, even at the expense of their own personal state of holiness.

The priestly blessing in a synagogue in Ofra

5 They shall not shave smooth any part of their heads, or cut the side-growth of their beards, or make gashes in their flesh.

ה לֹא־יִקְרְחֻ [יִקְרְחוּ] קָרְחָה בְּרֹאשָׁם וּפְאַת זְקָנָם לֹא יְגַלֵּחוּ וּבִבְשָׂרָם לֹא יִשְׂרְטוּ שָׂרָטֶת:

6 They shall be holy to their God and not profane the name of their God; for they offer *Hashem*'s offerings by fire, the food of their God, and so must be holy.

ו קְדֹשִׁים יִהְיוּ לֵאלֹהֵיהֶם וְלֹא יְחַלְּלוּ שֵׁם אֱלֹהֵיהֶם כִּי אֶת־אִשֵּׁי יְהֹוָה לֶחֶם אֱלֹהֵיהֶם הֵם מַקְרִיבִם וְהָיוּ קֹדֶשׁ:

7 They shall not marry a woman defiled by harlotry, nor shall they marry one divorced from her husband. For they are holy to their God

ז אִשָּׁה זֹנָה וַחֲלָלָה לֹא יִקָּחוּ וְאִשָּׁה גְּרוּשָׁה מֵאִישָׁהּ לֹא יִקָּחוּ כִּי־קָדֹשׁ הוּא לֵאלֹהָיו:

8 and you must treat them as holy, since they offer the food of your God; they shall be holy to you, for I *Hashem* who sanctify you am holy.

ח וְקִדַּשְׁתּוֹ כִּי־אֶת־לֶחֶם אֱלֹהֶיךָ הוּא מַקְרִיב קָדֹשׁ יִהְיֶה־לָּךְ כִּי קָדוֹשׁ אֲנִי יְהֹוָה מְקַדִּשְׁכֶם:

9 When the daughter of a *Kohen* defiles herself through harlotry, it is her father whom she defiles; she shall be put to the fire.

ט וּבַת אִישׁ כֹּהֵן כִּי תֵחֵל לִזְנוֹת אֶת־אָבִיהָ הִיא מְחַלֶּלֶת בָּאֵשׁ תִּשָּׂרֵף:

10 The *Kohen* who is exalted above his fellows, on whose head the anointing oil has been poured and who has been ordained to wear the vestments, shall not bare his head or rend his vestments.

י וְהַכֹּהֵן הַגָּדוֹל מֵאֶחָיו אֲשֶׁר־יוּצַק עַל־רֹאשׁוֹ שֶׁמֶן הַמִּשְׁחָה וּמִלֵּא אֶת־יָדוֹ לִלְבֹּשׁ אֶת־הַבְּגָדִים אֶת־רֹאשׁוֹ לֹא יִפְרָע וּבְגָדָיו לֹא יִפְרֹם:

11 He shall not go in where there is any dead body; he shall not defile himself even for his father or mother.

יא וְעַל כָּל־נַפְשֹׁת מֵת לֹא יָבֹא לְאָבִיו וּלְאִמּוֹ לֹא יִטַּמָּא:

12 He shall not go outside the sanctuary and profane the sanctuary of his God, for upon him is the distinction of the anointing oil of his God, Mine *Hashem*'s.

יב וּמִן־הַמִּקְדָּשׁ לֹא יֵצֵא וְלֹא יְחַלֵּל אֵת מִקְדַּשׁ אֱלֹהָיו כִּי נֵזֶר שֶׁמֶן מִשְׁחַת אֱלֹהָיו עָלָיו אֲנִי יְהֹוָה:

13 He may marry only a woman who is a virgin.

יג וְהוּא אִשָּׁה בִבְתוּלֶיהָ יִקָּח:

14 A widow, or a divorced woman, or one who is degraded by harlotry – such he may not marry. Only a virgin of his own kin may he take to wife –

יד אַלְמָנָה וּגְרוּשָׁה וַחֲלָלָה זֹנָה אֶת־אֵלֶּה לֹא יִקָּח כִּי אִם־בְּתוּלָה מֵעַמָּיו יִקַּח אִשָּׁה:

15 that he may not profane his offspring among his kin, for I *Hashem* have sanctified him.

טו וְלֹא־יְחַלֵּל זַרְעוֹ בְּעַמָּיו כִּי אֲנִי יְהֹוָה מְקַדְּשׁוֹ:

16 *Hashem* spoke further to *Moshe*:

טז וַיְדַבֵּר יְהֹוָה אֶל־מֹשֶׁה לֵּאמֹר:

17 Speak to *Aharon* and say: No man of your offspring throughout the ages who has a defect shall be qualified to offer the food of his God.

יז דַּבֵּר אֶל־אַהֲרֹן לֵאמֹר אִישׁ מִזַּרְעֲךָ לְדֹרֹתָם אֲשֶׁר יִהְיֶה בוֹ מוּם לֹא יִקְרַב לְהַקְרִיב לֶחֶם אֱלֹהָיו:

18 No one at all who has a defect shall be qualified: no man who is blind, or lame, or has a limb too short or too long;

יח כִּי כָל־אִישׁ אֲשֶׁר־בּוֹ מוּם לֹא יִקְרָב אִישׁ עִוֵּר אוֹ פִסֵּחַ אוֹ חָרֻם אוֹ שָׂרוּעַ:

19 no man who has a broken leg or a broken arm;

יט אוֹ אִישׁ אֲשֶׁר־יִהְיֶה בוֹ שֶׁבֶר רָגֶל אוֹ שֶׁבֶר יָד:

20 or who is a hunchback, or a dwarf, or who has a growth in his eye, or who has a boil-scar, or scurvy, or crushed testes.

21 No man among the offspring of *Aharon* the *Kohen* who has a defect shall be qualified to offer *Hashem*'s offering by fire; having a defect, he shall not be qualified to offer the food of his God.

22 He may eat of the food of his God, of the most holy as well as of the holy;

23 but he shall not enter behind the curtain or come near the *Mizbayach*, for he has a defect. He shall not profane these places sacred to Me, for I *Hashem* have sanctified them.

24 Thus *Moshe* spoke to *Aharon* and his sons and to all the Israelites.

22 1 *Hashem* spoke to *Moshe*, saying:

2 Instruct *Aharon* and his sons to be scrupulous about the sacred donations that *B'nei Yisrael* consecrate to Me, lest they profane My holy name, Mine *Hashem*'s.

3 Say to them: Throughout the ages, if any man among your offspring, while in a state of uncleanness, partakes of any sacred donation that *B'nei Yisrael* may consecrate to *Hashem*, that person shall be cut off from before Me: I am *Hashem*.

4 No man of *Aharon*'s offspring who has an eruption or a discharge shall eat of the sacred donations until he is clean. If one touches anything made unclean by a corpse, or if a man has an emission of semen,

5 or if a man touches any swarming thing by which he is made unclean or any human being by whom he is made unclean – whatever his uncleanness –

6 the person who touches such shall be unclean until evening and shall not eat of the sacred donations unless he has washed his body in water.

7 As soon as the sun sets, he shall be clean; and afterward he may eat of the sacred donations, for they are his food.

8 He shall not eat anything that died or was torn by beasts, thereby becoming unclean: I am *Hashem*.

כ אוֹ־גִבֵּן אוֹ־דַק אוֹ תְּבַלֻּל בְּעֵינוֹ אוֹ גָרָב אוֹ יַלֶּפֶת אוֹ מְרוֹחַ אָשֶׁךְ:

כא כָּל־אִישׁ אֲשֶׁר־בּוֹ מוּם מִזֶּרַע אַהֲרֹן הַכֹּהֵן לֹא יִגַּשׁ לְהַקְרִיב אֶת־אִשֵּׁי יְהוָה מוּם בּוֹ אֵת לֶחֶם אֱלֹהָיו לֹא יִגַּשׁ לְהַקְרִיב:

כב לֶחֶם אֱלֹהָיו מִקָּדְשֵׁי הַקֳּדָשִׁים וּמִן־הַקֳּדָשִׁים יֹאכֵל:

כג אַךְ אֶל־הַפָּרֹכֶת לֹא יָבֹא וְאֶל־הַמִּזְבֵּחַ לֹא יִגַּשׁ כִּי־מוּם בּוֹ וְלֹא יְחַלֵּל אֶת־מִקְדָּשַׁי כִּי אֲנִי יְהוָה מְקַדְּשָׁם:

כד וַיְדַבֵּר מֹשֶׁה אֶל־אַהֲרֹן וְאֶל־בָּנָיו וְאֶל־כָּל־בְּנֵי יִשְׂרָאֵל:

כב א וַיְדַבֵּר יְהוָה אֶל־מֹשֶׁה לֵּאמֹר:

ב דַּבֵּר אֶל־אַהֲרֹן וְאֶל־בָּנָיו וְיִנָּזְרוּ מִקָּדְשֵׁי בְנֵי־יִשְׂרָאֵל וְלֹא יְחַלְּלוּ אֶת־שֵׁם קָדְשִׁי אֲשֶׁר הֵם מַקְדִּשִׁים לִי אֲנִי יְהוָה:

ג אֱמֹר אֲלֵהֶם לְדֹרֹתֵיכֶם כָּל־אִישׁ אֲשֶׁר־יִקְרַב מִכָּל־זַרְעֲכֶם אֶל־הַקֳּדָשִׁים אֲשֶׁר יַקְדִּישׁוּ בְנֵי־יִשְׂרָאֵל לַיהוָה וְטֻמְאָתוֹ עָלָיו וְנִכְרְתָה הַנֶּפֶשׁ הַהִוא מִלְּפָנַי אֲנִי יְהוָה:

ד אִישׁ אִישׁ מִזֶּרַע אַהֲרֹן וְהוּא צָרוּעַ אוֹ זָב בַּקֳּדָשִׁים לֹא יֹאכַל עַד אֲשֶׁר יִטְהָר וְהַנֹּגֵעַ בְּכָל־טְמֵא־נֶפֶשׁ אוֹ אִישׁ אֲשֶׁר־תֵּצֵא מִמֶּנּוּ שִׁכְבַת־זָרַע:

ה אוֹ־אִישׁ אֲשֶׁר יִגַּע בְּכָל־שֶׁרֶץ אֲשֶׁר יִטְמָא־לוֹ אוֹ בְאָדָם אֲשֶׁר יִטְמָא־לוֹ לְכֹל טֻמְאָתוֹ:

ו נֶפֶשׁ אֲשֶׁר תִּגַּע־בּוֹ וְטָמְאָה עַד־הָעָרֶב וְלֹא יֹאכַל מִן־הַקֳּדָשִׁים כִּי אִם־רָחַץ בְּשָׂרוֹ בַּמָּיִם:

ז וּבָא הַשֶּׁמֶשׁ וְטָהֵר וְאַחַר יֹאכַל מִן־הַקֳּדָשִׁים כִּי לַחְמוֹ הוּא:

ח נְבֵלָה וּטְרֵפָה לֹא יֹאכַל לְטָמְאָה־בָהּ אֲנִי יְהוָה:

Leviticus

9 They shall keep My charge, lest they incur guilt thereby and die for it, having committed profanation: I *Hashem* consecrate them.

ט וְשָׁמְרוּ אֶת־מִשְׁמַרְתִּי וְלֹא־יִשְׂאוּ עָלָיו חֵטְא וּמֵתוּ בוֹ כִּי יְחַלְּלֻהוּ אֲנִי יְהֹוָה מְקַדְּשָׁם:

10 No lay person shall eat of the sacred donations. No bound or hired laborer of a *Kohen* shall eat of the sacred donations;

י וְכָל־זָר לֹא־יֹאכַל קֹדֶשׁ תּוֹשַׁב כֹּהֵן וְשָׂכִיר לֹא־יֹאכַל קֹדֶשׁ:

11 but a person who is a *Kohen*'s property by purchase may eat of them; and those that are born into his household may eat of his food.

יא וְכֹהֵן כִּי־יִקְנֶה נֶפֶשׁ קִנְיַן כַּסְפּוֹ הוּא יֹאכַל בּוֹ וִילִיד בֵּיתוֹ הֵם יֹאכְלוּ בְלַחְמוֹ:

12 If a *Kohen*'s daughter marries a layman, she may not eat of the sacred gifts;

יב וּבַת־כֹּהֵן כִּי תִהְיֶה לְאִישׁ זָר הִוא בִּתְרוּמַת הַקֳּדָשִׁים לֹא תֹאכֵל:

13 but if the *Kohen*'s daughter is widowed or divorced and without offspring, and is back in her father's house as in her youth, she may eat of her father's food. No lay person may eat of it:

יג וּבַת־כֹּהֵן כִּי תִהְיֶה אַלְמָנָה וּגְרוּשָׁה וְזֶרַע אֵין לָהּ וְשָׁבָה אֶל־בֵּית אָבִיהָ כִּנְעוּרֶיהָ מִלֶּחֶם אָבִיהָ תֹּאכֵל וְכָל־זָר לֹא־יֹאכַל בּוֹ:

14 but if a man eats of a sacred donation unwittingly, he shall pay the *Kohen* for the sacred donation, adding one-fifth of its value.

יד וְאִישׁ כִּי־יֹאכַל קֹדֶשׁ בִּשְׁגָגָה וְיָסַף חֲמִשִׁיתוֹ עָלָיו וְנָתַן לַכֹּהֵן אֶת־הַקֹּדֶשׁ:

15 But [the *Kohanim*] must not allow the Israelites to profane the sacred donations that they set aside for *Hashem*,

טו וְלֹא יְחַלְּלוּ אֶת־קָדְשֵׁי בְּנֵי יִשְׂרָאֵל אֵת אֲשֶׁר־יָרִימוּ לַיהֹוָה:

16 or to incur guilt requiring a penalty payment, by eating such sacred donations: for it is I *Hashem* who make them sacred.

טז וְהִשִּׂיאוּ אוֹתָם עֲוֹן אַשְׁמָה בְּאָכְלָם אֶת־קָדְשֵׁיהֶם כִּי אֲנִי יְהֹוָה מְקַדְּשָׁם:

17 *Hashem* spoke to *Moshe*, saying:

יז וַיְדַבֵּר יְהֹוָה אֶל־מֹשֶׁה לֵּאמֹר:

18 Speak to *Aharon* and his sons, and to all *B'nei Yisrael*, and say to them: When any man of the house of *Yisrael* or of the strangers in *Yisrael* presents a burnt offering as his offering for any of the votive or any of the freewill offerings that they offer to *Hashem*,

יח דַּבֵּר אֶל־אַהֲרֹן וְאֶל־בָּנָיו וְאֶל כָּל־בְּנֵי יִשְׂרָאֵל וְאָמַרְתָּ אֲלֵהֶם אִישׁ אִישׁ מִבֵּית יִשְׂרָאֵל וּמִן־הַגֵּר בְּיִשְׂרָאֵל אֲשֶׁר יַקְרִיב קָרְבָּנוֹ לְכָל־נִדְרֵיהֶם וּלְכָל־נִדְבוֹתָם אֲשֶׁר־יַקְרִיבוּ לַיהֹוָה לְעֹלָה:

19 it must, to be acceptable in your favor, be a male without blemish, from cattle or sheep or goats.

יט לִרְצֹנְכֶם תָּמִים זָכָר בַּבָּקָר בַּכְּשָׂבִים וּבָעִזִּים:

20 You shall not offer any that has a defect, for it will not be accepted in your favor.

כ כֹּל אֲשֶׁר־בּוֹ מוּם לֹא תַקְרִיבוּ כִּי־לֹא לְרָצוֹן יִהְיֶה לָכֶם:

21 And when a man offers, from the herd or the flock, a sacrifice of well-being to *Hashem* for an explicit vow or as a freewill offering, it must, to be acceptable, be without blemish; there must be no defect in it.

כא וְאִישׁ כִּי־יַקְרִיב זֶבַח־שְׁלָמִים לַיהֹוָה לְפַלֵּא־נֶדֶר אוֹ לִנְדָבָה בַּבָּקָר אוֹ בַצֹּאן תָּמִים יִהְיֶה לְרָצוֹן כָּל־מוּם לֹא יִהְיֶה בּוֹ:

22 Anything blind, or injured, or maimed, or with a wen, boil-scar, or scurvy – such you shall not offer to *Hashem*; you shall not put any of them on the *Mizbayach* as offerings by fire to *Hashem*.

כב עִוֶּרֶת אוֹ שָׁבוּר אוֹ־חָרוּץ אוֹ־יַבֶּלֶת אוֹ גָרָב אוֹ יַלֶּפֶת לֹא־תַקְרִיבוּ אֵלֶּה לַיהוָה וְאִשֶּׁה לֹא־תִתְּנוּ מֵהֶם עַל־הַמִּזְבֵּחַ לַיהוָה:

23 You may, however, present as a freewill offering an ox or a sheep with a limb extended or contracted; but it will not be accepted for a vow.

כג וְשׁוֹר וָשֶׂה שָׂרוּעַ וְקָלוּט נְדָבָה תַּעֲשֶׂה אֹתוֹ וּלְנֵדֶר לֹא יֵרָצֶה:

24 You shall not offer to *Hashem* anything [with its testes] bruised or crushed or torn or cut. You shall have no such practices in your own land,

כד וּמָעוּךְ וְכָתוּת וְנָתוּק וְכָרוּת לֹא תַקְרִיבוּ לַיהוָה וּבְאַרְצְכֶם לֹא תַעֲשׂוּ:

25 nor shall you accept such [animals] from a foreigner for offering as food for your God, for they are mutilated, they have a defect; they shall not be accepted in your favor.

כה וּמִיַּד בֶּן־נֵכָר לֹא תַקְרִיבוּ אֶת־לֶחֶם אֱלֹהֵיכֶם מִכָּל־אֵלֶּה כִּי מָשְׁחָתָם בָּהֶם מוּם בָּם לֹא יֵרָצוּ לָכֶם:

26 *Hashem* spoke to *Moshe*, saying:

כו וַיְדַבֵּר יְהוָה אֶל־מֹשֶׁה לֵּאמֹר:

27 When an ox or a sheep or a goat is born, it shall stay seven days with its mother, and from the eighth day on it shall be acceptable as an offering by fire to *Hashem*.

כז שׁוֹר אוֹ־כֶשֶׂב אוֹ־עֵז כִּי יִוָּלֵד וְהָיָה שִׁבְעַת יָמִים תַּחַת אִמּוֹ וּמִיּוֹם הַשְּׁמִינִי וָהָלְאָה יֵרָצֶה לְקָרְבַּן אִשֶּׁה לַיהוָה:

28 However, no animal from the herd or from the flock shall be slaughtered on the same day with its young.

כח וְשׁוֹר אוֹ־שֶׂה אֹתוֹ וְאֶת־בְּנוֹ לֹא תִשְׁחֲטוּ בְּיוֹם אֶחָד:

29 When you sacrifice a thanksgiving offering to *Hashem*, sacrifice it so that it may be acceptable in your favor.

כט וְכִי־תִזְבְּחוּ זֶבַח־תּוֹדָה לַיהוָה לִרְצֹנְכֶם תִּזְבָּחוּ:

30 It shall be eaten on the same day; you shall not leave any of it until morning: I am *Hashem*.

ל בַּיּוֹם הַהוּא יֵאָכֵל לֹא־תוֹתִירוּ מִמֶּנּוּ עַד־בֹּקֶר אֲנִי יְהוָה:

31 You shall faithfully observe My commandments: I am *Hashem*.

לא וּשְׁמַרְתֶּם מִצְוֹתַי וַעֲשִׂיתֶם אֹתָם אֲנִי יְהוָה:

32 You shall not profane My holy name, that I may be sanctified in the midst of *B'nei Yisrael* – I *Hashem* who sanctify you,

לב וְלֹא תְחַלְּלוּ אֶת־שֵׁם קָדְשִׁי וְנִקְדַּשְׁתִּי בְּתוֹךְ בְּנֵי יִשְׂרָאֵל אֲנִי יְהוָה מְקַדִּשְׁכֶם:

v'-LO t'-kha-l'-LU et SHAYM ko-d'-SHEE v'-NIK-dash-TEE b'-TOKH b'-NAY yis-ra-AYL a-NEE a-do-NAI m'-ka-dish-KHEM

22:32 That I may be sanctified in the midst of the B'nei Yisrael This verse addresses the imperative to sanctify the name of *Hashem*. Rashi comments that the juxtaposition of the command to make *Hashem*'s name holy with the statement "I am *Hashem*…Who brought you out of the land of Egypt" implies that God took the Children of Israel out of Egypt on condition that they sanctify His name. According to the Talmud (*Yoma* 86a), the primary way to sanctify *Hashem*'s name is through ensuring that one's behavior re- flects positively upon *Hashem*. One must act in accordance with His commandments and treat others with kindness, consideration and honesty. The mandate to sanctify God's name guides the State of Israel, and thei IDF in particular, to hold itself to the highest standards of morality.

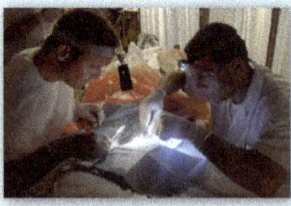

IDF doctors performing surgery at an IDF field hospital in Haiti, 2010

Leviticus

33 I who brought you out of the land of Egypt to be your God, I *Hashem*.

הַמּוֹצִיא אֶתְכֶם מֵאֶרֶץ מִצְרַיִם לִהְיוֹת לָכֶם לֵאלֹהִים אֲנִי יְהֹוָה: לג

ha-mo-TZEE at-KHEM may-E-retz mitz-RA-yim lih-YOT la-KHEM lay-lo-HEEM a-NEE a-do-NAI

23 ¹ *Hashem* spoke to *Moshe*, saying:

וַיְדַבֵּר יְהֹוָה אֶל־מֹשֶׁה לֵּאמֹר: א

² Speak to *B'nei Yisrael* and say to them: These are My fixed times, the fixed times of *Hashem*, which you shall proclaim as sacred occasions.

דַּבֵּר אֶל־בְּנֵי יִשְׂרָאֵל וְאָמַרְתָּ אֲלֵהֶם מוֹעֲדֵי יְהֹוָה אֲשֶׁר־תִּקְרְאוּ אֹתָם מִקְרָאֵי קֹדֶשׁ אֵלֶּה הֵם מוֹעֲדָי: ב

³ On six days work may be done, but on the seventh day there shall be a *Shabbat* of complete rest, a sacred occasion. You shall do no work; it shall be a *Shabbat* of *Hashem* throughout your settlements.

שֵׁשֶׁת יָמִים תֵּעָשֶׂה מְלָאכָה וּבַיּוֹם הַשְּׁבִיעִי שַׁבַּת שַׁבָּתוֹן מִקְרָא־קֹדֶשׁ כָּל־מְלָאכָה לֹא תַעֲשׂוּ שַׁבָּת הִוא לַיהֹוָה בְּכֹל מוֹשְׁבֹתֵיכֶם: ג

⁴ These are the set times of *Hashem*, the sacred occasions, which you shall celebrate each at its appointed time:

אֵלֶּה מוֹעֲדֵי יְהֹוָה מִקְרָאֵי קֹדֶשׁ אֲשֶׁר־תִּקְרְאוּ אֹתָם בְּמוֹעֲדָם: ד

⁵ In the first month, on the fourteenth day of the month, at twilight, there shall be a *Pesach* offering to *Hashem*,

בַּחֹדֶשׁ הָרִאשׁוֹן בְּאַרְבָּעָה עָשָׂר לַחֹדֶשׁ בֵּין הָעַרְבָּיִם פֶּסַח לַיהֹוָה: ה

⁶ and on the fifteenth day of that month *Hashem's* Feast of Unleavened Bread. You shall eat unleavened bread for seven days.

וּבַחֲמִשָּׁה עָשָׂר יוֹם לַחֹדֶשׁ הַזֶּה חַג הַמַּצּוֹת לַיהֹוָה שִׁבְעַת יָמִים מַצּוֹת תֹּאכֵלוּ: ו

⁷ On the first day you shall celebrate a sacred occasion: you shall not work at your occupations.

בַּיּוֹם הָרִאשׁוֹן מִקְרָא־קֹדֶשׁ יִהְיֶה לָכֶם כָּל־מְלֶאכֶת עֲבֹדָה לֹא תַעֲשׂוּ: ז

⁸ Seven days you shall make offerings by fire to *Hashem*. The seventh day shall be a sacred occasion: you shall not work at your occupations.

וְהִקְרַבְתֶּם אִשֶּׁה לַיהֹוָה שִׁבְעַת יָמִים בַּיּוֹם הַשְּׁבִיעִי מִקְרָא־קֹדֶשׁ כָּל־מְלֶאכֶת עֲבֹדָה לֹא תַעֲשׂוּ: ח

⁹ *Hashem* spoke to *Moshe*, saying:

וַיְדַבֵּר יְהֹוָה אֶל־מֹשֶׁה לֵּאמֹר: ט

¹⁰ Speak to *B'nei Yisrael* and say to them: When you enter the land that I am giving to you and you reap its harvest, you shall bring the first sheaf of your harvest to the *Kohen*.

דַּבֵּר אֶל־בְּנֵי יִשְׂרָאֵל וְאָמַרְתָּ אֲלֵהֶם כִּי־תָבֹאוּ אֶל־הָאָרֶץ אֲשֶׁר אֲנִי נֹתֵן לָכֶם וּקְצַרְתֶּם אֶת־קְצִירָהּ וַהֲבֵאתֶם אֶת־עֹמֶר רֵאשִׁית קְצִירְכֶם אֶל־הַכֹּהֵן: י

da-BAYR el b'-NAY yis-ra-AYL v'-a-mar-TA a-lay-HEM kee ta-VO-u el ha-A-retz a-SHER a-NEE no-TAYN la-KHEM uk-tzar-TEM et k'-tzee-RA va-ha-vay-TEM et O-mer ray-SHEET k'-tzee-r'-KHEM el ha-ko-HAYN

Barley growing in the western Negev

23:10 You shall bring the first sheaf of your harvest The *omer* is an offering of barley brought to the *Beit Hamikdash* in *Yerushalayim* on the second day of *Pesach*, corresponding to the sixteenth day of the month of *Nisan*. Only once this offering was brought, all grain that had taken root prior to the time of the offering may be eaten.

According to the Sages (*Kiddushin* 38a), it was on the sixteenth of *Nisan* that the Israelites ran out of manna after it ceased to fall following the death of *Moshe*. The offering of the first grain in the *Beit Hamikdash* on that day each year reminds us of the eternal lesson of the manna. We dedicate a portion of our crops to our Creator before

11 He shall elevate the sheaf before *Hashem* for acceptance in your behalf; the *Kohen* shall elevate it on the day after the *Shabbat*.

יא וְהֵנִיף אֶת־הָעֹמֶר לִפְנֵי יְהוָה לִרְצֹנְכֶם מִמָּחֳרַת הַשַּׁבָּת יְנִיפֶנּוּ הַכֹּהֵן:

12 On the day that you elevate the sheaf, you shall offer as a burnt offering to *Hashem* a lamb of the first year without blemish.

יב וַעֲשִׂיתֶם בְּיוֹם הֲנִיפְכֶם אֶת־הָעֹמֶר כֶּבֶשׂ תָּמִים בֶּן־שְׁנָתוֹ לְעֹלָה לַיהוָה:

13 The meal offering with it shall be two-tenths of a measure of choice flour with oil mixed in, an offering by fire of pleasing odor to *Hashem*; and the libation with it shall be of wine, a quarter of a *hin*.

יג וּמִנְחָתוֹ שְׁנֵי עֶשְׂרֹנִים סֹלֶת בְּלוּלָה בַשֶּׁמֶן אִשֶּׁה לַיהוָה רֵיחַ נִיחֹחַ וְנִסְכֹּה יַיִן רְבִיעִת הַהִין:

14 Until that very day, until you have brought the offering of your God, you shall eat no bread or parched grain or fresh ears; it is a law for all time throughout the ages in all your settlements.

יד וְלֶחֶם וְקָלִי וְכַרְמֶל לֹא תֹאכְלוּ עַד־ עֶצֶם הַיּוֹם הַזֶּה עַד הֲבִיאֲכֶם אֶת־קָרְבַּן אֱלֹהֵיכֶם חֻקַּת עוֹלָם לְדֹרֹתֵיכֶם בְּכֹל מֹשְׁבֹתֵיכֶם:

15 And from the day on which you bring the sheaf of elevation offering – the day after the *Shabbat* – you shall count off seven weeks. They must be complete:

טו וּסְפַרְתֶּם לָכֶם מִמָּחֳרַת הַשַּׁבָּת מִיּוֹם הֲבִיאֲכֶם אֶת־עֹמֶר הַתְּנוּפָה שֶׁבַע שַׁבָּתוֹת תְּמִימֹת תִּהְיֶינָה:

16 you must count until the day after the seventh week – fifty days; then you shall bring an offering of new grain to *Hashem*.

טז עַד מִמָּחֳרַת הַשַּׁבָּת הַשְּׁבִיעִת תִּסְפְּרוּ חֲמִשִּׁים יוֹם וְהִקְרַבְתֶּם מִנְחָה חֲדָשָׁה לַיהוָה:

17 You shall bring from your settlements two loaves of bread as an elevation offering; each shall be made of two-tenths of a measure of choice flour, baked after leavening, as first fruits to *Hashem*.

יז מִמּוֹשְׁבֹתֵיכֶם תָּבִיאוּ לֶחֶם תְּנוּפָה שְׁתַּיִם שְׁנֵי עֶשְׂרֹנִים סֹלֶת תִּהְיֶינָה חָמֵץ תֵּאָפֶינָה בִּכּוּרִים לַיהוָה:

18 With the bread you shall present, as burnt offerings to *Hashem*, seven yearling lambs without blemish, one bull of the herd, and two rams, with their meal offerings and libations, an offering by fire of pleasing odor to *Hashem*.

יח וְהִקְרַבְתֶּם עַל־הַלֶּחֶם שִׁבְעַת כְּבָשִׂים תְּמִימִם בְּנֵי שָׁנָה וּפַר בֶּן־בָּקָר אֶחָד וְאֵילִם שְׁנָיִם יִהְיוּ עֹלָה לַיהוָה וּמִנְחָתָם וְנִסְכֵּיהֶם אִשֶּׁה רֵיחַ־נִיחֹחַ לַיהוָה:

19 You shall also offer one he-goat as a sin offering and two yearling lambs as a sacrifice of well-being.

יט וַעֲשִׂיתֶם שְׂעִיר־עִזִּים אֶחָד לְחַטָּאת וּשְׁנֵי כְבָשִׂים בְּנֵי שָׁנָה לְזֶבַח שְׁלָמִים:

20 The *Kohen* shall elevate these – the two lambs – together with the bread of first fruits as an elevation offering before *Hashem*; they shall be holy to *Hashem*, for the *Kohen*.

כ וְהֵנִיף הַכֹּהֵן אֹתָם עַל לֶחֶם הַבִּכּוּרִים תְּנוּפָה לִפְנֵי יְהוָה עַל־שְׁנֵי כְּבָשִׂים קֹדֶשׁ יִהְיוּ לַיהוָה לַכֹּהֵן:

we eat from them ourselves, to remind us that no matter how hard we work the land, and despite the tremendous human effort required to produce it, our sustenance is really a gift from God in heaven.

21 On that same day you shall hold a celebration; it shall be a sacred occasion for you; you shall not work at your occupations. This is a law for all time in all your settlements, throughout the ages.

כא וּקְרָאתֶם בְּעֶצֶם הַיּוֹם הַזֶּה מִקְרָא־קֹדֶשׁ יִהְיֶה לָכֶם כָּל־מְלֶאכֶת עֲבֹדָה לֹא תַעֲשׂוּ חֻקַּת עוֹלָם בְּכָל־מוֹשְׁבֹתֵיכֶם לְדֹרֹתֵיכֶם:

22 And when you reap the harvest of your land, you shall not reap all the way to the edges of your field, or gather the gleanings of your harvest; you shall leave them for the poor and the stranger: I *Hashem* am your God.

כב וּבְקֻצְרְכֶם אֶת־קְצִיר אַרְצְכֶם לֹא־תְכַלֶּה פְּאַת שָׂדְךָ בְּקֻצְרֶךָ וְלֶקֶט קְצִירְךָ לֹא תְלַקֵּט לֶעָנִי וְלַגֵּר תַּעֲזֹב אֹתָם אֲנִי יְהֹוָה אֱלֹהֵיכֶם:

uv-kutz-r'-KHEM et k'-TZEER ar-tz'-KHEM lo t'-kha-LE p'-AT sa-d'-KHA b'-kutz-RE-kha v'-LE-ket k'-tzee-r'-KHA LO te-la-KAYT le-a-NEE v'-la-GAYR ta-a-ZOV o-TAM a-NEE a-do-NAI e-LO-hay-khem

23 *Hashem* spoke to *Moshe*, saying:

כג וַיְדַבֵּר יְהֹוָה אֶל־מֹשֶׁה לֵּאמֹר:

24 Speak to *B'nei Yisrael* thus: In the seventh month, on the first day of the month, you shall observe complete rest, a sacred occasion commemorated with loud blasts.

כד דַּבֵּר אֶל־בְּנֵי יִשְׂרָאֵל לֵאמֹר בַּחֹדֶשׁ הַשְּׁבִיעִי בְּאֶחָד לַחֹדֶשׁ יִהְיֶה לָכֶם שַׁבָּתוֹן זִכְרוֹן תְּרוּעָה מִקְרָא־קֹדֶשׁ:

da-BAYR el b'-NAY yis-ra-AYL lay-MOR ba-KHO-desh ha-sh'-vee-EE b'-e-KHAD la-KHO-desh yih-YEH la-KHEM sha-ba-TON zikh-RON t'-ru-AH mik-ra KO-desh

25 You shall not work at your occupations; and you shall bring an offering by fire to *Hashem*.

כה כָּל־מְלֶאכֶת עֲבֹדָה לֹא תַעֲשׂוּ וְהִקְרַבְתֶּם אִשֶּׁה לַיהֹוָה:

26 *Hashem* spoke to *Moshe*, saying:

כו וַיְדַבֵּר יְהֹוָה אֶל־מֹשֶׁה לֵּאמֹר:

27 Mark, the tenth day of this seventh month is *Yom Kippur*. It shall be a sacred occasion for you: you shall practice self-denial, and you shall bring an offering by fire to *Hashem*;

כז אַךְ בֶּעָשׂוֹר לַחֹדֶשׁ הַשְּׁבִיעִי הַזֶּה יוֹם הַכִּפֻּרִים הוּא מִקְרָא־קֹדֶשׁ יִהְיֶה לָכֶם וְעִנִּיתֶם אֶת־נַפְשֹׁתֵיכֶם וְהִקְרַבְתֶּם אִשֶּׁה לַיהֹוָה:

23:22 You shall not reap all the way to the edges of your field This verse describes some of the agricultural laws reflecting the biblical notion of charity. A farmer must leave a corner of his field unharvested, and may also not collect stalks of grain that fall during harvesting. Similarly, forgotten sheaves of grain and small grapes left on the vine must not be collected. Instead, each of these portions of the harvest must be left for the poor. These commandments only apply to farmers in Israel. Farmers outside of *Eretz Yisrael* may harvest their entire field, as reflected in the words "of your land," which refer specifically to the Land of Israel. This biblical imperative is still practiced in Israel today. Each season, farmers throughout Israel leave over millions of pounds of produce from the fields, which are collected by volunteers and distributed to poor people all over the country.

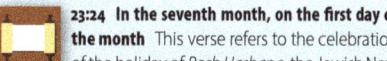
A tractor ploughing a field in the Negev desert

23:24 In the seventh month, on the first day of the month This verse refers to the celebration of the holiday of *Rosh Hashana*, the Jewish New Year and the first of the High Holidays. The story is told of a small, uneducated child who did not know Hebrew, and thus could not participate in the *Rosh Hashana* services. He desperately wanted to pray with the congregation on such a holy day, and so he entered the synagogue and hesitantly approached the Holy Ark. As the congregants looked at him in confusion, he called out to *Hashem* by simply reciting the letters of the Hebrew alphabet, the only Hebrew familiar to him. There was not a person in the room who wasn't moved by his pure desire to return to *Hashem*, and the gates of Heaven immediately opened to accept his prayers. Do not think that the road to heaven is closed to you, God is always ready to welcome anyone who sincerely desires to approach Him.

28 you shall do no work throughout that day. For it is *Yom Kippur*, on which expiation is made on your behalf before *Hashem* your God.

29 Indeed, any person who does not practice self-denial throughout that day shall be cut off from his kin;

30 and whoever does any work throughout that day, I will cause that person to perish from among his people.

31 Do no work whatever; it is a law for all time, throughout the ages in all your settlements.

32 It shall be a *Shabbat* of complete rest for you, and you shall practice self-denial; on the ninth day of the month at evening, from evening to evening, you shall observe this your *Shabbat*.

33 *Hashem* spoke to *Moshe*, saying:

34 Say to *B'nei Yisrael*: On the fifteenth day of this seventh month there shall be the festival of *Sukkot* to *Hashem*, [to last] seven days.

35 The first day shall be a sacred occasion: you shall not work at your occupations;

36 seven days you shall bring offerings by fire to *Hashem*. On the eighth day you shall observe a sacred occasion and bring an offering by fire to *Hashem*; it is a solemn gathering: you shall not work at your occupations.

37 Those are the set times of *Hashem* that you shall celebrate as sacred occasions, bringing offerings by fire to *Hashem* – burnt offerings, meal offerings, sacrifices, and libations, on each day what is proper to it –

38 apart from the *Shabbatot* of *Hashem*, and apart from your gifts and from all your votive offerings and from all your freewill offerings that you give to *Hashem*.

39 Mark, on the fifteenth day of the seventh month, when you have gathered in the yield of your land,

כח וְכָל־מְלָאכָה לֹא תַעֲשׂוּ בְּעֶצֶם הַיּוֹם הַזֶּה כִּי יוֹם כִּפֻּרִים הוּא לְכַפֵּר עֲלֵיכֶם לִפְנֵי יְהֹוָה אֱלֹהֵיכֶם:

כט כִּי כָל־הַנֶּפֶשׁ אֲשֶׁר לֹא־תְעֻנֶּה בְּעֶצֶם הַיּוֹם הַזֶּה וְנִכְרְתָה מֵעַמֶּיהָ:

ל וְכָל־הַנֶּפֶשׁ אֲשֶׁר תַּעֲשֶׂה כָּל־מְלָאכָה בְּעֶצֶם הַיּוֹם הַזֶּה וְהַאֲבַדְתִּי אֶת־הַנֶּפֶשׁ הַהִוא מִקֶּרֶב עַמָּהּ:

לא כָּל־מְלָאכָה לֹא תַעֲשׂוּ חֻקַּת עוֹלָם לְדֹרֹתֵיכֶם בְּכֹל מֹשְׁבֹתֵיכֶם:

לב שַׁבַּת שַׁבָּתוֹן הוּא לָכֶם וְעִנִּיתֶם אֶת־נַפְשֹׁתֵיכֶם בְּתִשְׁעָה לַחֹדֶשׁ בָּעֶרֶב מֵעֶרֶב עַד־עֶרֶב תִּשְׁבְּתוּ שַׁבַּתְּכֶם:

לג וַיְדַבֵּר יְהֹוָה אֶל־מֹשֶׁה לֵּאמֹר:

לד דַּבֵּר אֶל־בְּנֵי יִשְׂרָאֵל לֵאמֹר בַּחֲמִשָּׁה עָשָׂר יוֹם לַחֹדֶשׁ הַשְּׁבִיעִי הַזֶּה חַג הַסֻּכּוֹת שִׁבְעַת יָמִים לַיהֹוָה:

לה בַּיּוֹם הָרִאשׁוֹן מִקְרָא־קֹדֶשׁ כָּל־מְלֶאכֶת עֲבֹדָה לֹא תַעֲשׂוּ:

לו שִׁבְעַת יָמִים תַּקְרִיבוּ אִשֶּׁה לַיהֹוָה בַּיּוֹם הַשְּׁמִינִי מִקְרָא־קֹדֶשׁ יִהְיֶה לָכֶם וְהִקְרַבְתֶּם אִשֶּׁה לַיהֹוָה עֲצֶרֶת הִוא כָּל־מְלֶאכֶת עֲבֹדָה לֹא תַעֲשׂוּ:

לז אֵלֶּה מוֹעֲדֵי יְהֹוָה אֲשֶׁר־תִּקְרְאוּ אֹתָם מִקְרָאֵי קֹדֶשׁ לְהַקְרִיב אִשֶּׁה לַיהֹוָה עֹלָה וּמִנְחָה זֶבַח וּנְסָכִים דְּבַר־יוֹם בְּיוֹמוֹ:

לח מִלְּבַד שַׁבְּתֹת יְהֹוָה וּמִלְּבַד מַתְּנוֹתֵיכֶם וּמִלְּבַד כָּל־נִדְרֵיכֶם וּמִלְּבַד כָּל־נִדְבֹתֵיכֶם אֲשֶׁר תִּתְּנוּ לַיהֹוָה:

לט אַךְ בַּחֲמִשָּׁה עָשָׂר יוֹם לַחֹדֶשׁ הַשְּׁבִיעִי בְּאָסְפְּכֶם אֶת־תְּבוּאַת הָאָרֶץ תָּחֹגּוּ

23:39 On the first day you shall take One of the unique practices of the holiday of *Sukkot* is the taking of the four species. The Sages of the *Midrash* tell us that these four species symbolize four different personality types. The *etrog* (אתרוג), 'citron,' which is both fragrant and tasty, represents a person who knows

you shall observe the festival of *Hashem* [to last] seven days: a complete rest on the first day, and a complete rest on the eighth day.

אֶת־חַג־יְהֹוָה שִׁבְעַת יָמִים בַּיּוֹם הָרִאשׁוֹן שַׁבָּתוֹן וּבַיּוֹם הַשְּׁמִינִי שַׁבָּתוֹן:

AKH ba-kha-mi-SHAH a-SAR YOM la-KHO-desh ha-sh'-vee-EE b'-os-p'-KHEM et t'-vu-at ha-A-retz ta-KHO-gu et khag a-do-NAI shiv-AT ya-MEEM ba-YOM ha-ri-SHON sha-ba-TON u-va-YOM ha-sh'-mee-NEE sha-ba-TON

40 On the first day you shall take the product of hadar trees, branches of palm trees, boughs of leafy trees, and willows of the brook, and you shall rejoice before *Hashem* your God seven days.

מ וּלְקַחְתֶּם לָכֶם בַּיּוֹם הָרִאשׁוֹן פְּרִי עֵץ הָדָר כַּפֹּת תְּמָרִים וַעֲנַף עֵץ־עָבֹת וְעַרְבֵי־נָחַל וּשְׂמַחְתֶּם לִפְנֵי יְהֹוָה אֱלֹהֵיכֶם שִׁבְעַת יָמִים:

ul-kakh-TEM la-KHEM ba-YOM ha-ri-SHON p'-REE AYTZ ha-DAR ka-POT t'-ma-REEM va-a-NAF aytz a-VOT v'-ar-VAY NA-khal us-makh-TEM lif-NAY a-do-NAI e-lo-hay-KHEM shiv-AT ya-MEEM

41 You shall observe it as a festival of *Hashem* for seven days in the year; you shall observe it in the seventh month as a law for all time, throughout the ages.

מא וְחַגֹּתֶם אֹתוֹ חַג לַיהֹוָה שִׁבְעַת יָמִים בַּשָּׁנָה חֻקַּת עוֹלָם לְדֹרֹתֵיכֶם בַּחֹדֶשׁ הַשְּׁבִיעִי תָּחֹגּוּ אֹתוֹ:

42 You shall live in booths seven days; all citizens in *Yisrael* shall live in booths,

מב בַּסֻּכֹּת תֵּשְׁבוּ שִׁבְעַת יָמִים כָּל־הָאֶזְרָח בְּיִשְׂרָאֵל יֵשְׁבוּ בַּסֻּכֹּת:

43 in order that future generations may know that I made B'nei Yisrael live in booths when I brought them out of the land of Egypt, I *Hashem* your God.

מג לְמַעַן יֵדְעוּ דֹרֹתֵיכֶם כִּי בַסֻּכּוֹת הוֹשַׁבְתִּי אֶת־בְּנֵי יִשְׂרָאֵל בְּהוֹצִיאִי אוֹתָם מֵאֶרֶץ מִצְרָיִם אֲנִי יְהֹוָה אֱלֹהֵיכֶם:

l'-MA-an yay-d'-U do-ro-tay-KHEM KEE va-su-KOT ho-SHAV-tee et b'-NAY yis-ra-AYL b'-ho-tzee-EE o-TAM may-E-retz mitz-RA-yim a-NEE a-do-NAI e-lo-hay-KHEM

The four species

Torah and also performs good deeds. The *lulav* (לולב), 'palm branch,' has tasty fruit but no aroma, and thus represents a person who has knowledge of *Torah*, but does not perform good deeds. Conversely, the *hadas* (הדס), 'myrtle branch,' has a pleasant smell but no taste, representing a person who does good deeds, but lacks *Torah* knowledge. And the *arava* (ערבה), 'willow branch,' which lacks both smell and taste, represents a person who has neither *Torah* nor good deeds. By taking these different species and holding them together, we emphasize the importance of everyone, with all of their strengths and weaknesses, coming together and uniting in the service of the one true God.

23:40 You shall rejoice before *Hashem* your God seven days *Sukkot*, the Feast of Tabernacles, was the most joyous of the festivals observed in the *Beit Hamikdash*. However, according to the Sages (*Rosh Hashana* 16a), *Hashem* judges the people for water and determines how much rain will fall in the coming year on *Sukkot*. Given the fact that *Eretz Yisrael* is very dependent on rainfall, it seems that *Sukkot* should be a solemn time and not one of joyous celebration. What is the reason for such festivity? By making His people dependent on rainfall which comes from heaven, *Hashem* ensures that they must maintain a close connection with Him through prayer at all times. It is the constant connection with the Almighty, by virtue of His children's continued dependence on Him, which is the cause for great celebration on *Sukkot*.

23:43 In order that future generations may know The holiday of *Sukkot* recalls the protective shelter *Hashem* provided to the People of Israel in the desert. By following Him into the wilderness, they

A sukkah in Kibbutz Ein Hanatziv

44 So *Moshe* declared to the Israelites the set times of *Hashem*.

מד וַיְדַבֵּר מֹשֶׁה אֶת־מֹעֲדֵי יְהוָה אֶל־בְּנֵי יִשְׂרָאֵל:

4 1 *Hashem* spoke to *Moshe*, saying:

כד א וַיְדַבֵּר יְהוָה אֶל־מֹשֶׁה לֵּאמֹר:

2 Command *B'nei Yisrael* to bring you clear oil of beaten olives for lighting, for kindling lamps regularly.

ב צַו אֶת־בְּנֵי יִשְׂרָאֵל וְיִקְחוּ אֵלֶיךָ שֶׁמֶן זַיִת זָךְ כָּתִית לַמָּאוֹר לְהַעֲלֹת נֵר תָּמִיד:

3 *Aharon* shall set them up in the Tent of Meeting outside the curtain of the Pact [to burn] from evening to morning before *Hashem* regularly; it is a law for all time throughout the ages.

ג מִחוּץ לְפָרֹכֶת הָעֵדֻת בְּאֹהֶל מוֹעֵד יַעֲרֹךְ אֹתוֹ אַהֲרֹן מֵעֶרֶב עַד־בֹּקֶר לִפְנֵי יְהוָה תָּמִיד חֻקַּת עוֹלָם לְדֹרֹתֵיכֶם:

4 He shall set up the lamps on the pure *menorah* before *Hashem* [to burn] regularly.

ד עַל הַמְּנֹרָה הַטְּהֹרָה יַעֲרֹךְ אֶת־הַנֵּרוֹת לִפְנֵי יְהוָה תָּמִיד:

5 You shall take choice flour and bake of it twelve loaves, two-tenths of a measure for each loaf.

ה וְלָקַחְתָּ סֹלֶת וְאָפִיתָ אֹתָהּ שְׁתֵּים עֶשְׂרֵה חַלּוֹת שְׁנֵי עֶשְׂרֹנִים יִהְיֶה הַחַלָּה הָאֶחָת:

6 Place them on the pure table before *Hashem* in two rows, six to a row.

ו וְשַׂמְתָּ אוֹתָם שְׁתַּיִם מַעֲרָכוֹת שֵׁשׁ הַמַּעֲרָכֶת עַל הַשֻּׁלְחָן הַטָּהֹר לִפְנֵי יְהוָה:

7 With each row you shall place pure frankincense, which is to be a token offering for the bread, as an offering by fire to *Hashem*.

ז וְנָתַתָּ עַל־הַמַּעֲרֶכֶת לְבֹנָה זַכָּה וְהָיְתָה לַלֶּחֶם לְאַזְכָּרָה אִשֶּׁה לַיהוָה:

8 He shall arrange them before *Hashem* regularly every *Shabbat* day – it is a commitment for all time on the part of the Israelites.

ח בְּיוֹם הַשַּׁבָּת בְּיוֹם הַשַּׁבָּת יַעַרְכֶנּוּ לִפְנֵי יְהוָה תָּמִיד מֵאֵת בְּנֵי־יִשְׂרָאֵל בְּרִית עוֹלָם:

b'-YOM ha-sha-BAT b'-YOM ha-sha-BAT ya-ar-KHE-nu lif-NAY a-do-NAI ta-MEED may-AYT b'-nay yis-ra-AYL b'-REET o-LAM

9 They shall belong to *Aharon* and his sons, who shall eat them in the sacred precinct; for they are his as most holy things from *Hashem*'s offerings by fire, a due for all time.

ט וְהָיְתָה לְאַהֲרֹן וּלְבָנָיו וַאֲכָלֻהוּ בְּמָקוֹם קָדֹשׁ כִּי קֹדֶשׁ קָדָשִׁים הוּא לוֹ מֵאִשֵּׁי יְהוָה חָק־עוֹלָם:

demonstrated their unshakable faith in the Lord and their unwavering love for Him, as it says in *Yirmiyahu* (2:2) "Thus said *Hashem*: I accounted to your favor the devotion of your youth, your love as a bride, how you followed Me in the wilderness, in a land not sown." By leaving their sturdy homes and eating and sleeping in a *sukkah* for the seven days of the holiday, future generations demonstrate their unshakeable trust in *Hashem* and their faith that He will continue to take care of them throughout all of their challenges and tribulations, just as He did in the wilderness.

24:8 He shall arrange them before *Hashem* regularly Just as *Aharon* arranges the candles of the Temple *menorah* (Numbers 8:2–3), he is to arrange the twelve loaves of bread every *Shabbat* as a "commitment for all time." On the day that the Children of

Israel desist from activities related to earning their livelihood and focus instead on their relationship with the Almighty, *Aharon* sets the bread before *Hashem*, reflecting the understanding that it is He who ultimately provides mankind with their physical sustenance. Both the *menorah* and the *lechem hapanim* (לחם הפנים) 'bread of display,' or 'shewbread,' are a constant presence in the *Beit Hamikdash*. The light of the lamp symbolizes the spiritual life of the people, while bread symbolizes the physical realm. When the People of Israel rest on the *Shabbat* and focus on matters of the soul, God ensures that their physical well-being will be taken care of as well.

Mother and daughter lighting the *Shabbat* candles

Leviticus

10 There came out among the Israelites one whose mother was Israelite and whose father was Egyptian. And a fight broke out in the camp between that half-Israelite and a certain Israelite.

יֹ וַיֵּצֵא בֶּן־אִשָּׁה יִשְׂרְאֵלִית וְהוּא בֶּן־אִישׁ מִצְרִי בְּתוֹךְ בְּנֵי יִשְׂרָאֵל וַיִּנָּצוּ בַּמַּחֲנֶה בֶּן הַיִּשְׂרְאֵלִית וְאִישׁ הַיִּשְׂרְאֵלִי:

11 The son of the Israelite woman pronounced the Name in blasphemy, and he was brought to *Moshe* – now his mother's name was Shelomith daughter of Dibri of the tribe of *Dan* –

יא וַיִּקֹּב בֶּן־הָאִשָּׁה הַיִּשְׂרְאֵלִית אֶת־הַשֵּׁם וַיְקַלֵּל וַיָּבִיאוּ אֹתוֹ אֶל־מֹשֶׁה וְשֵׁם אִמּוֹ שְׁלֹמִית בַּת־דִּבְרִי לְמַטֵּה־דָן:

12 and he was placed in custody, until the decision of *Hashem* should be made clear to them.

יב וַיַּנִּיחֻהוּ בַּמִּשְׁמָר לִפְרֹשׁ לָהֶם עַל־פִּי יְהֹוָה:

13 And *Hashem* spoke to *Moshe*, saying:

יג וַיְדַבֵּר יְהֹוָה אֶל־מֹשֶׁה לֵּאמֹר:

14 Take the blasphemer outside the camp; and let all who were within hearing lay their hands upon his head, and let the whole community stone him.

יד הוֹצֵא אֶת־הַמְקַלֵּל אֶל־מִחוּץ לַמַּחֲנֶה וְסָמְכוּ כָל־הַשֹּׁמְעִים אֶת־יְדֵיהֶם עַל־רֹאשׁוֹ וְרָגְמוּ אֹתוֹ כָּל־הָעֵדָה:

15 And to *B'nei Yisrael* speak thus: Anyone who blasphemes his God shall bear his guilt;

טו וְאֶל־בְּנֵי יִשְׂרָאֵל תְּדַבֵּר לֵאמֹר אִישׁ אִישׁ כִּי־יְקַלֵּל אֱלֹהָיו וְנָשָׂא חֶטְאוֹ:

16 if he also pronounces the name *Hashem*, he shall be put to death. The whole community shall stone him; stranger or citizen, if he has thus pronounced the Name, he shall be put to death.

טז וְנֹקֵב שֵׁם־יְהֹוָה מוֹת יוּמָת רָגוֹם יִרְגְּמוּ־בוֹ כָּל־הָעֵדָה כַּגֵּר כָּאֶזְרָח בְּנָקְבוֹ־שֵׁם יוּמָת:

17 If anyone kills any human being, he shall be put to death.

יז וְאִישׁ כִּי יַכֶּה כָּל־נֶפֶשׁ אָדָם מוֹת יוּמָת:

18 One who kills a beast shall make restitution for it: life for life.

יח וּמַכֵּה נֶפֶשׁ־בְּהֵמָה יְשַׁלְּמֶנָּה נֶפֶשׁ תַּחַת נָפֶשׁ:

19 If anyone maims his fellow, as he has done so shall it be done to him:

יט וְאִישׁ כִּי־יִתֵּן מוּם בַּעֲמִיתוֹ כַּאֲשֶׁר עָשָׂה כֵּן יֵעָשֶׂה לּוֹ:

20 fracture for fracture, eye for eye, tooth for tooth. The injury he inflicted on another shall be inflicted on him.

כ שֶׁבֶר תַּחַת שֶׁבֶר עַיִן תַּחַת עַיִן שֵׁן תַּחַת שֵׁן כַּאֲשֶׁר יִתֵּן מוּם בָּאָדָם כֵּן יִנָּתֶן בּוֹ:

21 One who kills a beast shall make restitution for it; but one who kills a human being shall be put to death.

כא וּמַכֵּה בְהֵמָה יְשַׁלְּמֶנָּה וּמַכֵּה אָדָם יוּמָת:

22 You shall have one standard for stranger and citizen alike: for I *Hashem* am your God.

כב מִשְׁפַּט אֶחָד יִהְיֶה לָכֶם כַּגֵּר כָּאֶזְרָח יִהְיֶה כִּי אֲנִי יְהֹוָה אֱלֹהֵיכֶם:

23 *Moshe* spoke thus to the Israelites. And they took the blasphemer outside the camp and pelted him with stones. The Israelites did as *Hashem* had commanded *Moshe*.

כג וַיְדַבֵּר מֹשֶׁה אֶל־בְּנֵי יִשְׂרָאֵל וַיּוֹצִיאוּ אֶת־הַמְקַלֵּל אֶל־מִחוּץ לַמַּחֲנֶה וַיִּרְגְּמוּ אֹתוֹ אָבֶן וּבְנֵי־יִשְׂרָאֵל עָשׂוּ כַּאֲשֶׁר צִוָּה יְהֹוָה אֶת־מֹשֶׁה:

ויקרא   כה

בהר

5 ¹ Hashem spoke to *Moshe* on *Har Sinai*:

כה א וַיְדַבֵּר יְהֹוָה אֶל־מֹשֶׁה בְּהַר סִינַי לֵאמֹר:

² Speak to *B'nei Yisrael* and say to them: When you enter the land that I assign to you, the land shall observe a *Shabbat* of *Hashem*.

ב דַּבֵּר אֶל־בְּנֵי יִשְׂרָאֵל וְאָמַרְתָּ אֲלֵהֶם כִּי תָבֹאוּ אֶל־הָאָרֶץ אֲשֶׁר אֲנִי נֹתֵן לָכֶם וְשָׁבְתָה הָאָרֶץ שַׁבָּת לַיהֹוָה:

³ Six years you may sow your field and six years you may prune your vineyard and gather in the yield.

ג שֵׁשׁ שָׁנִים תִּזְרַע שָׂדֶךָ וְשֵׁשׁ שָׁנִים תִּזְמֹר כַּרְמֶךָ וְאָסַפְתָּ אֶת־תְּבוּאָתָהּ:

⁴ But in the seventh year the land shall have a *Shabbat* of complete rest, a *Shabbat* of *Hashem*: you shall not sow your field or prune your vineyard.

ד וּבַשָּׁנָה הַשְּׁבִיעִת שַׁבַּת שַׁבָּתוֹן יִהְיֶה לָאָרֶץ שַׁבָּת לַיהֹוָה שָׂדְךָ לֹא תִזְרָע וְכַרְמְךָ לֹא תִזְמֹר:

⁵ You shall not reap the aftergrowth of your harvest or gather the grapes of your untrimmed vines; it shall be a year of complete rest for the land.

ה אֵת סְפִיחַ קְצִירְךָ לֹא תִקְצוֹר וְאֶת־עִנְּבֵי נְזִירֶךָ לֹא תִבְצֹר שְׁנַת שַׁבָּתוֹן יִהְיֶה לָאָרֶץ:

⁶ But you may eat whatever the land during its *Shabbat* will produce – you, your male and female slaves, the hired and bound laborers who live with you,

ו וְהָיְתָה שַׁבַּת הָאָרֶץ לָכֶם לְאָכְלָה לְךָ וּלְעַבְדְּךָ וְלַאֲמָתֶךָ וְלִשְׂכִירְךָ וּלְתוֹשָׁבְךָ הַגָּרִים עִמָּךְ:

⁷ and your cattle and the beasts in your land may eat all its yield.

ז וְלִבְהֶמְתְּךָ וְלַחַיָּה אֲשֶׁר בְּאַרְצֶךָ תִּהְיֶה כָל־תְּבוּאָתָהּ לֶאֱכֹל:

⁸ You shall count off seven weeks of years – seven times seven years – so that the period of seven weeks of years gives you a total of forty-nine years.

ח וְסָפַרְתָּ לְךָ שֶׁבַע שַׁבְּתֹת שָׁנִים שֶׁבַע שָׁנִים שֶׁבַע פְּעָמִים וְהָיוּ לְךָ יְמֵי שֶׁבַע שַׁבְּתֹת הַשָּׁנִים תֵּשַׁע וְאַרְבָּעִים שָׁנָה:

⁹ Then you shall sound the *shofar* loud; in the seventh month, on the tenth day of the month – the Day of Atonement – you shall have the *shofar* sounded throughout your land

ט וְהַעֲבַרְתָּ שׁוֹפַר תְּרוּעָה בַּחֹדֶשׁ הַשְּׁבִעִי בֶּעָשׂוֹר לַחֹדֶשׁ בְּיוֹם הַכִּפֻּרִים תַּעֲבִירוּ שׁוֹפָר בְּכָל־אַרְצְכֶם:

¹⁰ and you shall hallow the fiftieth year. You shall proclaim release throughout the land for all its inhabitants. It shall be a jubilee for you: each of you shall return to his holding and each of you shall return to his family.

י וְקִדַּשְׁתֶּם אֵת שְׁנַת הַחֲמִשִּׁים שָׁנָה וּקְרָאתֶם דְּרוֹר בָּאָרֶץ לְכָל־יֹשְׁבֶיהָ יוֹבֵל הִוא תִּהְיֶה לָכֶם וְשַׁבְתֶּם אִישׁ אֶל־אֲחֻזָּתוֹ וְאִישׁ אֶל־מִשְׁפַּחְתּוֹ תָּשֻׁבוּ:

v'-ki-dash-TEM AYT sh'-NAT ha-kha-mi-SHEEM sha-NAH uk-ra-TEM d'-ROR ba-A-retz l'-khol yo-sh'-VE-ha yo-VAYL HEE tih-YEH la-KHEM v'-shav-TEM EESH el a-khu-za-TO v'-EESH el mish-pakh-TO ta-SHU-vu

25:10 You shall proclaim release throughout the land The Liberty Bell is an icon of American independence. Commissioned in 1751 for the Pennsylvania State House, the bell was cast with the words "proclaim liberty throughout all the land unto all the inhabitants thereof," taken from this verse. Because of this inscription, it was made a symbol of freedom by the abolitionists in the 1830s, when it was also given the name 'Liberty Bell.' It has remained a symbol of freedom and liberty ever since. In recognition of their shared Judeo-Christian values, the State of Israel built a replica of the Liberty Bell and placed it in the center of Jerusalem as a symbol the special bond between the two countries.

Liberty Bell Park in *Yerushalayim*

11 That fiftieth year shall be a jubilee for you: you shall not sow, neither shall you reap the aftergrowth or harvest the untrimmed vines,

יא יוֹבֵ֣ל הִ֗וא שְׁנַ֛ת הַחֲמִשִּׁ֥ים שָׁנָ֖ה תִּהְיֶ֣ה לָכֶ֑ם לֹ֣א תִזְרָ֗עוּ וְלֹ֤א תִקְצְרוּ֙ אֶת־סְפִיחֶ֔יהָ וְלֹ֥א תִבְצְר֖וּ אֶת־נְזִרֶֽיהָ׃

12 for it is a jubilee. It shall be holy to you: you may only eat the growth direct from the field.

יב כִּ֚י יוֹבֵ֣ל הִ֔וא קֹ֖דֶשׁ תִּהְיֶ֣ה לָכֶ֑ם מִן־הַ֨שָּׂדֶ֔ה תֹּאכְל֖וּ אֶת־תְּבוּאָתָֽהּ׃

13 In this year of jubilee, each of you shall return to his holding.

יג בִּשְׁנַ֥ת הַיּוֹבֵ֖ל הַזֹּ֑את תָּשֻׁ֕בוּ אִ֖ישׁ אֶל־אֲחֻזָּתֽוֹ׃

14 When you sell property to your neighbor, or buy any from your neighbor, you shall not wrong one another.

יד וְכִֽי־תִמְכְּר֤וּ מִמְכָּר֙ לַעֲמִיתֶ֔ךָ א֥וֹ קָנֹ֖ה מִיַּ֣ד עֲמִיתֶ֑ךָ אַל־תּוֹנ֖וּ אִ֥ישׁ אֶת־אָחִֽיו׃

15 In buying from your neighbor, you shall deduct only for the number of years since the jubilee; and in selling to you, he shall charge you only for the remaining crop years:

טו בְּמִסְפַּ֤ר שָׁנִים֙ אַחַ֣ר הַיּוֹבֵ֔ל תִּקְנֶ֖ה מֵאֵ֣ת עֲמִיתֶ֑ךָ בְּמִסְפַּ֥ר שְׁנֵֽי־תְבוּאֹ֖ת יִמְכָּר־לָֽךְ׃

16 the more such years, the higher the price you pay; the fewer such years, the lower the price; for what he is selling you is a number of harvests.

טז לְפִ֣י ׀ רֹ֣ב הַשָּׁנִ֗ים תַּרְבֶּה֙ מִקְנָת֔וֹ וּלְפִ֕י מְעֹ֣ט הַשָּׁנִ֔ים תַּמְעִ֖יט מִקְנָת֑וֹ כִּ֚י מִסְפַּ֣ר תְּבוּאֹ֔ת ה֥וּא מֹכֵ֖ר לָֽךְ׃

17 Do not wrong one another, but fear your God; for I *Hashem* am your God.

יז וְלֹ֤א תוֹנוּ֙ אִ֣ישׁ אֶת־עֲמִית֔וֹ וְיָרֵ֖אתָ מֵֽאֱלֹהֶ֑יךָ כִּ֛י אֲנִ֥י יְהֹוָ֖ה אֱלֹהֵיכֶֽם׃

18 You shall observe My laws and faithfully keep My rules, that you may live upon the land in security;

יח וַעֲשִׂיתֶם֙ אֶת־חֻקֹּתַ֔י וְאֶת־מִשְׁפָּטַ֥י תִּשְׁמְר֖וּ וַעֲשִׂיתֶ֣ם אֹתָ֑ם וִֽישַׁבְתֶּ֥ם עַל־הָאָ֖רֶץ לָבֶֽטַח׃

19 the land shall yield its fruit and you shall eat your fill, and you shall live upon it in security.

יט וְנָתְנָ֤ה הָאָ֙רֶץ֙ פִּרְיָ֔הּ וַאֲכַלְתֶּ֖ם לָשֹׂ֑בַע וִֽישַׁבְתֶּ֥ם לָבֶ֖טַח עָלֶֽיהָ׃

20 And should you ask, "What are we to eat in the seventh year, if we may neither sow nor gather in our crops?"

כ וְכִ֣י תֹאמְר֔וּ מַה־נֹּאכַ֖ל בַּשָּׁנָ֣ה הַשְּׁבִיעִ֑ת הֵ֚ן לֹ֣א נִזְרָ֔ע וְלֹ֥א נֶאֱסֹ֖ף אֶת־תְּבוּאָתֵֽנוּ׃

21 I will ordain My blessing for you in the sixth year, so that it shall yield a crop sufficient for three years.

כא וְצִוִּ֤יתִי אֶת־בִּרְכָתִי֙ לָכֶ֔ם בַּשָּׁנָ֖ה הַשִּׁשִּׁ֑ית וְעָשָׂת֙ אֶת־הַתְּבוּאָ֔ה לִשְׁלֹ֖שׁ הַשָּׁנִֽים׃

v'-tzi-VEE-tee et bir-kha-TEE la-KHEM ba-sha-NAH ha-shi-SHEET
v'-a-SAT et ha-t'-vu-AH lish-LOSH ha-sha-NEEM

25:21 I will ordain My blessing for you in the sixth year
Chapter 25 describes the blessing of the Sabbatical year, which is often cited as one of the proofs of the Divinity of the Bible. Verses 20–21 state, "And should you ask, 'What are we to eat in the seventh year, if we may neither sow nor gather in our crops?' I will ordain My blessing for you in the sixth year, so that it shall yield a crop sufficient for three years." No human being would ever make such an audacious guarantee – essentially sentencing the entire nation to starve every seventh year. Certainly, after one failed cycle, no one would obey the Sabbatical restrictions again. Only the one true God could make and keep such a grandiose promise.

A field in the Galilee

22 When you sow in the eighth year, you will still be eating old grain of that crop; you will be eating the old until the ninth year, until its crops come in.

כב וּזְרַעְתֶּ֗ם אֵ֚ת הַשָּׁנָ֣ה הַשְּׁמִינִ֔ת וַאֲכַלְתֶּ֖ם מִן־הַתְּבוּאָ֣ה יָשָׁ֑ן עַ֣ד ׀ הַשָּׁנָ֣ה הַתְּשִׁיעִ֗ת עַד־בּוֹא֙ תְּבֽוּאָתָ֔הּ תֹּאכְל֖וּ יָשָֽׁן׃

23 But the land must not be sold beyond reclaim, for the land is Mine; you are but strangers resident with Me.

כג וְהָאָ֗רֶץ לֹ֤א תִמָּכֵר֙ לִצְמִתֻ֔ת כִּי־לִ֖י הָאָ֑רֶץ כִּֽי־גֵרִ֧ים וְתוֹשָׁבִ֛ים אַתֶּ֖ם עִמָּדִֽי׃

24 Throughout the land that you hold, you must provide for the redemption of the land.

כד וּבְכֹ֖ל אֶ֣רֶץ אֲחֻזַּתְכֶ֑ם גְּאֻלָּ֖ה תִּתְּנ֥וּ לָאָֽרֶץ׃

25 If your kinsman is in straits and has to sell part of his holding, his nearest redeemer shall come and redeem what his kinsman has sold.

כה כִּֽי־יָמ֣וּךְ אָחִ֔יךָ וּמָכַ֖ר מֵאֲחֻזָּת֑וֹ וּבָ֤א גֹֽאֲלוֹ֙ הַקָּרֹ֣ב אֵלָ֔יו וְגָאַ֕ל אֵ֖ת מִמְכַּ֥ר אָחִֽיו׃

26 If a man has no one to redeem for him, but prospers and acquires enough to redeem with,

כו וְאִ֕ישׁ כִּ֛י לֹ֥א יִֽהְיֶה־לּ֖וֹ גֹּאֵ֑ל וְהִשִּׂ֣יגָה יָד֔וֹ וּמָצָ֖א כְּדֵ֥י גְאֻלָּתֽוֹ׃

27 he shall compute the years since its sale, refund the difference to the man to whom he sold it, and return to his holding.

כז וְחִשַּׁב֙ אֶת־שְׁנֵ֣י מִמְכָּר֔וֹ וְהֵשִׁיב֙ אֶת־הָ֣עֹדֵ֔ף לָאִ֖ישׁ אֲשֶׁ֣ר מָֽכַר־ל֑וֹ וְשָׁ֖ב לַאֲחֻזָּתֽוֹ׃

28 If he lacks sufficient means to recover it, what he sold shall remain with the purchaser until the jubilee; in the jubilee year it shall be released, and he shall return to his holding.

כח וְאִ֨ם לֹֽא־מָצְאָ֜ה יָד֗וֹ דֵּי֮ הָשִׁ֣יב לוֹ֒ וְהָיָ֣ה מִמְכָּר֗וֹ בְּיַד֙ הַקֹּנֶ֣ה אֹת֔וֹ עַ֖ד שְׁנַ֣ת הַיּוֹבֵ֑ל וְיָצָא֙ בַּיֹּבֵ֔ל וְשָׁ֖ב לַאֲחֻזָּתֽוֹ׃

29 If a man sells a dwelling house in a walled city, it may be redeemed until a year has elapsed since its sale; the redemption period shall be a year.

כט וְאִ֗ישׁ כִּֽי־יִמְכֹּ֤ר בֵּית־מוֹשַׁב֙ עִ֣יר חוֹמָ֔ה וְהָיְתָה֙ גְּאֻלָּת֔וֹ עַד־תֹּ֖ם שְׁנַ֣ת מִמְכָּר֑וֹ יָמִ֖ים תִּהְיֶ֥ה גְאֻלָּתֽוֹ׃

30 If it is not redeemed before a full year has elapsed, the house in the walled city shall pass to the purchaser beyond reclaim throughout the ages; it shall not be released in the jubilee.

ל וְאִ֣ם לֹֽא־יִגָּאֵ֗ל עַד־מְלֹ֨את לוֹ֮ שָׁנָ֣ה תְמִימָה֒ וְ֠קָ֠ם הַבַּ֨יִת אֲשֶׁר־בָּעִ֜יר אֲשֶׁר־ל֣וֹ [לוֹ֩] חֹמָ֡ה לַצְּמִיתֻ֨ת לַקֹּנֶ֥ה אֹת֛וֹ לְדֹרֹתָ֖יו לֹ֥א יֵצֵ֖א בַּיֹּבֵֽל׃

31 But houses in villages that have no encircling walls shall be classed as open country: they may be redeemed, and they shall be released through the jubilee.

לא וּבָתֵּ֣י הַחֲצֵרִ֗ים אֲשֶׁ֨ר אֵֽין־לָהֶ֤ם חֹמָה֙ סָבִ֔יב עַל־שְׂדֵ֥ה הָאָ֖רֶץ יֵחָשֵׁ֑ב גְּאֻלָּה֙ תִּהְיֶה־לּ֔וֹ וּבַיֹּבֵ֖ל יֵצֵֽא׃

32 As for the cities of the *Leviim*, the houses in the cities they hold – the *Leviim* shall forever have the right of redemption.

לב וְעָרֵי֙ הַלְוִיִּ֔ם בָּתֵּ֖י עָרֵ֣י אֲחֻזָּתָ֑ם גְּאֻלַּ֥ת עוֹלָ֖ם תִּהְיֶ֥ה לַלְוִיִּֽם׃

33 Such property as may be redeemed from the *Leviim* – houses sold in a city they hold – shall be released through the jubilee; for the houses in the cities of the *Leviim* are their holding among the Israelites.

לג וַאֲשֶׁ֤ר יִגְאַל֙ מִן־הַלְוִיִּ֔ם וְיָצָ֧א מִמְכַּר־בַּ֛יִת וְעִ֥יר אֲחֻזָּת֖וֹ בַּיֹּבֵ֑ל כִּ֣י בָתֵּ֞י עָרֵ֣י הַלְוִיִּ֗ם הִ֚וא אֲחֻזָּתָ֔ם בְּת֖וֹךְ בְּנֵ֥י יִשְׂרָאֵֽל׃

34 But the unenclosed land about their cities cannot be sold, for that is their holding for all time.

לד וּשְׂדֵה מִגְרַשׁ עָרֵיהֶם לֹא יִמָּכֵר כִּי־אֲחֻזַּת עוֹלָם הוּא לָהֶם:

35 If your kinsman, being in straits, comes under your authority, and you hold him as though a resident alien, let him live by your side:

לה וְכִי־יָמוּךְ אָחִיךָ וּמָטָה יָדוֹ עִמָּךְ וְהֶחֱזַקְתָּ בּוֹ גֵּר וְתוֹשָׁב וָחַי עִמָּךְ:

36 do not exact from him advance or accrued interest, but fear your God. Let him live by your side as your kinsman.

לו אַל־תִּקַּח מֵאִתּוֹ נֶשֶׁךְ וְתַרְבִּית וְיָרֵאתָ מֵאֱלֹהֶיךָ וְחֵי אָחִיךָ עִמָּךְ:

37 Do not lend him your money at advance interest, or give him your food at accrued interest.

לז אֶת־כַּסְפְּךָ לֹא־תִתֵּן לוֹ בְּנֶשֶׁךְ וּבְמַרְבִּית לֹא־תִתֵּן אָכְלֶךָ:

38 I *Hashem* am your God, who brought you out of the land of Egypt, to give you the land of Canaan, to be your God.

לח אֲנִי יְהֹוָה אֱלֹהֵיכֶם אֲשֶׁר־הוֹצֵאתִי אֶתְכֶם מֵאֶרֶץ מִצְרָיִם לָתֵת לָכֶם אֶת־אֶרֶץ כְּנַעַן לִהְיוֹת לָכֶם לֵאלֹהִים:

39 If your kinsman under you continues in straits and must give himself over to you, do not subject him to the treatment of a slave.

לט וְכִי־יָמוּךְ אָחִיךָ עִמָּךְ וְנִמְכַּר־לָךְ לֹא־תַעֲבֹד בּוֹ עֲבֹדַת עָבֶד:

40 He shall remain with you as a hired or bound laborer; he shall serve with you only until the jubilee year.

מ כְּשָׂכִיר כְּתוֹשָׁב יִהְיֶה עִמָּךְ עַד־שְׁנַת הַיֹּבֵל יַעֲבֹד עִמָּךְ:

41 Then he and his children with him shall be free of your authority; he shall go back to his family and return to his ancestral holding. –

מא וְיָצָא מֵעִמָּךְ הוּא וּבָנָיו עִמּוֹ וְשָׁב אֶל־מִשְׁפַּחְתּוֹ וְאֶל־אֲחֻזַּת אֲבֹתָיו יָשׁוּב:

42 For they are My servants, whom I freed from the land of Egypt; they may not give themselves over into servitude. –

מב כִּי־עֲבָדַי הֵם אֲשֶׁר־הוֹצֵאתִי אֹתָם מֵאֶרֶץ מִצְרָיִם לֹא יִמָּכְרוּ מִמְכֶּרֶת עָבֶד:

43 You shall not rule over him ruthlessly; you shall fear your God.

מג לֹא־תִרְדֶּה בוֹ בְּפָרֶךְ וְיָרֵאתָ מֵאֱלֹהֶיךָ:

44 Such male and female slaves as you may have – it is from the nations round about you that you may acquire male and female slaves.

מד וְעַבְדְּךָ וַאֲמָתְךָ אֲשֶׁר יִהְיוּ־לָךְ מֵאֵת הַגּוֹיִם אֲשֶׁר סְבִיבֹתֵיכֶם מֵהֶם תִּקְנוּ עֶבֶד וְאָמָה:

45 You may also buy them from among the children of aliens resident among you, or from their families that are among you, whom they begot in your land. These shall become your property:

מה וְגַם מִבְּנֵי הַתּוֹשָׁבִים הַגָּרִים עִמָּכֶם מֵהֶם תִּקְנוּ וּמִמִּשְׁפַּחְתָּם אֲשֶׁר עִמָּכֶם אֲשֶׁר הוֹלִידוּ בְּאַרְצְכֶם וְהָיוּ לָכֶם לַאֲחֻזָּה:

46 you may keep them as a possession for your children after you, for them to inherit as property for all time. Such you may treat as slaves. But as for your Israelite kinsmen, no one shall rule ruthlessly over the other.

מו וְהִתְנַחַלְתֶּם אֹתָם לִבְנֵיכֶם אַחֲרֵיכֶם לָרֶשֶׁת אֲחֻזָּה לְעֹלָם בָּהֶם תַּעֲבֹדוּ וּבְאַחֵיכֶם בְּנֵי־יִשְׂרָאֵל אִישׁ בְּאָחִיו לֹא־תִרְדֶּה בוֹ בְּפָרֶךְ:

47 If a resident alien among you has prospered, and your kinsman being in straits, comes under his authority and gives himself over to the resident alien among you, or to an offshoot of an alien's family,

מז וְכִי תַשִּׂיג יַד גֵּר וְתוֹשָׁב עִמָּךְ וּמָךְ אָחִיךָ עִמּוֹ וְנִמְכַּר לְגֵר תּוֹשָׁב עִמָּךְ אוֹ לְעֵקֶר מִשְׁפַּחַת גֵּר:

48 he shall have the right of redemption even after he has given himself over. One of his kinsmen shall redeem him,

מח אַחֲרֵי נִמְכַּר גְּאֻלָּה תִּהְיֶה־לּוֹ אֶחָד מֵאֶחָיו יִגְאָלֶנּוּ:

49 or his uncle or his uncle's son shall redeem him, or anyone of his family who is of his own flesh shall redeem him; or, if he prospers, he may redeem himself.

מט אוֹ־דֹדוֹ אוֹ בֶן־דֹדוֹ יִגְאָלֶנּוּ אוֹ־מִשְּׁאֵר בְּשָׂרוֹ מִמִּשְׁפַּחְתּוֹ יִגְאָלֶנּוּ אוֹ־הִשִּׂיגָה יָדוֹ וְנִגְאָל:

50 He shall compute with his purchaser the total from the year he gave himself over to him until the jubilee year; the price of his sale shall be applied to the number of years, as though it were for a term as a hired laborer under the other's authority.

נ וְחִשַּׁב עִם־קֹנֵהוּ מִשְּׁנַת הִמָּכְרוֹ לוֹ עַד שְׁנַת הַיֹּבֵל וְהָיָה כֶּסֶף מִמְכָּרוֹ בְּמִסְפַּר שָׁנִים כִּימֵי שָׂכִיר יִהְיֶה עִמּוֹ:

51 If many years remain, he shall pay back for his redemption in proportion to his purchase price;

נא אִם־עוֹד רַבּוֹת בַּשָּׁנִים לְפִיהֶן יָשִׁיב גְּאֻלָּתוֹ מִכֶּסֶף מִקְנָתוֹ:

52 and if few years remain until the jubilee year, he shall so compute: he shall make payment for his redemption according to the years involved.

נב וְאִם־מְעַט נִשְׁאַר בַּשָּׁנִים עַד־שְׁנַת הַיֹּבֵל וְחִשַּׁב־לוֹ כְּפִי שָׁנָיו יָשִׁיב אֶת־גְּאֻלָּתוֹ:

53 He shall be under his authority as a laborer hired by the year; he shall not rule ruthlessly over him in your sight.

נג כִּשְׂכִיר שָׁנָה בְּשָׁנָה יִהְיֶה עִמּוֹ לֹא־יִרְדֶּנּוּ בְּפֶרֶךְ לְעֵינֶיךָ:

54 If he has not been redeemed in any of those ways, he and his children with him shall go free in the jubilee year.

נד וְאִם־לֹא יִגָּאֵל בְּאֵלֶּה וְיָצָא בִּשְׁנַת הַיֹּבֵל הוּא וּבָנָיו עִמּוֹ:

55 For it is to Me that the Israelites are servants: they are My servants, whom I freed from the land of Egypt, I *Hashem* your God.

נה כִּי־לִי בְנֵי־יִשְׂרָאֵל עֲבָדִים עֲבָדַי הֵם אֲשֶׁר־הוֹצֵאתִי אוֹתָם מֵאֶרֶץ מִצְרָיִם אֲנִי יְהוָה אֱלֹהֵיכֶם:

6 1 You shall not make idols for yourselves, or set up for yourselves carved images or pillars, or place figured stones in your land to worship upon, for I *Hashem* am your God.

כו א לֹא־תַעֲשׂוּ לָכֶם אֱלִילִם וּפֶסֶל וּמַצֵּבָה לֹא־תָקִימוּ לָכֶם וְאֶבֶן מַשְׂכִּית לֹא תִתְּנוּ בְּאַרְצְכֶם לְהִשְׁתַּחֲוֹת עָלֶיהָ כִּי אֲנִי יְהוָה אֱלֹהֵיכֶם:

2 You shall keep My *Shabbatot* and venerate My sanctuary, Mine, *Hashem's*.

ב אֶת־שַׁבְּתֹתַי תִּשְׁמֹרוּ וּמִקְדָּשִׁי תִּירָאוּ אֲנִי יְהוָה:

3 If you follow My laws and faithfully observe My commandments,

ג אִם־בְּחֻקֹּתַי תֵּלֵכוּ וְאֶת־מִצְוֹתַי תִּשְׁמְרוּ וַעֲשִׂיתֶם אֹתָם:

im b'-khu-ko-TAI tay-LAY-khu v'-et mitz-vo-TAI tish-m'-RU va-a-see-TEM o-TAM

Leviticus

4 I will grant your rains in their season, so that the earth shall yield its produce and the trees of the field their fruit.

ד וְנָתַתִּי גִשְׁמֵיכֶם בְּעִתָּם וְנָתְנָה הָאָרֶץ יְבוּלָהּ וְעֵץ הַשָּׂדֶה יִתֵּן פִּרְיוֹ:

*v'-na-ta-TEE gish-may-KHEM b'-i-TAM v'-na-t'-NAH ha-A-retz
y'-vu-LAH v'-AYTZ ha-sa-DEH yi-TAYN pir-YO*

5 Your threshing shall overtake the vintage, and your vintage shall overtake the sowing; you shall eat your fill of bread and dwell securely in your land.

ה וְהִשִּׂיג לָכֶם דַּיִשׁ אֶת־בָּצִיר וּבָצִיר יַשִּׂיג אֶת־זָרַע וַאֲכַלְתֶּם לַחְמְכֶם לָשֹׂבַע וִישַׁבְתֶּם לָבֶטַח בְּאַרְצְכֶם:

6 I will grant peace in the land, and you shall lie down untroubled by anyone; I will give the land respite from vicious beasts, and no sword shall cross your land.

ו וְנָתַתִּי שָׁלוֹם בָּאָרֶץ וּשְׁכַבְתֶּם וְאֵין מַחֲרִיד וְהִשְׁבַּתִּי חַיָּה רָעָה מִן־הָאָרֶץ וְחֶרֶב לֹא־תַעֲבֹר בְּאַרְצְכֶם:

*v'-na-ta-TEE sha-LOM ba-A-retz ush-khav-TEM v'-AYN
ma-kha-REED v'-hish-ba-TEE kha-YAH ra-AH min
ha-A-retz v'-KHE-rev lo ta-a-VOR b'-ar-tz'-KHEM*

7 You shall give chase to your enemies, and they shall fall before you by the sword.

ז וּרְדַפְתֶּם אֶת־אֹיְבֵיכֶם וְנָפְלוּ לִפְנֵיכֶם לֶחָרֶב:

8 Five of you shall give chase to a hundred, and a hundred of you shall give chase to ten thousand; your enemies shall fall before you by the sword.

ח וְרָדְפוּ מִכֶּם חֲמִשָּׁה מֵאָה וּמֵאָה מִכֶּם רְבָבָה יִרְדֹּפוּ וְנָפְלוּ אֹיְבֵיכֶם לִפְנֵיכֶם לֶחָרֶב:

9 I will look with favor upon you, and make you fertile and multiply you; and I will maintain My covenant with you.

ט וּפָנִיתִי אֲלֵיכֶם וְהִפְרֵיתִי אֶתְכֶם וְהִרְבֵּיתִי אֶתְכֶם וַהֲקִימֹתִי אֶת־בְּרִיתִי אִתְּכֶם:

10 You shall eat old grain long stored, and you shall have to clear out the old to make room for the new.

י וַאֲכַלְתֶּם יָשָׁן נוֹשָׁן וְיָשָׁן מִפְּנֵי חָדָשׁ תּוֹצִיאוּ:

11 I will establish My abode in your midst, and I will not spurn you.

יא וְנָתַתִּי מִשְׁכָּנִי בְּתוֹכְכֶם וְלֹא־תִגְעַל נַפְשִׁי אֶתְכֶם:

12 I will be ever present in your midst: I will be your God, and you shall be My people.

יב וְהִתְהַלַּכְתִּי בְּתוֹכְכֶם וְהָיִיתִי לָכֶם לֵאלֹהִים וְאַתֶּם תִּהְיוּ־לִי לְעָם:

13 I *Hashem* am your God who brought you out from the land of the Egyptians to be their slaves no more, who broke the bars of your yoke and made you walk erect.

יג אֲנִי יְהוָה אֱלֹהֵיכֶם אֲשֶׁר הוֹצֵאתִי אֶתְכֶם מֵאֶרֶץ מִצְרַיִם מִהְיֹת לָהֶם עֲבָדִים וָאֶשְׁבֹּר מֹטֹת עֻלְּכֶם וָאוֹלֵךְ אֶתְכֶם קוֹמְמִיּוּת:

14 But if you do not obey Me and do not observe all these commandments,

יד וְאִם־לֹא תִשְׁמְעוּ לִי וְלֹא תַעֲשׂוּ אֵת כָּל־הַמִּצְוֺת הָאֵלֶּה:

Winter in Israel: an origami boat sails in a puddle of rainwater

26:4 I will grant your rains in their season Israel depends heavily on rain in order to grow its crops, as it does not have an independent body of water which can provide sufficient irrigation. Water can be the source of great blessing, but at the wrong times, too much or too little water can also be a curse. In this verse, *Hashem* promises that if the Children of Israel follow His commandments and do what He asks of them, He will bless them with the right amount of water at the right times, in order to provide an abundance of crops. In Hebrew, this rain is called *gishmay b'racha* (גשמי ברכה), 'rain of blessing' (Ezekiel 34:26).

15 if you reject My laws and spurn My rules, so that you do not observe all My commandments and you break My covenant,

16 I in turn will do this to you: I will wreak misery upon you – consumption and fever, which cause the eyes to pine and the body to languish; you shall sow your seed to no purpose, for your enemies shall eat it.

17 I will set My face against you: you shall be routed by your enemies, and your foes shall dominate you. You shall flee though none pursues.

18 And if, for all that, you do not obey Me, I will go on to discipline you sevenfold for your sins,

19 and I will break your proud glory. I will make your skies like iron and your earth like copper,

20 so that your strength shall be spent to no purpose. Your land shall not yield its produce, nor shall the trees of the land yield their fruit.

21 And if you remain hostile toward Me and refuse to obey Me, I will go on smiting you sevenfold for your sins.

22 I will loose wild beasts against you, and they shall bereave you of your children and wipe out your cattle. They shall decimate you, and your roads shall be deserted.

23 And if these things fail to discipline you for Me, and you remain hostile to Me,

24 I too will remain hostile to you: I in turn will smite you sevenfold for your sins.

25 I will bring a sword against you to wreak vengeance for the covenant; and if you withdraw into your cities, I will send pestilence among you, and you shall be delivered into enemy hands.

26 When I break your staff of bread, ten women shall bake your bread in a single oven; they shall dole out your bread by weight, and though you eat, you shall not be satisfied.

27 But if, despite this, you disobey Me and remain hostile to Me,

28 I will act against you in wrathful hostility; I, for My part, will discipline you sevenfold for your sins.

29 You shall eat the flesh of your sons and the flesh of your daughters.

טו וְאִם־בְּחֻקֹּתַי תִּמְאָסוּ וְאִם אֶת־מִשְׁפָּטַי תִּגְעַל נַפְשְׁכֶם לְבִלְתִּי עֲשׂוֹת אֶת־כָּל־מִצְוֺתַי לְהַפְרְכֶם אֶת־בְּרִיתִי:

טז אַף־אֲנִי אֶעֱשֶׂה־זֹּאת לָכֶם וְהִפְקַדְתִּי עֲלֵיכֶם בֶּהָלָה אֶת־הַשַּׁחֶפֶת וְאֶת־הַקַּדַּחַת מְכַלּוֹת עֵינַיִם וּמְדִיבֹת נָפֶשׁ וּזְרַעְתֶּם לָרִיק זַרְעֲכֶם וַאֲכָלֻהוּ אֹיְבֵיכֶם:

יז וְנָתַתִּי פָנַי בָּכֶם וְנִגַּפְתֶּם לִפְנֵי אֹיְבֵיכֶם וְרָדוּ בָכֶם שֹׂנְאֵיכֶם וְנַסְתֶּם וְאֵין־רֹדֵף אֶתְכֶם:

יח וְאִם־עַד־אֵלֶּה לֹא תִשְׁמְעוּ לִי וְיָסַפְתִּי לְיַסְּרָה אֶתְכֶם שֶׁבַע עַל־חַטֹּאתֵיכֶם:

יט וְשָׁבַרְתִּי אֶת־גְּאוֹן עֻזְּכֶם וְנָתַתִּי אֶת־שְׁמֵיכֶם כַּבַּרְזֶל וְאֶת־אַרְצְכֶם כַּנְּחֻשָׁה:

כ וְתַם לָרִיק כֹּחֲכֶם וְלֹא־תִתֵּן אַרְצְכֶם אֶת־יְבוּלָהּ וְעֵץ הָאָרֶץ לֹא יִתֵּן פִּרְיוֹ:

כא וְאִם־תֵּלְכוּ עִמִּי קֶרִי וְלֹא תֹאבוּ לִשְׁמֹעַ לִי וְיָסַפְתִּי עֲלֵיכֶם מַכָּה שֶׁבַע כְּחַטֹּאתֵיכֶם:

כב וְהִשְׁלַחְתִּי בָכֶם אֶת־חַיַּת הַשָּׂדֶה וְשִׁכְּלָה אֶתְכֶם וְהִכְרִיתָה אֶת־בְּהֶמְתְּכֶם וְהִמְעִיטָה אֶתְכֶם וְנָשַׁמּוּ דַּרְכֵיכֶם:

כג וְאִם־בְּאֵלֶּה לֹא תִוָּסְרוּ לִי וַהֲלַכְתֶּם עִמִּי קֶרִי:

כד וְהָלַכְתִּי אַף־אֲנִי עִמָּכֶם בְּקֶרִי וְהִכֵּיתִי אֶתְכֶם גַּם־אָנִי שֶׁבַע עַל־חַטֹּאתֵיכֶם:

כה וְהֵבֵאתִי עֲלֵיכֶם חֶרֶב נֹקֶמֶת נְקַם־בְּרִית וְנֶאֱסַפְתֶּם אֶל־עָרֵיכֶם וְשִׁלַּחְתִּי דֶבֶר בְּתוֹכְכֶם וְנִתַּתֶּם בְּיַד־אוֹיֵב:

כו בְּשִׁבְרִי לָכֶם מַטֵּה־לֶחֶם וְאָפוּ עֶשֶׂר נָשִׁים לַחְמְכֶם בְּתַנּוּר אֶחָד וְהֵשִׁיבוּ לַחְמְכֶם בַּמִּשְׁקָל וַאֲכַלְתֶּם וְלֹא תִשְׂבָּעוּ:

כז וְאִם־בְּזֹאת לֹא תִשְׁמְעוּ לִי וַהֲלַכְתֶּם עִמִּי בְּקֶרִי:

כח וְהָלַכְתִּי עִמָּכֶם בַּחֲמַת־קֶרִי וְיִסַּרְתִּי אֶתְכֶם אַף־אָנִי שֶׁבַע עַל־חַטֹּאתֵיכֶם:

כט וַאֲכַלְתֶּם בְּשַׂר בְּנֵיכֶם וּבְשַׂר בְּנֹתֵיכֶם תֹּאכֵלוּ:

Leviticus

30 I will destroy your cult places and cut down your incense stands, and I will heap your carcasses upon your lifeless fetishes. I will spurn you.

ל וְהִשְׁמַדְתִּי אֶת־בָּמֹתֵיכֶם וְהִכְרַתִּי אֶת־חַמָּנֵיכֶם וְנָתַתִּי אֶת־פִּגְרֵיכֶם עַל־פִּגְרֵי גִּלּוּלֵיכֶם וְגָעֲלָה נַפְשִׁי אֶתְכֶם:

31 I will lay your cities in ruin and make your sanctuaries desolate, and I will not savor your pleasing odors.

לא וְנָתַתִּי אֶת־עָרֵיכֶם חָרְבָּה וַהֲשִׁמּוֹתִי אֶת־מִקְדְּשֵׁיכֶם וְלֹא אָרִיחַ בְּרֵיחַ נִיחֹחֲכֶם:

32 I will make the land desolate, so that your enemies who settle in it shall be appalled by it.

לב וַהֲשִׁמֹּתִי אֲנִי אֶת־הָאָרֶץ וְשָׁמְמוּ עָלֶיהָ אֹיְבֵיכֶם הַיֹּשְׁבִים בָּהּ:

*va-ha-shi-mo-TEE a-NEE et ha-A-retz v'-sha-ma-MU
a-LE-ha o-y'-vay-KHEM ha-yo-sh'-VEEM bah*

33 And you I will scatter among the nations, and I will unsheath the sword against you. Your land shall become a desolation and your cities a ruin.

לג וְאֶתְכֶם אֱזָרֶה בַגּוֹיִם וַהֲרִיקֹתִי אַחֲרֵיכֶם חָרֶב וְהָיְתָה אַרְצְכֶם שְׁמָמָה וְעָרֵיכֶם יִהְיוּ חָרְבָּה:

34 Then shall the land make up for its *Shabbat* years throughout the time that it is desolate and you are in the land of your enemies; then shall the land rest and make up for its *Shabbat* years.

לד אָז תִּרְצֶה הָאָרֶץ אֶת־שַׁבְּתֹתֶיהָ כֹּל יְמֵי הָשַּׁמָּה וְאַתֶּם בְּאֶרֶץ אֹיְבֵיכֶם אָז תִּשְׁבַּת הָאָרֶץ וְהִרְצָת אֶת־שַׁבְּתֹתֶיהָ:

35 Throughout the time that it is desolate, it shall observe the rest that it did not observe in your *Shabbat* years while you were dwelling upon it.

לה כָּל־יְמֵי הָשַּׁמָּה תִּשְׁבֹּת אֵת אֲשֶׁר לֹא־שָׁבְתָה בְּשַׁבְּתֹתֵיכֶם בְּשִׁבְתְּכֶם עָלֶיהָ:

36 As for those of you who survive, I will cast a faintness into their hearts in the land of their enemies. The sound of a driven leaf shall put them to flight. Fleeing as though from the sword, they shall fall though none pursues.

לו וְהַנִּשְׁאָרִים בָּכֶם וְהֵבֵאתִי מֹרֶךְ בִּלְבָבָם בְּאַרְצֹת אֹיְבֵיהֶם וְרָדַף אֹתָם קוֹל עָלֶה נִדָּף וְנָסוּ מְנֻסַת־חֶרֶב וְנָפְלוּ וְאֵין רֹדֵף:

37 With no one pursuing, they shall stumble over one another as before the sword. You shall not be able to stand your ground before your enemies,

לז וְכָשְׁלוּ אִישׁ־בְּאָחִיו כְּמִפְּנֵי־חֶרֶב וְרֹדֵף אָיִן וְלֹא־תִהְיֶה לָכֶם תְּקוּמָה לִפְנֵי אֹיְבֵיכֶם:

38 but shall perish among the nations; and the land of your enemies shall consume you.

לח וַאֲבַדְתֶּם בַּגּוֹיִם וְאָכְלָה אֶתְכֶם אֶרֶץ אֹיְבֵיכֶם:

26:32 I will make the land desolate Though this verse is frightening, *Nachmanides* explains that it is actually a blessing in disguise. "I will make the land desolate; so that your enemies who settle in it will be appalled by it" implies that throughout the ages, no matter how many foreign empires occupy Israel, the land will not cooperate to bring forth its bounty. Indeed, in his book *Innocents Abroad*, Mark

Balloons flying over a field of flowers on an Israeli kibbutz

Twain wrote about his visit to Palestine in the 1860s: "A desolation is here that not even imagination can grace with the pomp of life and action.... Palestine is desolate and unlovely." Only when the Jewish People return to the Land of Israel does it give forth its blessing and return to its former glory. Today, thanks to the return of its indigenous Jewish population, *Eretz Yisrael* is once again thriving and prosperous.

39 Those of you who survive shall be heartsick over their iniquity in the land of your enemies; more, they shall be heartsick over the iniquities of their fathers;

לט וְהַנִּשְׁאָרִים בָּכֶם יִמַּקּוּ בַּעֲוֺנָם בְּאַרְצֹת אֹיְבֵיכֶם וְאַף בַּעֲוֺנֹת אֲבֹתָם אִתָּם יִמָּקּוּ:

40 and they shall confess their iniquity and the iniquity of their fathers, in that they trespassed against Me, yea, were hostile to Me.

מ וְהִתְוַדּוּ אֶת־עֲוֺנָם וְאֶת־עֲוֺן אֲבֹתָם בְּמַעֲלָם אֲשֶׁר מָעֲלוּ־בִי וְאַף אֲשֶׁר־הָלְכוּ עִמִּי בְּקֶרִי:

41 When I, in turn, have been hostile to them and have removed them into the land of their enemies, then at last shall their obdurate heart humble itself, and they shall atone for their iniquity.

מא אַף־אֲנִי אֵלֵךְ עִמָּם בְּקֶרִי וְהֵבֵאתִי אֹתָם בְּאֶרֶץ אֹיְבֵיהֶם אוֹ־אָז יִכָּנַע לְבָבָם הֶעָרֵל וְאָז יִרְצוּ אֶת־עֲוֺנָם:

42 Then will I remember My covenant with *Yaakov*; I will remember also My covenant with *Yitzchak*, and also My covenant with *Avraham*; and I will remember the land.

מב וְזָכַרְתִּי אֶת־בְּרִיתִי יַעֲקוֹב וְאַף אֶת־בְּרִיתִי יִצְחָק וְאַף אֶת־בְּרִיתִי אַבְרָהָם אֶזְכֹּר וְהָאָרֶץ אֶזְכֹּר:

v'-za-khar-TEE et b'-ree-TEE ya-a-KOV v'-AF et b'-ree-TEE yitz-KHAK
v'-AF et b'-ree-TEE av-ra-HAM ez-KOR v'-ha-A-retz ez-KOR

43 For the land shall be forsaken of them, making up for its *Shabbat* years by being desolate of them, while they atone for their iniquity; for the abundant reason that they rejected My rules and spurned My laws.

מג וְהָאָרֶץ תֵּעָזֵב מֵהֶם וְתִרֶץ אֶת־שַׁבְּתֹתֶיהָ בָּהְשַׁמָּה מֵהֶם וְהֵם יִרְצוּ אֶת־עֲוֺנָם יַעַן וּבְיַעַן בְּמִשְׁפָּטַי מָאָסוּ וְאֶת־חֻקֹּתַי גָּעֲלָה נַפְשָׁם:

44 Yet, even then, when they are in the land of their enemies, I will not reject them or spurn them so as to destroy them, annulling My covenant with them: for I *Hashem* am their God.

מד וְאַף־גַּם־זֹאת בִּהְיוֹתָם בְּאֶרֶץ אֹיְבֵיהֶם לֹא־מְאַסְתִּים וְלֹא־גְעַלְתִּים לְכַלֹּתָם לְהָפֵר בְּרִיתִי אִתָּם כִּי אֲנִי יְהוָה אֱלֹהֵיהֶם:

45 I will remember in their favor the covenant with the ancients, whom I freed from the land of Egypt in the sight of the nations to be their God: I, *Hashem*.

מה וְזָכַרְתִּי לָהֶם בְּרִית רִאשֹׁנִים אֲשֶׁר הוֹצֵאתִי־אֹתָם מֵאֶרֶץ מִצְרַיִם לְעֵינֵי הַגּוֹיִם לִהְיֹת לָהֶם לֵאלֹהִים אֲנִי יְהוָה:

46 These are the laws, rules, and instructions that *Hashem* established, through *Moshe* on *Har Sinai*, between Himself and *B'nei Yisrael*.

מו אֵלֶּה הַחֻקִּים וְהַמִּשְׁפָּטִים וְהַתּוֹרֹת אֲשֶׁר נָתַן יְהוָה בֵּינוֹ וּבֵין בְּנֵי יִשְׂרָאֵל בְּהַר סִינַי בְּיַד־מֹשֶׁה:

27 1 *Hashem* spoke to *Moshe*, saying:

כז א וַיְדַבֵּר יְהוָה אֶל־מֹשֶׁה לֵּאמֹר:

26:42 And I will remember the land This passage lists the curses that will be brought upon the People of Israel if they fail to follow *Hashem*'s commandments. If His children's sins become too great, God promises to exile the people from the Promised Land, and to destroy the land itself. Following these curses, however, *Hashem* promises that He will never give up on His people and that ultimately, there will be a redemption. In this verse, He promises that he will remember not only the People of Is- rael, but also the Land of Israel itself. He will return His chosen people to the chosen land, and this land will flourish. How fortunate is our genera- tion to witness *Hashem* "remembering the land" as this verse promises.

A sunburst over the Old City of *Yerushalayim*

Leviticus

2 Speak to *B'nei Yisrael* and say to them: When anyone explicitly vows to *Hashem* the equivalent for a human being,

ב דַּבֵּר אֶל־בְּנֵי יִשְׂרָאֵל וְאָמַרְתָּ אֲלֵהֶם אִישׁ כִּי יַפְלִא נֶדֶר בְּעֶרְכְּךָ נְפָשֹׁת לַיהוָה:

3 the following scale shall apply: If it is a male from twenty to sixty years of age, the equivalent is fifty *shekalim* of silver by the sanctuary weight;

ג וְהָיָה עֶרְכְּךָ הַזָּכָר מִבֶּן עֶשְׂרִים שָׁנָה וְעַד בֶּן־שִׁשִּׁים שָׁנָה וְהָיָה עֶרְכְּךָ חֲמִשִּׁים שֶׁקֶל כֶּסֶף בְּשֶׁקֶל הַקֹּדֶשׁ:

4 if it is a female, the equivalent is thirty *shekalim*.

ד וְאִם־נְקֵבָה הִוא וְהָיָה עֶרְכְּךָ שְׁלֹשִׁים שָׁקֶל:

5 If the age is from five years to twenty years, the equivalent is twenty *shekalim* for a male and ten *shekalim* for a female.

ה וְאִם מִבֶּן־חָמֵשׁ שָׁנִים וְעַד בֶּן־עֶשְׂרִים שָׁנָה וְהָיָה עֶרְכְּךָ הַזָּכָר עֶשְׂרִים שְׁקָלִים וְלַנְּקֵבָה עֲשֶׂרֶת שְׁקָלִים:

6 If the age is from one month to five years, the equivalent for a male is five *shekalim* of silver, and the equivalent for a female is three *shekalim* of silver.

ו וְאִם מִבֶּן־חֹדֶשׁ וְעַד בֶּן־חָמֵשׁ שָׁנִים וְהָיָה עֶרְכְּךָ הַזָּכָר חֲמִשָּׁה שְׁקָלִים כָּסֶף וְלַנְּקֵבָה עֶרְכְּךָ שְׁלֹשֶׁת שְׁקָלִים כָּסֶף:

7 If the age is sixty years or over, the equivalent is fifteen *shekalim* in the case of a male and ten *shekalim* for a female.

ז וְאִם מִבֶּן־שִׁשִּׁים שָׁנָה וָמַעְלָה אִם־זָכָר וְהָיָה עֶרְכְּךָ חֲמִשָּׁה עָשָׂר שָׁקֶל וְלַנְּקֵבָה עֲשָׂרָה שְׁקָלִים:

8 But if one cannot afford the equivalent, he shall be presented before the *Kohen*, and the *Kohen* shall assess him; the *Kohen* shall assess him according to what the vower can afford.

ח וְאִם־מָךְ הוּא מֵעֶרְכֶּךָ וְהֶעֱמִידוֹ לִפְנֵי הַכֹּהֵן וְהֶעֱרִיךְ אֹתוֹ הַכֹּהֵן עַל־פִּי אֲשֶׁר תַּשִּׂיג יַד הַנֹּדֵר יַעֲרִיכֶנּוּ הַכֹּהֵן:

9 If [the vow concerns] any animal that may be brought as an offering to *Hashem*, any such that may be given to *Hashem* shall be holy.

ט וְאִם־בְּהֵמָה אֲשֶׁר יַקְרִיבוּ מִמֶּנָּה קָרְבָּן לַיהוָה כֹּל אֲשֶׁר יִתֵּן מִמֶּנּוּ לַיהוָה יִהְיֶה־קֹּדֶשׁ:

10 One may not exchange or substitute another for it, either good for bad, or bad for good; if one does substitute one animal for another, the thing vowed and its substitute shall both be holy.

י לֹא יַחֲלִיפֶנּוּ וְלֹא־יָמִיר אֹתוֹ טוֹב בְּרָע אוֹ־רַע בְּטוֹב וְאִם־הָמֵר יָמִיר בְּהֵמָה בִּבְהֵמָה וְהָיָה־הוּא וּתְמוּרָתוֹ יִהְיֶה־קֹּדֶשׁ:

11 If [the vow concerns] any unclean animal that may not be brought as an offering to *Hashem*, the animal shall be presented before the *Kohen*,

יא וְאִם כָּל־בְּהֵמָה טְמֵאָה אֲשֶׁר לֹא־יַקְרִיבוּ מִמֶּנָּה קָרְבָּן לַיהוָה וְהֶעֱמִיד אֶת־הַבְּהֵמָה לִפְנֵי הַכֹּהֵן:

12 and the *Kohen* shall assess it. Whether high or low, whatever assessment is set by the *Kohen* shall stand;

יב וְהֶעֱרִיךְ הַכֹּהֵן אֹתָהּ בֵּין טוֹב וּבֵין רָע כְּעֶרְכְּךָ הַכֹּהֵן כֵּן יִהְיֶה:

13 and if he wishes to redeem it, he must add one-fifth to its assessment.

יג וְאִם־גָּאֹל יִגְאָלֶנָּה וְיָסַף חֲמִישִׁתוֹ עַל־עֶרְכֶּךָ:

14 If anyone consecrates his house to *Hashem*, the *Kohen* shall assess it. Whether high or low, as the *Kohen* assesses it, so it shall stand;

יד וְאִישׁ כִּי־יַקְדִּשׁ אֶת־בֵּיתוֹ קֹדֶשׁ לַיהוָה וְהֶעֱרִיכוֹ הַכֹּהֵן בֵּין טוֹב וּבֵין רָע כַּאֲשֶׁר יַעֲרִיךְ אֹתוֹ הַכֹּהֵן כֵּן יָקוּם:

15 and if he who has consecrated his house wishes to redeem it, he must add one-fifth to the sum at which it was assessed, and it shall be his.

טו וְאִם־הַמַּקְדִּישׁ יִגְאַל אֶת־בֵּיתוֹ וְיָסַף חֲמִישִׁית כֶּסֶף־עֶרְכְּךָ עָלָיו וְהָיָה לוֹ:

16 If anyone consecrates to *Hashem* any land that he holds, its assessment shall be in accordance with its seed requirement: fifty *shekalim* of silver to a *chomer* of barley seed.

טז וְאִם מִשְּׂדֵה אֲחֻזָּתוֹ יַקְדִּישׁ אִישׁ לַיהוה וְהָיָה עֶרְכְּךָ לְפִי זַרְעוֹ זֶרַע חֹמֶר שְׂעֹרִים בַּחֲמִשִּׁים שֶׁקֶל כָּסֶף:

17 If he consecrates his land as of the jubilee year, its assessment stands.

יז אִם מִשְּׁנַת הַיֹּבֵל יַקְדִּישׁ שָׂדֵהוּ כְּעֶרְכְּךָ יָקוּם:

18 But if he consecrates his land after the jubilee, the *Kohen* shall compute the price according to the years that are left until the jubilee year, and its assessment shall be so reduced;

יח וְאִם אַחַר הַיֹּבֵל יַקְדִּישׁ שָׂדֵהוּ וְחִשַּׁב לוֹ הַכֹּהֵן אֶת הַכֶּסֶף עַל פִּי הַשָּׁנִים הַנּוֹתָרֹת עַד שְׁנַת הַיֹּבֵל וְנִגְרַע מֵעֶרְכֶּךָ:

19 and if he who consecrated the land wishes to redeem it, he must add one-fifth to the sum at which it was assessed, and it shall pass to him.

יט וְאִם גָּאֹל יִגְאַל אֶת הַשָּׂדֶה הַמַּקְדִּישׁ אֹתוֹ וְיָסַף חֲמִשִׁית כֶּסֶף עֶרְכְּךָ עָלָיו וְקָם לוֹ:

20 But if he does not redeem the land, and the land is sold to another, it shall no longer be redeemable:

כ וְאִם לֹא יִגְאַל אֶת הַשָּׂדֶה וְאִם מָכַר אֶת הַשָּׂדֶה לְאִישׁ אַחֵר לֹא יִגָּאֵל עוֹד:

21 when it is released in the jubilee, the land shall be holy to *Hashem*, as land proscribed; it becomes the *Kohen*'s holding.

כא וְהָיָה הַשָּׂדֶה בְּצֵאתוֹ בַיֹּבֵל קֹדֶשׁ לַיהוה כִּשְׂדֵה הַחֵרֶם לַכֹּהֵן תִּהְיֶה אֲחֻזָּתוֹ:

22 If he consecrates to *Hashem* land that he purchased, which is not land of his holding,

כב וְאִם אֶת שְׂדֵה מִקְנָתוֹ אֲשֶׁר לֹא מִשְּׂדֵה אֲחֻזָּתוֹ יַקְדִּישׁ לַיהוה:

23 the *Kohen* shall compute for him the proportionate assessment up to the jubilee year, and he shall pay the assessment as of that day, a sacred donation to *Hashem*.

כג וְחִשַּׁב לוֹ הַכֹּהֵן אֵת מִכְסַת הָעֶרְכְּךָ עַד שְׁנַת הַיֹּבֵל וְנָתַן אֶת הָעֶרְכְּךָ בַּיּוֹם הַהוּא קֹדֶשׁ לַיהוה:

24 In the jubilee year the land shall revert to him from whom it was bought, whose holding the land is.

כד בִּשְׁנַת הַיּוֹבֵל יָשׁוּב הַשָּׂדֶה לַאֲשֶׁר קָנָהוּ מֵאִתּוֹ לַאֲשֶׁר לוֹ אֲחֻזַּת הָאָרֶץ:

25 All assessments shall be by the sanctuary weight, the *shekel* being twenty *geira*.

כה וְכָל עֶרְכְּךָ יִהְיֶה בְּשֶׁקֶל הַקֹּדֶשׁ עֶשְׂרִים גֵּרָה יִהְיֶה הַשָּׁקֶל:

26 A firstling of animals, however, which – as a firstling – is *Hashem*'s, cannot be consecrated by anybody; whether ox or sheep, it is *Hashem*'s.

כו אַךְ בְּכוֹר אֲשֶׁר יְבֻכַּר לַיהוה בִּבְהֵמָה לֹא יַקְדִּישׁ אִישׁ אֹתוֹ אִם שׁוֹר אִם שֶׂה לַיהוה הוּא:

27 But if it is of unclean animals, it may be ransomed as its assessment, with one-fifth added; if it is not redeemed, it shall be sold at its assessment.

כז וְאִם בַּבְּהֵמָה הַטְּמֵאָה וּפָדָה בְעֶרְכֶּךָ וְיָסַף חֲמִשִׁתוֹ עָלָיו וְאִם לֹא יִגָּאֵל וְנִמְכַּר בְּעֶרְכֶּךָ:

28 But of all that anyone owns, be it man or beast or land of his holding, nothing that he has proscribed for *Hashem* may be sold or redeemed; every proscribed thing is totally consecrated to *Hashem*.

כח אַךְ כָּל חֵרֶם אֲשֶׁר יַחֲרִם אִישׁ לַיהוה מִכָּל אֲשֶׁר לוֹ מֵאָדָם וּבְהֵמָה וּמִשְּׂדֵה אֲחֻזָּתוֹ לֹא יִמָּכֵר וְלֹא יִגָּאֵל כָּל חֵרֶם קֹדֶשׁ קָדָשִׁים הוּא לַיהוה:

29 No human being who has been proscribed can be ransomed: he shall be put to death.

כט כָּל חֵרֶם אֲשֶׁר יָחֳרַם מִן הָאָדָם לֹא יִפָּדֶה מוֹת יוּמָת:

30 All tithes from the land, whether seed from the ground or fruit from the tree, are *Hashem*'s; they are holy to *Hashem*.

לוְכָל־מַעְשַׂר הָאָרֶץ מִזֶּרַע הָאָרֶץ מִפְּרִי הָעֵץ לַיהֹוָה הוּא קֹדֶשׁ לַיהֹוָה:

v'-khol ma-SAR ha-A-retz mi-ZE-ra ha-A-retz mi-p'-REE ha-AYTZ la-do-NAI HU KO-desh la-do-NAI

31 If anyone wishes to redeem any of his tithes, he must add one-fifth to them.

לאוְאִם־גָּאֹל יִגְאַל אִישׁ מִמַּעֲשְׂרוֹ חֲמִשִׁיתוֹ יֹסֵף עָלָיו:

32 All tithes of the herd or flock – of all that passes under the shepherd's staff, every tenth one – shall be holy to *Hashem*.

לבוְכָל־מַעְשַׂר בָּקָר וָצֹאן כֹּל אֲשֶׁר־יַעֲבֹר תַּחַת הַשָּׁבֶט הָעֲשִׂירִי יִהְיֶה־קֹּדֶשׁ לַיהֹוָה:

33 He must not look out for good as against bad, or make substitution for it. If he does make substitution for it, then it and its substitute shall both be holy: it cannot be redeemed.

לגלֹא יְבַקֵּר בֵּין־טוֹב לָרַע וְלֹא יְמִירֶנּוּ וְאִם־הָמֵר יְמִירֶנּוּ וְהָיָה־הוּא וּתְמוּרָתוֹ יִהְיֶה־קֹּדֶשׁ לֹא יִגָּאֵל:

34 These are the commandments that *Hashem* gave *Moshe* for *B'nei Yisrael* on *Har Sinai*.

לדאֵלֶּה הַמִּצְוֹת אֲשֶׁר צִוָּה יְהֹוָה אֶת־מֹשֶׁה אֶל־בְּנֵי יִשְׂרָאֵל בְּהַר סִינָי:

Produce of the Land: ripe persimmon fruit hanging from a branch

27:30 All tithes from the land The laws of the tithes serve as another reminder that our successes in life should be attributed to *Hashem*, the source of everything in this world. This verse describes the second tithe, one tenth of a farmer's produce that is to be separated after the first tithe is set aside for the *Leviim*. This tithe must be eaten in *Yerushalayim*, or redeemed for coins with which to purchase and eat food in the holy city. By separating one tenth of his produce and bringing it to *Hashem*'s capital city, the farmer is forced to remember that all of his produce is a gift from God; not merely the result of his own efforts.

List of Transliterated Words in *The Israel Bible*

The following is a list of nouns which have been transliterated into Hebrew in the English translation and commentary of *The Israel Bible*:

Hebrew Name	English Name	Pronunciation	Hebrew
Achan	Achan	a-KHAN	עָכָן
Achav	Ahab	akh-AV	אַחְאָב
Achaz	Ahaz	a-KHAZ	אָחָז
Achazyahu	Ahaziah	a-khaz-YA-hu	אֲחַזְיָהוּ
Achiezer	Ahiezer	a-khee-E-zer	אֲחִיעֶזֶר
Achihud	Ahihud	a-khee-HUD	אֲחִיהוּד
Achikam	Ahikam	a-khee-KAM	אֲחִיקָם
Achilud	Ahilud	a-khee-LUD	אֲחִילוּד
Achimelech	Ahimelech	a-khee-ME-lekh	אֲחִימֶלֶךְ
Achira	Ahira	a-khee-RA	אֲחִירַע
Achisamach	Ahisamach	a-khee-sa-MAKH	אֲחִיסָמָךְ
Achitofel	Ahithophel	a-khee-TO-fel	אֲחִיתֹפֶל
Achituv	Ahitub	a-khee-TUV	אֲחִיטוּב
Achiya	Ahijah	a-khi-YAH	אֲחִיָּה
Adam	Adam	a-DAM	אָדָם
Adar	Adar	a-DAR	אֲדָר
Adoniyahu	Adonijah	a-do-ni-YA-hu	אֲדֹנִיָּהוּ
Adulam	Adullam	a-du-LAM	עֲדֻלָּם
Agur	Agur	a-GUR	אָגוּר
Aharon	Aaron	a-ha-RON	אַהֲרֹן
Amasa	Amasa	a-ma-SA	עֲמָשָׂא
Amatzya	Amaziah	a-matz-YAH	אֲמַצְיָה
Amen	Amen	a-MAYN	אָמֵן
Amiel	Ammiel	a-mee-AYL	עַמִּיאֵל
Aminadav	Amminadab	a-mee-na-DAV	עַמִּינָדָב
Amitai	Amittai	a-mi-TAI	אֲמִתַּי
Amnon	Amnon	am-NON	אַמְנֹן

Hebrew Name	English Name	Pronunciation	Hebrew
Amon	Amon	a-MON	אָמוֹן
Amos	Amos	a-MOS	עָמוֹס
Amotz	Amoz	a-MOTZ	אָמוֹץ
Amram	Amram	am-RAM	עַמְרָם
Anatot	Anathoth	a-na-TOT	עֲנָתוֹת
Aron	Ark	a-RON	אָרוֹן
Aron HaBrit	Ark of the Covenant	a-RON ha-b'-REET	אֲרוֹן הַבְּרִית
Arpachshad	Arpachshad	ar-pakh-SHAD	אַרְפַּכְשַׁד
Asa	Asa	a-SA	אָסָא
Asael	Asahel	a-sah-AYL	עֲשָׂהאֵל
Asaf	Asaph	a-SAF	אָסָף
Ashdod	Ashdod	ash-DOD	אַשְׁדּוֹד
Asher	Asher	a-SHAYR	אָשֵׁר
Ashkelon	Ashkelon	ash-k'-LON	אַשְׁקְלוֹן
Atalya	Athaliah	a-tal-YAH	עֲתַלְיָה
Avdon	Abdon	av-DON	עַבְדּוֹן
Avichayil	Abihail	a-vee-KHA-yil	אֲבִיחַיִל
Avidan	Abidan	a-vee-DAN	אֲבִידָן
Avigail	Abigail	a-vee-GA-yil	אֲבִיגַיִל
Avihu	Abihu	a-vee-HU	אֲבִיהוּא
Avimelech	Abimelech	a-vee-ME-lekh	אֲבִימֶלֶךְ
Avinadav	Abinadab	a-vee-na-DAV	אֲבִינָדָב
Aviram	Abiram	a-vee-RAM	אֲבִירָם
Avishai	Abishai	a-vee-SHAI	אֲבִישַׁי
Aviya	Abijah	a-vi-YAH	אֲבִיָה
Aviyam	Abijam	a-vi-YAM	אֲבִיָם
Avner	Abner	av-NAYR	אַבְנֵר
Avraham	Abraham	av-ra-HAM	אַבְרָהָם
Avram	Abram	av-RAM	אַבְרָם
Avshalom	Absalom	av-sha-LOM	אַבְשָׁלוֹם
Azarya	Azariah	a-zar-YAH	עֲזַרְיָה
Azeika	Azekah	a-zay-KAH	עֲזֵקָה
Azza	Gaza	a-ZAH	עַזָּה

Hebrew Name	English Name	Pronunciation	Hebrew
B'nei Yisrael	The Children of Israel	b'-NAY yis-ra-AYL	בְּנֵי יִשְׂרָאֵל
Barak	Barak	ba-rakh-AYL	בָּרָק
Baruch	Baruch	ba-RUKH	בָּרוּךְ
Barzilai	Barzillai	bar-zi-LAI	בַּרְזִלַּי
Basha	Baasa	ba-SHA	בַּעְשָׁא
Batsheva	Bath-sheba	bat-SHE-va	בַּת־שֶׁבַע
Be'er Sheva	Beer-sheba	b'-AYR SHE-va	בְּאֵר שֶׁבַע
Be'eri	Beeri	b'-ay-REE	בְּאֵרִי
Beit Aven	Beth-aven	bayt A-ven	בֵּית אָוֶן
Beit El	Beth-el	bayt el	בֵּית אֵל
Beit Hamikdash	Temple	bayt ha-mik-DASH	בֵּית הַמִּקְדָּשׁ
Beit Lechem	Beth-lehem	bayt LE-khem	בֵּית לֶחֶם
Beit Shean	Beth-shean	bayt sh'-AN	בֵּית שְׁאָן
Beit Shemesh	Beth-shemesh	bayt SHE-mesh	בֵּית שָׁמֶשׁ
Berechya	Berechiah	be-rekh-YAH	בֶּרֶכְיָה
Betzalel	Bezalel	b'-tzal-AYL	בְּצַלְאֵל
Bilha	Bilhah	bil-HAH	בִּלְהָה
Binyamin	Benjamin	bin-ya-MIN	בִּנְיָמִין
Boaz	Boaz	BO-az	בֹּעַז
Buki	Bukki	bu-KEE	בֻּקִּי
Buzi	Buzi	bu-ZEE	בּוּזִי
Carmel	Carmel	kar-MEL	כַּרְמֶל
Chachalya	Hacaliah	kha-khal-YAH	חֲכַלְיָה
Chagai	Haggai	kha-GAI	חַגַּי
Chana	Hannah	kha-NAH	חַנָּה
Chanamel	Hanamel	kha-nam-AYL	חֲנַמְאֵל
Chanani	Hanani	kha-NA-nee	חֲנָנִי
Chananya	Hananiah	kha-nan-YAH	חֲנַנְיָה
Chaniel	Hanniel	kha-nee-AYL	חַנִּיאֵל
Chanoch	Enoch	kha-NOKH	חֲנוֹךְ
Chava	Eve	kha-VAH	חַוָּה
Chavakuk	Habakkuk	kha-va-KUK	חֲבַקּוּק
Chermon	Hermon	kher-MON	חֶרְמוֹן

Hebrew Name	English Name	Pronunciation	Hebrew
Chetzron	Hezron	khetz-RON	חֶצְרוֹן
Chever	Heber	KHE-ver	חֶבֶר
Chevron	Hebron	khev-RON	חֶבְרוֹן
Chilkiyahu	Hilkiah	khil-ki-YA-hu	חִלְקִיָּהוּ
Chizkiyahu	Hezekiah	khiz-ki-YA-hu	חִזְקִיָּהוּ
Chofni	Hophni	khof-NEE	חָפְנִי
Chogla	Hoglah	khog-LAH	חָגְלָה
Chulda	Hulda	khul-DAH	חֻלְדָּה
Chur	Hur	Khur	חוּר
Dan	Dan	Dan	דָּן
Daniel	Daniel	da-ni-YAYL	דָּנִיֵּאל
Datan	Dathan	da-TAN	דָּתָן
David	David	da-VID	דָּוִד
Devora	Deborah	d'-vo-RAH	דְּבוֹרָה
Dina	Dinah	DEE-nah	דִּינָה
Doeg Ha'adomi	Doeg the Edomite	do-AYG ha-a-do-MEE	דּוֹאֵג הָאֲדֹמִי
Efraim	Ephraim	ef-RA-yim	אֶפְרַיִם
Efrat	Ephrat	ef-RAT	אֶפְרָתָה
Efrat	Ephrathah	ef-RA-tah	אֶפְרָתָה
Ehud	Ehud	ay-HUD	אֵהוּד
Eila	Elah	AY-lah	אֵלָה
Eilon	Elon	ay-LON	אֵילוֹן
Ein Gedi	En-gedi	ayn GE-dee	עֵין גֶּדִי
Elazar	Eleazar	el-a-ZAR	אֶלְעָזָר
Elchanan	Elhanan	el-kha-NAN	אֶלְחָנָן
Eli	Eli	ay-LEE	עֵלִי
Eliav	Eliab	e-lee-AV	אֱלִיאָב
Elidad	Elidad	e-lee-DAD	אֱלִידָד
Eliezer	Eliezer	e-lee-E-zer	אֱלִיעֶזֶר
Elimelech	Elimelech	e-lee-ME-lekh	אֱלִימֶלֶךְ
Elisha	Elisha	e-lee-SHA	אֱלִישָׁע
Elishama	Elishama	e-lee-sha-MA	אֱלִישָׁמָע
Elisheva	Elisheba	e-lee-SHE-va	אֱלִישֶׁבַע

Hebrew Name	English Name	Pronunciation	Hebrew
Elitzafan	Eli-zaphan	e-lee-tza-FAN	אֱלִיצָפָן
Elitzur	Elizur	e-lee-TZUR	אֱלִיצוּר
Eliyahu	Elijah	ay-li-YA-hu	אֵלִיָּהוּ
Elkana	Elkanah	el-ka-NAH	אֶלְקָנָה
Elyasaf	Eliasaph	el-ya-SAF	אֶלְיָסָף
Elyashiv	Eliashib	el-ya-SHEEV	אֶלְיָשִׁיב
Enosh	Enosh	e-NOSH	אֱנוֹשׁ
Er	Er	ayr	עֵר
Eshtaol	Eshtaol	esh-ta-OL	אֶשְׁתָּאֹל
Esther	Esther	es-TAYR	אֶסְתֵּר
Eved Melech	Ebed-melech	E-ved ME-lekh	עֶבֶד־מֶלֶךְ
Even Ha-Ezer	Eben-Ezer	E-ven ha-E-zer	אֶבֶן הָעֵזֶר
Ever	Eber	AY-ver	עֵבֶר
Evyatar	Abiathar	ev-ya-TAR	אֶבְיָתָר
Ezra	Ezra	ez-RA	עֶזְרָא
Gad	Gad	gad	גָּד
Gadi	Gaddi	ga-DEE	גַּדִּי
Gadiel	Gaddiel	ga-dee-AYL	גַּדִּיאֵל
Gamliel	Gamaliel	gam-lee-AYL	גַּמְלִיאֵל
Gedalia	Gedaliah	g'-dal-YA (hu)	גְּדַלְיָהוּ
Gedera	Gederah	g'-day-RAH	גְּדֵרָה
Gershom	Gershom	gay-r'-SHOM	גֵּרְשֹׁם
Gershon	Gershon	gay-r'-SHON	גֵּרְשׁוֹן
Geshem	Geshem	GE-shem	גֶּשֶׁם
Geuel	Geuel	g'-u-AYL	גְּאוּאֵל
Gidon	Gideon	gid-ON	גִּדְעוֹן
Gilad	Gilead	gil-AD	גִּלְעָד
Gilgal	Gilgal	gil-GAL	גִּלְגָּל
Giva	Gibeah	giv-AH	גִּבְעָה
Givon	Gibeon	giv-ON	גִּבְעוֹן
Hadassa	Hadassah	ha-da-SAH	הֲדַסָּה
Har Eival	Mount Ebal	ay-VAL	הַר עֵיבָל
Har Gerizim	Mount Gerizim	g'-ri-ZEEM	הַר גְּרִזִים

Hebrew Name	English Name	Pronunciation	Hebrew
Har HaBayit	Temple Mount	har ha-BA-yit	הַר הַבַּיִת
Har HaZeitim	the Mount of Olives	har ha-zay-TEEM	הַר הַזֵּיתִים
Hashem	Lord/God		
Hayman	Heman	hay-MAN	הֵימָן
Hoshea	Hosea	ho-SHAY-a	הוֹשֵׁעַ
Ido	Iddo	i-DO	עִדּוֹ
Imanu-El	Immanuel	i-MA-nu ayl	עִמָּנוּ אֵל
Ish-boshet	Ish-bosheth	eesh BO-shet	אִישׁ־בֹּשֶׁת
Itamar	Ithamar	ee-ta-MAR	אִיתָמָר
Itiel	Ithiel	ee-tee-AYL	אִיתִיאֵל
Ivtzan	Ibzan	iv-TZAN	אִבְצָן
Iyov	Job	i-YOV	אִיּוֹב
Kadmiel	Kadmiel	kad-mee-AYL	קַדְמִיאֵל
Kalev	Caleb	ka-LAYV	כָּלֵב
Keesh	Kish	keesh	קִישׁ
Kehat	Kohath	k'-HAT	קְהָת
Keinan	Kenan	kay-NAN	קֵינָן
Kemuel	Kemuel	k'-mu-AYL	קְמוּאֵל
Keruvim	Cherubim	k'-ru-VEEM	כְּרוּבִים
Kilyon	Chilion	kil-YON	כִּלְיוֹן
Kiryat Arba	Kiriath-arba	keer-YAT AR-bah	קִרְיַת אַרְבַּע
Kiryat Sefer	Kiriath-sepher	keer-YAT SAY-fer	קִרְיַת־סֵפֶר
Kiryat Ye'arim	Kiriath-jearim	keer-YAT y'-a-REEM	קִרְיַת יְעָרִים
Kislev	Chislev	kis-LAYV	כִּסְלֵו
Kohanim	Priests	ko-ha-NEEM	כֹּהֲנִים
Kohelet	Koheleth	ko-HE-let	קֹהֶלֶת
Kohen	Priest	ko-HAYN	כֹּהֵן
Kohen Gadol	High Priest	ko-HAYN ga-DOL	כֹּהֵן גָּדוֹל
Korach	Korah	KO-rakh	קֹרַח
Kushi	Cushi	ku-SHEE	כּוּשִׁי
Lachish	Lachish	la-KHEESH	לָכִישׁ
Leah	Leah	lay-AH	לֵאָה
Lemech	Lamech	LE-mekh	לֶמֶךְ

Hebrew Name	English Name	Pronunciation	Hebrew
Lemuel	Lemuel	l'-mu-AYL	לְמוֹאֵל
Levi	Levi	lay-VEE	לֵוִי
Leviim	Levites	l'-vee-IM	לְוִיִם
Machla	Mahlah	makh-LAH	מַחְלָה
Machlon	Mahlon	makh-LON	מַחְלוֹן
Machseya	Mahseiah	makh-say-YAH	מַחְסֵיָה
Malachi	Malachi	mal-a-KHEE	מַלְאָכִי
Manoach	Manoah	ma-NO-akh	מָנוֹחַ
Mashiach	Messiah	ma-SHEE-akh	מָשִׁיחַ
Mefiboshet	Mephibosheth	m'-fee-VO-shet	מְפִיבֹשֶׁת
Mehalalel	Mahalalel	ma-ha-lal-AYL	מַהֲלַלְאֵל
Menachem	Menahem	m'-na-KHAYM	מְנַחֵם
Menashe	Menasseh	m'-na-SHEH	מְנַשֶּׁה
Menorah	Candlestick	m'-no-RAH	מְנֹרָה
Merari	Merari	m'-ra-REE	מְרָרִי
Metushelach	Methusaleh	m'-tu-SHE-lakh	מְתוּשָׁלַח
Micha	Micah	mee-KHAH	מִיכָה
Michael	Michael	mee-kha-AYL	מִיכָאֵל
Michaihu	Micaiah	mee-KHAI-hu	מִיכָיְהוּ
Michal	Michal	mee-KHAL	מִיכַל
Milka	Milcah	mil-KAH	מִלְכָּה
Miriam	Miriam	mir-YAM	מִרְיָם
Mishael	Mishael	mee-sha-AYL	מִישָׁאֵל
Mishkan	Tabernacle	mish-KAN	מִשְׁכָּן
Mitzpa	Mizpah	mitz-PAH	מִצְפָּה
Mizbayach	Altar	miz-BAY-akh	מִזְבֵּחַ
Mordechai	Mordecai	mor-d'-KHAI	מָרְדְּכַי
Moriah	Moriah	mo-ri-YAH	מוֹרִיָּה
Moshe	Moses	mo-SHEH	מֹשֶׁה
Nachbi	Nahbi	nakh-BEE	נַחְבִּי
Nachor	Nahor	na-KHOR	נָחוֹר
Nachshon	Nahshon	nakh-SHON	נַחְשׁוֹן
Nachum	Nahum	na-KHUM	נַחוּם

Hebrew Name	English Name	Pronunciation	Hebrew
Nadav	Nadab	na-DAV	נָדָב
Naftali	Naphtali	naf-ta-LEE	נַפְתָּלִי
Naomi	Naomi	na-o-MEE	נָעֳמִי
Natan	Nathan	na-TAN	נָתָן
Naval	Nabal	na-VAL	נָבָל
Navi	Prophet	na-VEE	נָבִיא
Navot	Naboth	na-VAL	נָבָל
Nechemya	Nehemiah	n'-khem-YAH	נְחֶמְיָה
Negev	Negeb	NE-gev	נֶגֶב
Nerya	Neriah	nay-ri-YAH	נֵרִיָּה
Netanel	Nethanel	n'-tan-AYL	נְתַנְאֵל
Neviah	Prophetess	n'-vee-AH	נְבִיאָה
Neviim	Prophets	n'-vee-EEM	נְבִיאִים
Nisan	Nisan	nee-SAN	נִיסָן
Noa	Noah	no-AH	נֹעָה
Noach	Noah	NO-akh	נֹחַ
Nov	Nob	nov	נֹב
Nun	Nun	nun	נוּן
Oded	Oded	o-DAYD	עוֹדֵד
Ohola	Oholah	a-ho-LAH	אָהֳלָה
Oholiav	Oholiab	o-ha-lee-AV	אָהֳלִיאָב
Oholiva	Oholibah	a-ho-lee-VAH	אָהֳלִיבָה
Omri	Omri	om-REE	עָמְרִי
Onan	Onan	o-NAN	אוֹנָן
Otniel	Othniel	ot-nee-AYL	עָתְנִיאֵל
Ovadya	Obadiah	o-vad-YAH	עֹבַדְיָה
Oved	Obed	o-VAYD	עוֹבֵד
Oved Edom	Obed Edom	o-VAYD e-DOM	עוֹבֵד אֱדֹום
Pagiel	Pagiel	pag-ee-AYL	פַּגְעִיאֵל
Palti	Palti	pal-TEE	פַּלְטִי
Paltiel	Paltiel	pal-tee-AYL	פַּלְטִיאֵל
Pekach	Pekah	PE-kakh	פֶּקַח
Pedael	Pedahel	p'-da-AYL	פְּדַהְאֵל

Hebrew Name	English Name	Pronunciation	Hebrew
Pekachya	Pekahiah	p'-kakh-YAH	פְּקַחְיָה
Peleg	Peleg	PE-leg	פֶּלֶג
Penina	Peninnah	p'-ni-NAH	פְּנִנָּה
Peretz	Perez	PE-retz	פֶּרֶץ
Petuel	Pethuel	p'-tu-AYL	פְּתוּאֵל
Pinchas	Phinehas	peen-KHAS	פִּינְחָס
Rachel	Rachel	ra-KHAYL	רָחֵל
Ram	Ram	ram	רָם
Rama	Ramah	ra-MAH	רָמָה
Re'u	Reu	r'-U	רְעוּ
Rechovam	Rehoboam	r'-khav-AM	רְחַבְעָם
Reuven	Reuben	r'-u-VAYN	רְאוּבֵן
Rivka	Rebecca	riv-KAH	רִבְקָה
Rut	Ruth	rut	רוּת
Salma	Salmon/Salmah	sal-MAH	שַׂלְמָה
Salmon	Salmon	sal-MON	שַׂלְמוֹן
Sara	Sarah	sa-RAH	שָׂרָה
Sarai	Sarai	sa-RAI	שָׂרַי
Selah	Selah	SE-lah	סֶלָה
Seraya	Seraiah	s'-ra-YAH	שְׂרָיָה
Serug	Serug	s'-RUG	שְׂרוּג
Setur	Sethur	s'-TUR	סְתוּר
Shaarayim	Shaaraim	sha-a-RA-yim	שַׁעֲרַיִם
Shabbat	Sabbath	sha-BAT	שַׁבָּת
Shabbatot	Sabbaths	sha-ba-TOT	שַׁבָּתוֹת
Shafan	Shaphan	sha-FAN	שָׁפָן
Shafat	Shaphat	sha-FAT	שָׁפָט
Shalem	Salem	sha-LAYM	שָׁלֵם
Shalum	Shallum	sha-LUM	שַׁלּוּם
Shamgar	Shamgar	sham-GAR	שַׁמְגַּר
Shamua	Shammua	sha-MU-a	שַׁמּוּעַ
Shaul	Saul	sha-UL	שָׁאוּל
Shealtiel	Shealtiel	sh'-al-tee-AYL	שְׁאַלְתִּיאֵל

Hebrew Name	English Name	Pronunciation	Hebrew
Shear Yashuv	Shear-Jashub	sh'-AR ya-SHUV	שְׁאָר יָשׁוּב
Shechanya	Shecaniah	sh'-khan-YAH	שְׁכַנְיָה
Shechem	Shechem	sh'-KHEM	שְׁכֶם
Sheila	Shelah	shay-LAH	שֵׁלָה
Shelach	Shelah	SHE-lakh	שָׁלַח
Shelumiel	Shelumiel	sh'-lu-mee-AYL	שְׁלֻמִיאֵל
Shem	Shem	Shaym	שֵׁם
Shemaya	Shemaiah	sh'-ma-YAH	שְׁמַעְיָה
Sheshbatzar	Sheshbazzar	shaysh-ba-TZAR	שֵׁשְׁבַּצַּר
Shet	Seth	Shayt	שֵׁת
Shevat	Shebat	sh'-VAT	שְׁבָט
Shilo	Shiloh	shi-LOH	שִׁלֹה
Shim'i	Shimei	shim-EE	שִׁמְעִי
Shimon	Simeon	shim-ON	שִׁמְעוֹן
Shimshon	Samson	shim-SHON	שִׁמְשׁוֹן
Shlomo	Solomon	sh'-lo-MOH	שְׁלֹמֹה
Shmuel	Samuel	sh'-mu-AYL	שְׁמוּאֵל
Shofar	Horn	sho-FAR	שׁוֹפָר
Shofarot	Horns	sho-fa-ROT	שׁוֹפָרוֹת
Shomron	Samaria	sho-m'-RON	שֹׁמְרוֹן
Sivan	Sivan	see-VAN	סִיוָן
Tamar	Tamar	ta-MAR	תָּמָר
Tanakh	Hebrew Bible	ta-NAKH	תָּנָ"ךְ
Tapuach	Tappuah	ta-PU-akh	תַּפּוּחַ
Tavor	Tabor	ta-VOR	תָּבוֹר
Tekoa	Tekoa	t'-KO-a	תְּקוֹעָה
Terach	Terah	TE-rakh	תֶּרַח
Teveria	Tiberias	t'-ver-YAH	טְבֶרְיָה
Tevet	Tebeth	tay-VAYT	טֵבֵת
Tirtza	Tirzah	tir-TZAH	תִּרְצָה
Tola	Tola	to-LA	תּוֹלָע
Tzadok	Zadok	tza-DOK	צָדוֹק
Tzefanya	Zephaniah	tz'-fan-YAH	צְפַנְיָה

Hebrew Name	English Name	Pronunciation	Hebrew
Tzelofchad	Zelophehad	tz'-lo-f-KHAD	צְלָפְחָד
Tzeruya	Zeruiah	tz'-ru-YAH	צְרוּיָה
Tzfat	Safed	tz'-FAT	צְפַת
Tzidkiyahu	Zedekiah	tzid-ki-YA-hu	צִדְקִיָּהוּ
Tziklag	Ziklag	tzi-k'-LAG	צִקְלַג
Tzion	Zion	tzi-YON	צִיּוֹן
Tzipora	Zipporah	tzi-po-RAH	צִפֹּרָה
Tzora	Zorah	tzor-AH	צָרְעָה
Tzuriel	Zuriel	tzu-ree-AYL	צוּרִיאֵל
Ukal	Ucal	u-KAL	אֻכָל
Uri	Uri	u-REE	אוּרִי
Uriya	Uriah	u-ri-YAH	אוּרִיָּה
Utz	Uz	Utz	עוּץ
Uzziyahu	Uzziah	u-zi-YA-hu	עֻזִּיָּהוּ
Yaakov	Jacob	ya-a-KOV	יַעֲקֹב
Yachaziel	Jahaziel	ya-kha-zee-AYL	יַחֲזִיאֵל
Yael	Jael	ya-AYL	יָעֵל
Yaffo	Joppa/Jaffa	ya-FO	יָפוֹ
Yair	Jair	ya-EER	יָאִיר
Yakeh	Jakeh	ya-KEH	יָקֶה
Yarden	Jordan	yar-DAYN	יַרְדֵּן
Yarmut	Jarmuth	yar-MUT	יַרְמוּת
Yechezkel	Ezekiel	y'-khez-KAYL	יְחֶזְקֵאל
Yechiel	Jehiel	y'-khee-AYL	יְחִיאֵל
Yechonya	Jeconiah	y'-khon-YAH	יְכָנְיָה
Yedutun	Jeduthun	y'-du-TUN	יְדוּתוּן
Yehoachaz	Jehoahaz	y'-ho-a-KHAZ	יְהוֹאָחָז
Yehoash	Jehoash	y'-ho-ASH	יְהוֹאָשׁ
Yehochanan	Jehohanan	y'-ho-kha-NAN	יְהוֹחָנָן
Yehonatan	Jonathan	y'-ho-na-TAN	יְהוֹנָתָן
Yehoram	Jehoram	y'-ho-RAM	יְהוֹרָם
Yehoshafat	Jehoshaphat	y'-ho-sha-FAT	יְהוֹשָׁפָט
Yehoshavat	Jehoshabeath	y'-ho-shav-AT	יְהוֹשַׁבְעַת

Hebrew Name	English Name	Pronunciation	Hebrew
Yehosheva	Jehosheba	y-ho-SHE-va	יְהוֹשֶׁבַע
Yehoshua	Joshua	y'-ho-SHU-a	יְהוֹשֻׁעַ
Yehotzadak	Jehozadak	y'-ho-tza-DAK	יְהוֹצָדָק
Yehoyachin	Jehoiachin	y'-ho-ya-KHEEN	יְהוֹיָכִין
Yehoyada	Jehoiada	y'-ho-ya-DA	יְהוֹיָדָע
Yehoyakim	Jehoiakim	y'-ho-ya-KEEM	יְהוֹיָקִים
Yehu	Jehu	yay-HU	יֵהוּא
Yehuda	Judah	y'-hu-DAH	יְהוּדָה
Yehudi	Jew	y'-hu-DEE	יְהוּדִי
Yehudim	Jews	y'-hu-DEEM	יְהוּדִים
Yered	Jared	YE-red	יֶרֶד
Yericho	Jericho	y'-ree-KHO	יְרִיחוֹ
Yerovam	Jeroboam	ya-rov-AM	יָרָבְעָם
Yerubaal	Jerubbaal	y'-ru-BA-al	יְרֻבַּעַל
Yerushalayim	Jerusalem	y'-ru-sha-LA-yim	יְרוּשָׁלַיִם
Yeshayahu	Isaiah	y'-sha-YA-hu	יְשַׁעְיָהוּ
Yeshua	Jeshua	yay-SHU-a	יֵשׁוּעַ
Yiftach	Jephthah	yif-TAKH	יִפְתָּח
Yigal	Igal	yig-AL	יִגְאָל
Yirmiyahu	Jeremiah	yir-m'-YA-hu	יִרְמְיָהוּ
Yishai	Jesse	yi-SHAI	יִשַׁי
Yisrael	Israel	yis-ra-AYL	יִשְׂרָאֵל
Yissachar	Issachar	yi-sa-KHAR	יִשָּׂשכָר
Yitzchak	Issac	yitz-KHAK	יִצְחָק
Yizrael	Jezreel	yiz-r'-EL	יִזְרְעֶאל
Yoash	Joash	yo-ASH	יוֹאָש
Yoav	Joab	yo-AV	יוֹאָב
Yochanan	Johanan	yo-kha-NAN	יוֹחָנָן
Yocheved	Jochebed	yo-KHE-ved	יוֹכֶבֶד
Yoel	Joel	yo-AYL	יוֹאֵל
Yona	Jonah	yo-NAH	יוֹנָה
Yonadav	Jonadab	yo-na-DAV	יוֹנָדָב
Yonatan	Jonathan	yo-na-TAN	יוֹנָתָן

Hebrew Name	English Name	Pronunciation	Hebrew
Yoram	Joram	yo-RAM	יוֹרָם
Yosef	Joseph	yo-SAYF	יוֹסֵף
Yoshiyahu	Josiah	yo-shi-YA-hu	יֹאשִׁיָהוּ
Yotam	Jotham	yo-TAM	יוֹתָם
Yotzadak	Jozadak	yo-tza-DAK	יוֹצָדָק
Yozavad	Jozabad	yo-za-VAD	יוֹזָבָד
Zanoach	Zanoah	za-NO-akh	זָנוֹחַ
Zecharya	Zechariah	z'-khar-YAH	זְכַרְיָה
Zerach	Zerah	ZE-rakh	זֶרַח
Zerubavel	Zerubbabel	z'-ru-ba-VEL	זְרֻבָּבֶל
Zevulun	Zebulun	z'-vu-LUN	זְבוּלֻן
Zilpa	Zilpah	zil-PAH	זִלְפָּה
Zimri	Zimri	zim-REE	זִמְרִי

Jewish Holidays

Chanukah	Hanukkah	kha-nu-KAH	חֲנוּכָּה
Pesach	Passover	PE-sakh	פֶּסַח
Purim	Purim	pu-REEM	פּוּרִים
Rosh Hashana	Jewish New Year	rosh ha-sha-NAH	רֹאש הַשָּׁנָה
Shavuot	Feast of Weeks	sha-vu-OT	שָׁבוּעוֹת
Shemini Atzeret	Eight Day of Assembly	sh'-mee-NEE a-TZE-ret	שְׁמִינִי עֲצֶרֶת
Sukkot	Feast of Tabernacles	su-KOT	סֻכּוֹת
Yom Kippur	Day of Atonement	yom kee-PUR	יוֹם כִּיפּוֹר

Biblical Measurements

Amah	Cubit	a-MAH	אַמָּה
Amot	Cubits	a-MOT	אַמּוֹת
Bat	Bath	bat	בַּת
Batim	Baths	ba-TEEM	בָּתִּים
Beka	half-shekel	BE-ka	בֶּקַע
Chomarim	Homers	kho-ma-REEM	חֳמָרִים
Chomer	Homer	KHO-mer	חֹמֶר
Efah	Ephah	ay-FAH	אֵיפָה
Geira	Gerah	gay-RAH	גֵּרָה

Hebrew Name	English Name	Pronunciation	Hebrew
Gomed	Gomed	GO- med	גֹּמֶד
Hin	Hin	heen	הִין
Kav	kab	kav	קַב
Kesita	kesitah	k'-see-TAH	קְשִׂיטָה
Kikar	talent	ki-KAR	כִּכָּר
Kikarim	talents	ki-ka-RIM	כִּכָּרִים
Kor	kor	kor	כֹּר
Letek	lethech	LE-tek	לֶתֶךְ
Log	Log	log	לֹג
Maneh	Mina	ma-NEH	מָנֶה
Manim	Minas	ma-NEEM	מָנִים
Omer	Omer	O-mer	עֹמֶר
Pim	Pim	peem	פִּים
Se'ah	Seah	say-AH	סְאָה
Se'eem	Seahs	s'-EEM	סְאִים
Shekalim	Shekels	sh'-ka-LEEM	שְׁקָלִים
Shekel	Shekel	SHE-kel	שֶׁקֶל
Tefach	Handbreadth	TE-fakh	טֶפַח
Zeret	Span	ZE-ret	זֶרֶת

Photo Credits

1:2 John Theodor/Shutterstock.com, **2:1** Alla Khananashvili/Shutterstock.com, **3:1** Noam Chen via goisrael.com, **4:13** Rawpixel.com/Shutterstock.com, **5:15** By Wilson44691 – Own work, Public Domain, https://commons.wikimedia.org/w/index.php?curid=7586805, **6:5** David via Wikimedia Commons, **7:12** Sergei25/Shutterstock.com, **8:3** Boris Diakovsky/Shutterstock.com, **9:23** Mboesch via Wikimedia Commons, **10:3** By David Shankbone – Own work, CC BY-SA 3.0, https://commons.wikimedia.org/w/index.php?curid=3272456, **11:45** AlexDonin/Shutterstock.com, **12:3** Ya'akov Sa'ar Government Press Office (Israel), **13:59** SJ Travel Photo and Video/Shutterstock.com, **15:12** Avishai Teicher via Wikimedia Commons, **16:2** Andrew Shiva via Wikimedia Commons, **17:4** Mark Neyman Government Press Office (Israel), **18:3** Boris Diakovsky/Shutterstock.com, **20:22** tomertu/Shutterstock.com, **21:1** By בקעי – https://commons.wikimedia.org/wiki/File:KohanimOfra242.jpg, CC BY-SA 3.0, https://commons.wikimedia.org/w/index.php?curid=36185538, **22:32** By Israel Defense Forces – IDF Medical Aid Team Performing Surgery in Haiti Field Hospital, CC BY 2.0, https://commons.wikimedia.org/w/index.php?curid=34362392, **23:10** Ya'akov Gefen Government Press Office (Israel), **23:22** PhotoStock-Israel/Shutterstock.com, **23:39** blueeyes/Shutterstock.com, **23:43** Danny W via Wikimedia Commons, **24:8** Monkey Business Images/Shutterstock.com, **25:10** Avi Deror via Wikimedia Commons, **25:21** xnir Photography/Shutterstock.com, **26:4** Shabtay/Shutterstock.com, **26:32** kavram/Shutterstock.com, **26:42** John Theodor/Shutterstock.com **27:30** Emma Grimberg/Shutterstock.com

Map of Modern-Day Israel and its Neighbors

The following is a map of modern-day Israel and the surrounding countries

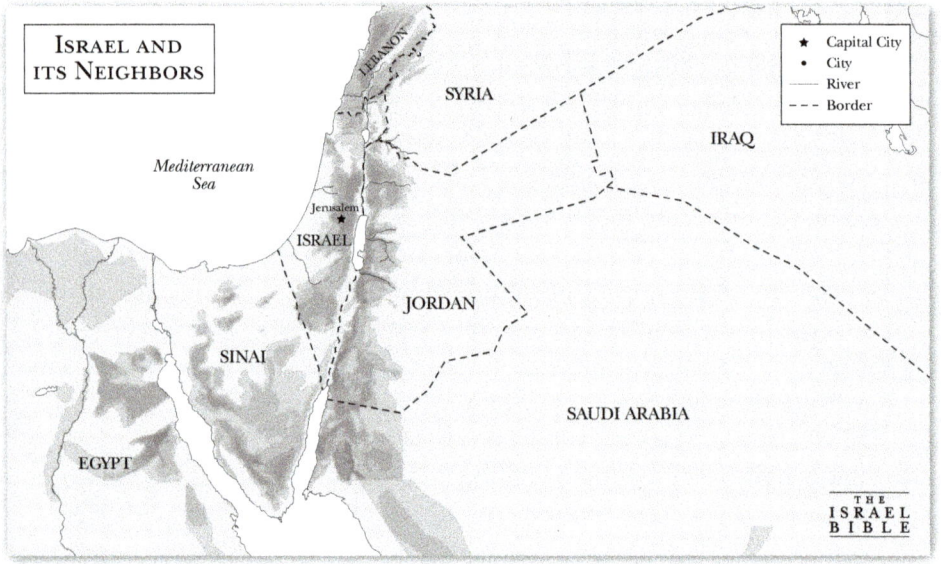

NOTES

NOTES

NOTES

NOTES

NOTES

For more inspiring commentary,
interactive maps, educational videos,
vivid photographs and more,
please visit our website

www.TheIsraelBible.com

THE
ISRAEL
BIBLE